HOME FRONT DIARY 1944

A FAMILY'S AWAKENING TO TRUTH AND COURAGE

B.G. WEBB

authorHOUSE®

AuthorHouse™
1663 Liberty Drive
Bloomington, IN 47403
www.authorhouse.com
Phone: 1 (800) 839-8640

Published by AuthorHouse 01/20/2017

ISBN: 978-1-5246-6035-2 (sc)
ISBN: 978-1-5246-6034-5 (e)

Library of Congress Control Number: 2017900835

Print information available on the last page.

Any people depicted in stock imagery provided by Thinkstock are models, and such images are being used for illustrative purposes only. Certain stock imagery © Thinkstock.

This book is printed on acid-free paper.

Because of the dynamic nature of the Internet, any web addresses or links contained in this book may have changed since publication and may no longer be valid. The views expressed in this work are solely those of the author and do not necessarily reflect the views of the publisher, and the publisher hereby disclaims any responsibility for them.

to Truth and Courage

DEDICATION

TO ALL THE BRAVE AND COURAGEOUS MEN AND WOMEN
IN WORLD WAR II WHO GAVE THEIR LIVES
IN THE FIGHT AGAINST FASCISM SO THAT WE
MIGHT ENJOY THE BLESSINGS OF
FREEDOM AND LIBERTY

FOREWORD

In 1985 I was asked by my Great Aunt Rebecca Johnson to help her go through her papers -- both financial and personal. During the course of doing this, I came upon parts of a diary kept by her deceased son Mark David Johnson. The section that I found most revealing was the section that covered the year 1944. The diary gives a vivid account of what it was like to be on the home front during World War II. It relates the way people lived at that time and how they dealt with their ups and downs. Also, it gives a highly personal account of a young man coming into manhood and dealing with a totally unexpected challenge. The events of the war literally changed the course of Mark's life and those of his neighbors forever.

When I first read the diary, I felt that it should be published. However, when I proposed the idea, Aunt Rebecca objected because of the very personal nature of the account. Therefore, I waited until after her death to attempt to interest publishers in Mark's story. Now, after years of trying to have it appear in print, it is now out in the light of day for all to see. I hope that the readers will not only find that it brings to life an era that is gone forever, but some insight into how the people -- particularly the Johnson family and Mark in particular -- reacted in a time of crisis.

When I edited the diary I made every effort to keep it as close to the original as possible -- including the uneven grammar and spelling. For example, Mark usually never wrote out numbers. I have kept them that way. I also kept the material that he added in round "()" brackets. In reading the diary I discovered that certain sections contained numbers and punctuation marks. I concluded that Mark had worked out a code to keep certain personal observations secret. It took a long time to translate the code. And, I confess that I probably never would have been able to do it if I had not discovered the key on a folded piece of paper in one of Mark's German dictionaries that he had used in high school. I have indicated in the text what parts were in code. My translation is within square "[]" brackets.

Mark made weekly entries in his diary. I have added titles to them in order to give the reader an idea of some of the more important topics covered in each account. I have also added in square "[]" brackets within the text explanations of certain terms or references made by Mark. One of Mark's favorite pastimes was drawing small sketches of things that interested him. I found some in his diary and others in a special folder. I have included a lot of these sketches in the diary because they relate to things that he writes about.

In reading the diary I hope that people will find the work not only interesting in terms of history but in terms of how the people of that era tried to answer those age-old questions about the meaning of life.

B.G. Webb, Editor

Mark's Description of Himself and His Town and Neighborhood

So, how should I begin this diary? I guess with my name which is Mark David Johnson. I'm writing this first entry as I sit in my room located in my father's house on 11th Avenue in Milltown, Illinois. It is 7:30 P.M.

I decided to keep this diary because I agree with Mrs. Roosevelt that we are living in unusual times. We are all involved in the struggle to defeat Germany and Japan. It remains to be seen if we will be successful. We are only certain of two things -- that we are preoccupied daily with the war and that the result of the war will not only effect us but generations to come.

When I told my English teacher Miss Hennings about my idea to keep this diary, she thought it was a good one. Of course, she has always encouraged my desire to become a political journalist. She feels that the diary will help me learn a lot about what she calls "the human condition." She urged me to carefully observe and to listen to my surroundings -- that includes both things and people. -- and then to write down in detail what I have observed and what I think about what I have observed. Also, she told me to be sure to stress how people are reacting to situations. She finally said, "Mark, be sure to include yourself in this. Try to describe how you are reacting to people and to events. Be honest and describe everything. In order for you to develop as a writer, you must be honest with yourself and with the reader." I promised to share some of my entries with her in order to get her reaction and suggestions as to how I might improve my weekly accounts.

Well, for my first entry I want to tell you something about myself and the town I live in. As I indicated above I live in Milltown, Illinois which has increased its population to about 32,000 thanks to the many people who have moved to the city to work in the war industries. Milltown is located along the Mississippi River in Thoreau County. About 250 miles east of Milltown is Chicago, and Iowa City is about 100 miles west. The main industry in Milltown is farm equipment; the town's biggest employer is the Henry Boone Company. Of course, right now the company is producing more than farm implements. Like a lot of companies it is producing weapons of war or at least things that will assist in the war effort.

Most of the industrial plants in Milltown are located along the river. The main business district is located further up from the factories. On the steep hills or bluffs overlooking the river you find most of the people living in frame houses along tree-lined streets. Milltown is especially known for its beautiful tall elm trees that provide plenty of shade in the summer and brilliant shades of yellow in the autumn. Naturally, even up on the hills you find small business districts; each usually has a grocery store along with a hardware store, a movie theatre, tavern, restaurant, ice cream parlor, barber shop,

1

and beauty parlor. In most neighborhoods you will find a "mom and pop grocery" where people can buy a lot of basic food and household items along with catching up with the lastest gossip of the day.

Up the river on the Illinois side you find Andersonville (40,000). Down the river on the Illinois side you then find Milltown, East Milltown(17,000), and Rockville(3,000). In the middle of the river is a large island where the Arsenal is located. The Arsenal can be reached by several special bridges that are restricted only to those who have the proper military clearance. I have been told that it is the largest arsenal in the country. It certainly produces plenty of war materials; we often see railroad flat cars loaded down with cannons, tanks, jeeps, and military trucks. Some of these items are probably being produced by some of the Henry Boone plants. It is hard to know what items are coming from where.

Across the river in Iowa you find small cities like Bennington (3,000) and larger ones like Keyport (50,000). There is a suspension bridge that connects Bennington with Milltown. The bridge is one of the most beautiful man-made landmarks in the area; it was built during the 1930s as part of Roosevelt's New Deal program to put people back to work. The bridge provides a marvelous view of the Mississippi River. Whenever I go over it with my family and we stop to pay the toll, I always feel so small as I look down at the river and then look to the right and then to the left to see how the river flows through the valley. There is also an older bridge further up the river that connects Andersonville with Keyport.

I guess it is about time that I describe myself. I'm 17 years old and attend William McKinley High School. I'm only 5'8" tall but have a big-boned, muscular, compact body. I weigh in at 150 in the nude. I was named after both of my grandfathers -- Mark Johnson and David Mendell. I have been told by my Grandmother Mendell that I favor her side of the family -- the Goldmans. I have blond hair and black eyes. Grandma told me that my blond hair will eventually turn from a flaxen color to a golden auburn as I get into my 20s. That's what happened to all of Goldman children. I have what my grandmother calls a "man's nose" (meaning prominent) and a square jaw which I got from my father. I have been told that I have a friendly and wide smile when and if I decide to bestow one on someone. I'll admit that I tend to be a bit shy and reserved around people -- especially strangers. I'll also admit that I have a temper. I feel that I don't get angry unless I'm really pushed into defending my rights. But, I have been known to come out swinging if someone crosses me one too many times. Dad keeps telling me that it is alright to get angry but that I should keep my temper under control and try to find a positive way to solve problems rather than using my fists.

Some people think I'm smart because I take difficult courses and usually know the answers to questions that the teachers ask. One student gave me the nickname of "why" because I seem (at least to this girl) to always have the answer to the why questions in class. Actually, it comes from a lot of studying. Besides, if she could see me in chemistry class where I really have to struggle to maintain a low B average, she would know that her nickname for me doesn't fit.

Since I'm short and not very heavy, I have a hard time with such team sports as basketball and football. When I have gone out for sports, I have been more successful at swimming, playing baseball, and wrestling. I really enjoy water polo and wrestling. Both are really action sports that challenge a person to maintain one's body. I work out regularly and take great pride in my well developed body and hard muscles. Besides being in those sports, I am also on the newspaper (**The McKinley Herald**) staff and the annual (**The Mc**) staff. While I do some writing for both, I have been assigned mainly to work on layout and selling ads.

The only outside organization that I belong to besides the Riverside Presbyterian Church is the Boy Scouts. Frankly, while I like scouting, I don't care to go to meetings. Why? Because some of the bigger guys in the troop horse around too much. For example, they like to "depants" the new guys in the troop, and sometimes do more than that. Instead of going to Scout meetings, I would rather see a movie, listen to a comedy radio show, draw stekches of things that interest me, read a **Life** or **Time** magazine, or listen to a news analysis by H. V. Kaltenborn or my idol Edward R. Murrow. But, I go to Scout meetings because my parents -- especially Dad -- insists on my going. Dad keeps telling me "to set a good example" and "to stand up for the new comers." I do my best but it is easier to say those things than do them. But, to please Dad I try.

My neighborhood is called Hilltop Place by the people who live in it. Why? Because it is located on the very edge of one of the high hills or bluffs overlooking Milltown. The area contains a real mixture of people. There are individuals of great wealth and at the same time people who are barely getting by. There are professionals as well as blue collar workers living within the boundaries of Hilltop Place. While a few of the ladies in the neighborhood work, most stay at home and are homemakers. And, the latter are very proud to be described as a "homemakers" and can be very critical of those ladies who have recently taken jobs in the factories due to the need for more workers to produce goods for the war effort. While they realize that these ladies are supporting the war effort and at the same time are making good money -- especially if they work overtime --, they feel that these same ladies are neglecting their husbands and children. The "homemakers" are not so critical of those unmarried women who have to work to support themselves. But, they feel a certain amount of pity for them because they have not had the opportunity to marry and experience the joy of motherhood.

Hilltop place is the area within 16th Street on the West, 19th Street on the East, 11th Avenue on the North and 12th Avenue on the South. The area is partially bordered by a dense wooded area that is mostly in the northeast corner of the neighborhood. The woods mainly cover the steep hills and ravines found in the area. The kids like to go into the woods to built secret camps and engage in mock battles between the Americans and Japs or Americans and Germans. Before the war the battles were between the U.S. Cavalry and Indians but that has all changed now. Even some of the adults take to the woods to dig for worms, shoot squirrels, and pick wild flowers.

There are about twenty-five houses within the area. Most were built between

Map of Hilltop Place

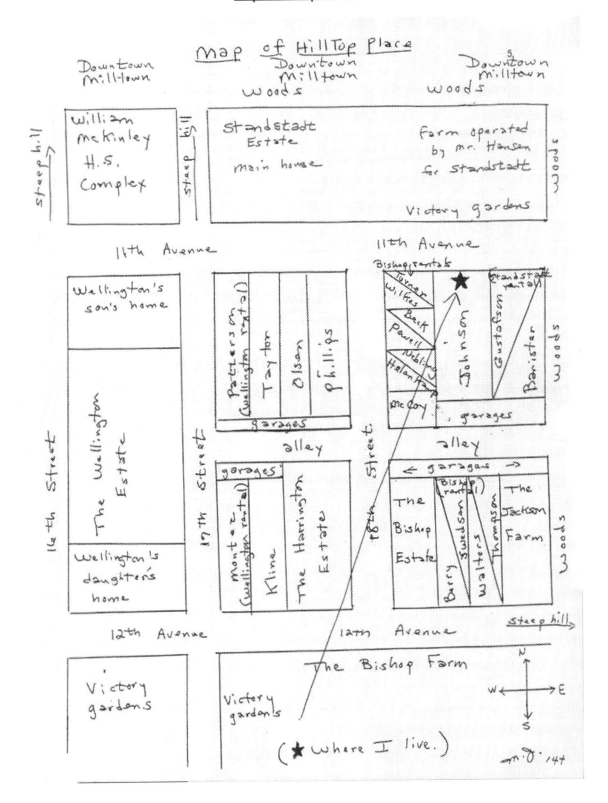

1900 to 1925. All are two story homes with large front porches and gabled roofs. Most are frame homes; a few of them have fireplaces. There are several large estates within the boundaries of the neighborhood. In fact, the land occupied now by private homes and rental houses used to belong to the ancestors of those living in the grand mansions on the estates. Also, some of the houses within Hilltop have been made into apartments; there are about eight houses like that. Finally, you find three small farms in the area. Two of them are used to supply vegetables and fruit for two of the estates. However, since the war started both have been used for Victory gardens. Every person in the neighborhood who expressed a desire to have Victory garden has been given a small plot on one of the farms connected with the estates. [I have included Mark's map of the area showing how the streets and avenues run, where various families live, where the great estates and farms are found, and finally where the woods are located.]

The thing that dominates all of our lives is the war. We are all wrapped up in the events going on in the world to beat the Nazis and Japs. I think that most of us sense how important the war is. Dad who is a veteran of World War I feels that the result of the war will determine the course of history for a hundred years -- maybe more. If the Fascists win, liberty as we know it will be like a long-forgotten dream. Ordinary people will exist to serve the rule of a military elite. Dad feels that this state of affairs will stiffle human creativity and progress not to mention the happiness of each individual to pursue whatever he wants. Dad compares the present situation facing mankind with the struggle against the South in 1860 and to the struggle against Napoleon in 1814. He exclaimed only the other day, "Holy Cow! (Dad's favorite phrase) If the South would have won the Civil War, the United States never would have become the influential nation that it is today. And, if Napoleon would have been allowed to dominate Europe, the course of history would have been greatly changed. The egomaniac would have probably hastened the development of the philosophy of Fascism."

Most of us have relatives serving overseas. Even a few of our neighbors are gone now because they have been drafted. We get plenty of war news over the radio, at the movies in the form of newsreels, at school in books, projects, and classroom discussions, and in our daily hometown newspaper **The Daily Herald** and magazines like **Life** (which Dad gets). Our daily newspaper is filled with maps, large photographs, and accounts of battles. Small protographs of local men and women killed, missing, or taken prisoner are a daily reality.

We all feel that we are part of the great effort for Victory because we buy war bonds, plant Victory gardens, give blood donations, save cans for the scrap drives, keep newspapers for the paper drives, dye our margarine to look like butter, go through mock airraids, collect fats and greases to make glycerin for high explosives, and do volunteer work to help with the war effort. Some of the women help out at the hospital and others at the Red Cross. Neighborhood kids have shows and circuses to raise money for veteran hospitals. We all use our ration books for such things as sugar, meat, gas, and shoes. Those families with members in the armed services display small flags with blue stars representing the sons and daughters engaged in the military effort to defeat the Germans and Japs If a star is gold, it indicates that a son or daughter has been killed. Most of us express our anger when he hear about people using the Black Market to get ration stamps, retread tires, butter, and sugar. While most workers are fully employed and make good money, they aren't spending it on consumer goods because they are in short supply. So, they have appliances, cars, etc. repaired if needed. This is nothing new. Ever since the Depression most of us are accustomed to keeping things up, improvising, and hoping that the quality named brand of coffee pot, waffle iron, stove, and refrigerator will last

Of course, sometimes things can't be fixed because of the lack of parts. So, what do you do? Well, you borrow from your neighbor or you car pool or you ride a Victory Bicycle to work. That's what. We are encouraged to do this by the OPA [Office of Price Administration]. One poster that we see a lot of is this: "Use it up/ Wear it out/ Make it do/ or Do without."

The Passing Parade

News Stories: "Yanks Driving on Cassino" and "Berlin Hit in Two Big Raids"

Song: Dinah Shore singing "I'll Walk Alone"

Movie: "Lassie Come Home" with Roddy McDowall (My little brother Buddy saw it twice.)

MARK'S FAMILY AND THE JOHNSON HOME ON 11TH AVENUE

As usual the newspapers have been filled with stories about the war. One that caught my eye was about how our men were trying to trick the Japs. It is a big thing if a Jap kills or captures an American officer. In order to protect themselves, the officers wear no insignia of any kind. Also, the privates are told to call their officers by their first names to protect them from Jap snipers.

I want to tell you about my family. Let me start with my father. His full name is Frederick Mark Johnson but everyone knows him as Fred Johnson. He grew up around Iowa City, Iowa. He has two older sisters named Emma and Maude and a younger brother named John. They still live in and around Iowa City. He works as a marketing consultant at the Henry Boone Farm Equipment Company. He was fresh out of the University of Iowa when he was hired there in 1925. He is 6'2", big-boned, with curly grey hair, blue eyes, and a firm square jaw. He is very out-going and approachable. He has a warm broad smile, a hearty laugh, and a welcoming handshake. He seems to be in command at all times. Dad says that his confidence came as a result of his experiences in World War I. He was only eighteen years old when he enlisted and quickly made sergeant as a result of what he calls "necessity." The officers in his unit were killed by German machine-gun fire and someone had to tell the men what to do. Dad did just that, and was rewarded with promotions. A month before the Armistice, Dad was severely wounded by a shell; you can still see the scars where the hot, sharp pieces of metal entered his body. When he strips down to put his swim suit on at the Milltown Public Pool or to use the shower in the basement, I have seen his body up close. There are scars on his back, arms and buttock. He was in a veteran's hospital for four months before he was released. He often says that he "had to grow up fast" when he was in the army and then usually adds that he doesn't "wish the experience on anyone."

Dad has a lot of interests, but the thing that really keeps him going is politics. He was elected to the Milltown City Council four years ago and expects to be reelected again this year. What is remarkable about his winning is that he is a Democrat and there aren't that many in Milltown. It is basically a Republican town. But, Dad got out there and campaigned and a lot of his friends (many fellow Masons) who are normally Republicans joined his campaign to spread the good word about him. So, he won about 52% of the vote. And, now he is on the Council and doing such a great job that he expects to be reelected. Dad's other interests are going fishing, playing poker with his buddies, working out cross-word puzzles, following the Chicago Cubs baseball team, reading biographies of political leaders, and taking care of his Victory garden.

He likes to take the family on trips to National Parks (Yellowstone) and historical places (Lincoln's home and tomb) but that is all in the past now with gas rationing. He could get a "B" sticker which would entitled him to have more gas than the average citizen. A few politicans even have "X" stickers for unlimited gas. But, Dad doesn't want to abuse his position as a Council member. So, he is content to have an "A" sticker like most people; it restricts him to 3 gallons a week.

Now, let me describe my mother. My mother's maiden name was Rebecca Mendell. She is called Becky by her many friends. She grew up in Chicago -- on the west side. She has a younger sister by the name of Ruth who still lives in Chicago. After attending business college she got a job at the Henry Boone Company and eventually met my father there. She was really taken with Dad. She told me that "he looked like a Greek god." According to Dad, Mom was gorgeous and reminded him of a blond Claudette Colbert -- the film star. Of course, when I look at the two of them, I do not see a Greek god or a Claudette Colbert. Both of them are now in their 40s; Dad is 45 and Mom is 41. Dad has a full head of hair but it has a lot of grey in it. Mom goes to a beauty parlor to keep her hair blond. Both wear glasses and have gained a few pounds since their courting days.

But, to get back to the story, Dad found himself very attracted to the young, slim, petite lady with the blond curly hair, large black eyes, and the ability to bring out the best in people with her friendly smile. The way he tells the story of their courtship, he decided that he was finished with shopping around for the right woman when he got to know Becky Mendell. And, I might add at this point that Dad had done a lot of shopping. When he was in France he had gotten to know to use his words "the pleasures of being with a woman." Anyway, once he got a taste of that experience, he wanted more and more and dated a lot. But, that all changed when he met Mom. After a short courtship they were married in a civil ceremony. Later, they both the joined the Riverside Presbyterian Church in Milltown and repeated their vows to each other in a private ceremony at the church.

What more can I say about her? She has a beautiful smile; she always greets people -- even total strangers -- with a smile. She wants to make a good impression and be liked. And does both. Grandma Mendell feels that Mom tries to appeal to the best side of every person she meets. Since Dad went into politics, Mom especially feels that it is her responsiblity to win over as many people as possible. She often says that she can identify with Mrs. Roosevelt and her efforts to help her husband by meeting all sorts of people and making friends with them.

Mom really seems to enjoy being a homemaker and doing volunteer work. If she has one interest outside of her family, it would be music. She plays the piano and organ for groups, weddings, and various Masonic related events. She is organist for her Order of Eastern Star and White Shrine chapters. Like her mother she enjoys gardening, quilting, crocheting, and reading fiction.

[Code: Mom seems very much in love with Dad and vice versa. My bedroom is next to theirs. At night, I often hear the sounds of the two of them making love -- the laughing and giggling before, Dad's heavy breathing as he plunges again and again into her, the bed springs moving along with their joined bodies, and finally the soft sounds of pleasure that come deep from within each of them.]

My little sister is named Carol, and she is 9 years old. Her full name is Carol Elizabeth Johnson. She is enrolled in the 4th grade at Willard Grade School. Carol does very well in school -- usually getting grades of "excellent" and "very good." She particularly likes reading and math. In fact, the other day she told me about one of the stories in her reader. It was about a family living in Norway and how they were part of the resistance movement. Then, in mathematics she said that they had to solve a problem about how many bottles of milk would be necessary to help feed twenty-five refugee families; the number of children in each family was given along with the average amount of milk consumed by a child per day. See what I mean. Everything is tied to the war in some way.

Carol, like me, has blond hair and black eyes but unlike me she is very petite. She has a real passion for horses; in fact, her dream is to own a horse someday. Naturally, she goes to every Gene Autry and Roy Rogers movie and collects pictures, books, and statues of horses. I have to admit that she knows a lot about them; in fact, she can name every type of horse and give you a detailed description of each one of them. Dad and Mom often take her out to Red Bud (a small town 25 miles from Milltown) to ride horses at a stable located on a nearby farm. Of course, she loves it. She has learned to ride a horse with the ease of someone born to the saddle.

Another thing that she dearly loves to do is to dress up -- really dress up -- to go to church or to the kids' Saturday matinee at the Roxy Theater up town on 15th Street. She usually wears a nice dressy blouse with a pleated shirt. Of course, she always wears some jewelry and takes her small patent leather purse. She is also very particular about the shoes she wears; she insists that they must match her purse and go with whatever outfit she has selected to wear. It is a miracle that she doesn't go the entire way and insist that she have a pair of white gloves. Mom and Dad feel that she is really cute when she does this. I think that she is just trying to be very fancy and put on airs. She probably hopes that she will be mistaken for the daughter of a millionaire. But, I'm in the minority about this. Even Grandma Mendell feels that I'm too critical of my little sister and joins Mom and Dad in thinking that Carol -- the all dressed up Carol -- is the cutest little girl that they have ever seen.

Buddy is my little brother. With his brown hair and blue eyes he looks like Dad. He is tall for his age so we think that he will someday be as tall as Dad. Buddy's full real name is Bernard Frederick Johnson. Of course, he got the Frederick from Dad. But, the Bernard came from the Mendell side. Bernard Mendell was my great grandfather's name. Mom wanted to call him "Bernie" for a nickname but Dad insisted on calling him "Buddy" after a comrade who died during the Great War. Dad won. "Buddy" it is. He is 7 years old and is enrolled in the 2nd grade at Willard. He really likes his current teacher -- Miss Lang. Why? Because she is always so patient and helpful. He had difficulty reading and Miss Lang spent a lot of extra time with him during recess and after school to help him sound out his words. Also, according to Buddy, she is always bringing things to class that he finds interesting. She brought an old electric train that she and her brothers had played with as children. She operated it on the floor of the classroom. I guess the class is studying different forms of transportation. Anyway, Buddy really enjoyed seeing Miss Lang's old train.

Buddy is in the Cub Scouts and really enjoys it. Recently, he became a Wolf after being a Bobcat. He especially likes making things after the regular line up activities (uniform inspection, giving the sign, motto, and salute, etc.) of the troop. Right now they are making wooden ducks for the lawn or garden. Buddy has three passions -- model planes, dogs, and peanut butter and mayomaise sandwiches. He spends hours in his room working with bamboo struts, balsa wood, wheels, and propellers to make his airplanes. Gluing the tissue paper to the assembled body of the plane takes a lot of time and patience. He has both. He enjoys flying his model planes outside on summer days. Dad often says that if Buddy dies, he hopes that God will have some materials to make model planes or to quote Dad, "Buddy will just pack up and leave." Buddy also collects statues of dogs and enjoys reading dog stories and seeing movies that feature dogs. He loved the movie featuring Lassie. Our dog Peggy often sleeps with Buddy when it storms outside. Peggy is very afraid of thunder and lightning and knows that Buddy's bed offers a safe haven.

At the present time Buddy is very much caught up with a Cub Scout project. The members of the troop are collecting discarded Christmas trees so that they can have a hugh bonfire. I think that they are planning to roast hot dogs and marshmellows after the initial blaze. Buddy goes from house to house asking for discarded trees. He always rings the doorbell and asks the home owner if he can have their Christmas tree that is usually parked next to the trash can or placed next to the house. If they say "yes" he drags the tree home to add it to the pile of trees that will be burned on the empty lot opposite our house. Actually, the lot is where Mr. Hansen grows vegetables for his employer Mr. Standstadt who lives in one of the large mansions nearby. Of course, a few people refuse to let Buddy take their trees; some of them like to use them as birdfeeders during the winter.

Mr. Hansen as the Cub Scout Master plans and supervises the actual burning of the trees. It is a sight to behold. Those kids usually collect about seventy-five trees. The neighbors often come in large numbers to witness the great event. You can smell the burning evergreen trees in the neighborhood for days afterward. The troop has been doing this for about five years now, and it has become a neighborhood tradition. Carol sometimes helps Buddy carry trees home if they are especially big ones. Naturally, she expects to be invited to the bonfire and the roasting of hot dogs that follow. In this she has never been disappointed.

To be honest, I often find both Buddy and Carol to be pests. I get tried of answering their many "why" questions. I have told them to stay out of my room so I can some privacy. They often come around when I'm talking with my buddies or a girl friend, and I usually tell them to leave. Mom doesn't like this. She feels that I should "be kind toward my little sister and brother." Dad usually sees my side to a certain extent. He'll say to Mom, "Holy Cow! A young man like Mark has to have some privacy." [Code: Another reason why I don't want Carol and Buddy coming into my room is because they may see me playing with my "cob." While I usually do this during the night, I sometimes have to do it in order to be able to concentrate on my studies. My penis sometimes gets so hard and ichy that I can't think of anything else but giving it -- to use one of my own creative phrases -- "a good husking." The darn thing gets so big, that it reminds me of a ear of corn surrounded by blond silks.] After a series of altercations between me and my brother and sister, Dad said that he had had enough. He met with Mom and Grandma to get their opinions and then called us all together and set down three rules for us to abide by. Here they are: We were all told to knock before we ever entered another person's bedroom. We were told to accept the person's decision to let us or not let us enter the room. And, the last rule was not to listen to telephone conversations or to private conversations.

Buddy and Carol get along pretty well. I guess it is because they are close to the same age. They walk to school together and have many of the same friends. Carol seems to like Buddy's company at the Roy Roger's movies and when she plays house. She orders him around a lot but he doesn't seem to mind as long as he is included in her latest project or mischief. The same goes for Carol. A lot of times she wants to be part of some of the games that Buddy has with his friends. It might be kick ball or making an army camp in the woods. All of this is fine with me since I find it difficult being an older brother to two small children. I love both of them but in small doses if you know what I mean.

My grandmother (my mother's mother) also lives with us. Her full name is Elizabeth Ruth Mendell and is close to 75 years old. She used to live in Chicago until Grandpa Mendell died in 1942. She spends most of her time reading, sewing, guilting, crocheting, and gardening in the summer. She is a very petite lady (5' 2", 100 lbs.) with white hair and black eyes. She wears gold-rimmed glasses with bifocals. She worked as a bookkeeper for about fifteen years back in the 1920s and 1930s. Dad has a lot of respect for her and says that "her mind is as sharp as a tack." Grandma is a modest, unassuming person with a warm smile and a willingness to listen. She is a hard worker too and does what she can to pull her weight. She doesn't want to be a burden. She has some money left from my grandfather's life insurance policies and from the sale of their home. Also, she receives a monthly check from Grandfather Mendell's business partner, Mr. Sherman Wisemann. The two men operated a drug store on the west side of Chicago for years. When Grandpa Mendell died, his partner offered to either buy out grandpa's half of the business or to share the profits with Grandma on a monthly basis. She decided on the monthly check, and she is happy that she went in that direction because the drug store has continued to be a money maker. She doesn't get 50% of the monthly profits because Mr. Wisemann and his sons are doing all of the work. However, she does receive 25% of the profits. So, right now she is getting about $200.00 a month. So, with that plus interest on the money that she has in the bank she is able to pay her way. And, she does so in a very generous manner. She pays for a percentage of our heating and grocery bills. While she is very religious, she only goes to our church occasionally. She usually stays home on Sunday in her room where she reads scripture and meditates.

The last member of my family is our dog Peggy. She is a toy fox terrier who has the run of the house. She is white with black ears and a small black spot on her forehead. She has one large black spot on her left side. Some of us call her "Duchess" because she has a mind of her own at times. While she is supposed to sleep in her own bed out in the hall on the second floor, she often, as I noted before, decides to sleep with Buddy -- especially if it rains and there is plenty of thunder.

1808 11 Avenue is our address. Our house sits on top of a small hill along with several others. Like a lot of houses in the area our house is a two story frame structure with a wrap around gingerbread front porch and a steep gable roof with dormers and a turret. We have some stained glass windows in the front door and in the formal living room on both sides of the fireplace which we seldom use since it gets so cold in the winter in Milltown. Besides the front parlor or formal living room we have a sitting room or informal parlor, a good size dining room, a large kitchen, and one bedroom on the first floor. Sliding wooden doors can be pulled out from the walls to separate the main rooms. We often do this during the winter months to save on coal and to make the living area warmer. Usually, we pull the sliding doors to close off the formal parlor from the rest of the rooms.

There is an open staircase that leads up to the second floor from the sitting room. Near the landing is a small table where our upright black telephone rests along with a phonebook and note pad. There are three bedrooms on the second floor along with a large bathroom. Also, there is a door leading up to the attic. It is sometimes used as a play room and an extra guest room if necessary. Sometimes relatives from Chicago and Iowa City visit. Dormer windows jut out from the attic on four sides and a person can get a good view of nearby houses and see neighbors coming and going. The imposing turret is on the right side of the house and is part of my parent's bedroom which faces 11th Avenue.

Grandma Mendell has the bedroom on the main floor while the rest of the family sleeps upstairs. Grandma has a chamber pot in the room in case "necessity" calls. Mom and Dad have the large front bedroom with the turret windows which give a person an excellent view of the Standstadt Estate. I have the small side bedroom on the second floor. My window overlooks the back of some of the rental houses on 18th street. Carol and Buddy share a large bedroom in the back of the house. Each has laid claim to one side of the room.

The house is decorated in a simple manner. Mom has kept the original walnut woodwork as it is; she refuses to have it painted. Dad with my help wallpapered the rooms in various colors and designs. We used floral patterns for most of the rooms. In the kitchen we used a pattern that features teapots and coffee pots. The wallpaper is ideal for older homes because it covers a lot of cracks in the plaster and gives the place a nice warm and friendly feeling. Our furniture is pretty basic; there are a lot of "hand-me-downs" and "make-me-overs" along with some fine antique pieces in various styles. We do have a handsome French provincial dining room set with a matching china cabinet made with cherry wood. We have a lot of old easy chairs and davenports that have been reupholstered with floral printed material. Our Turkish carpets are composed of elaborate designs in various shades of blue, beige and burgundy. They partially cover the walnut floors that mom insist be cleaned and waxed every four months at least. Of course our large RCA radio and Conn piano are in the informal or sitting room. We spend a lot of time in that room enjoying both of them., We also have a small radio in the kitchen to hear the morning and evening news while we eat. Also, I have a small wooden RCA radio in my room.

The kitchen has an oval table with six high back wooden chairs that have all been painted white. We have an old green colored gas stove that goes back to the early 1930s and a white refrigerator. The latter was purchased in 1941 and is one of Mom's special prides. It is certainly better than the old ice box that we used to have. Some of our neighbors still have ice boxes and rely on the ice man to bring them ice twice a week. Mom and Grandma do not mind the job of defrosting the refrigerator every 4th week or so. The kitchen has plenty of counter space for Mom and Grandma to prepare meals. The dishes and pots and pans are stored in built-in cupboards that have glass fronts. The kitchen floor is covered with a beige colored linoleum with squares going through it in a darker shade of brown--- more like cocoa.

Like a lot of people we haven't been able to buy a lot of replacements in our house because of the shortage of consumer goods due to the war. Because of the war a lot of people are making good money and are looking forward to spending it after the war on consumer goods. Meantime, we bank it and buy war bonds or both.

I should mention that like most of the houses in the neighborhood our garage is in the alley behind our house. Dad usually parks our 4-door black '39 Chevy there rather than in the front of the house. That way he doesn't have to walk up the cement stairs leading up to our house on the hill overlooking 11th Avenue. He also has a storage locker out in the garage for things pertaining to the car -- chains for the tires, oil, polish, etc. Also, we use the basement for a lot of things. Mom has her washing machine down there. It is a Maytag. It is old too; I think that it was purchased in the late 1930s. It is green and has a wringer. Mom has some extra tubs down there too. She uses them to rinse the clothes after they have been in the washing machine. Like most of the women in the neighborhood, she washes every Monday. Dad has a work bench in the basement and a cupboard for tools, fishing gear, and items (plumbing supplies, paint, etc.) that he may need to keep the house in good repair. Also, we store the storm windows and screens in the basement. Finally, there is a make-shift shower down there that is used only in the summer by Dad, Buddy, and me. It is a real help in making sure that everyone can take a bath or shower during the week. Usually, Mom and Grandma take their baths on Friday, while the rest of us take turns taking baths on Saturday and Sunday.

The Passing Parade

News Stories: "776 U.S. Wounded Brought Home from Africa on Floating Hospital" "Air-Bombarded Nazis Await Invasion"

Song: "Seems Like Old Times" by Guy Lombardo

Movie: "A Guy Named Joe" starring Spencer Tracy and Irene Dunne

Mark's Typical Day

I let Miss Hennings read my last week's entry and she especially liked the way I described my family. She told me "to keep up the good work." She liked the idea of including important news events in my accounts and noting what things -- like movies, songs, news stories -- were appearing.

During the week Carol sent a letter to President Roosevelt. She got the idea from Buddy. He had read a story in **The Daily Herald** about a 10 year old girl who wanted a cocker spaniel to keep her company while her dad was overseas in North Africa. Her mom could not afford to pay the high price for such a dog. The girl sent a letter to the President asking him to lower the price of dogs. President Roosevelt passed on the request to the O.P.A. [Office of Price Administration] and someone in that office provided her with a dog -- free. She named it Bamby. Carol sent a letter to the President about lowering the price of horses so that Dad could afford to buy one for her. She is probably hoping for a free one from the O.P.A. We'll have to see what happens. Of course, in Carol's case Dad isn't overseas.

Another newspaper story that Buddy saw was about a dog named "Chips" who won a Purple Heart and a D.S.C. [Distinguished Services Cross]. Why? Because he helped capture a machine-gun nest in Italy. Chips ran into the German bunker and attacked the Germans maning the machine-guns while the American troops finished the job. Buddy cut out Chip's picture and placed it on his bulletin board that is up on the wall in the bedroom that he shares with Carol.

I figure that if Eleanor Roosevelt can write about her day in her newspaper column, so can I. So, here is a running account of my typical day -- at least during the winter months.

6:45 A.M.   I get up and put on my heavy bathrobe and warm bedroom slippers and go down to put more coal in the furnace. Keeping the fire going down there is vital to the start of the day. The entire family likes a warm house to get up to. As I do this I usually put Peggy out in the fenced back yard. By the time I have the fire really going again, Peggy is ready to come back into the house and rejoin Buddy upstairs. Dad and I share the job of the furnace. It is easier to get it going again if there are some hot coals in it -- otherwise you have to start with newspapers and kindling. According to what the government has told us, we are supposed to set our thermostats at no more than 65 degrees in order to save on fuel. That's hard for us to do because we don't have a thermostat with our old heating system. Besides, it is very difficult to evenly heat our old two story house.

7:00 A.M.   I use the bathroom to shave and wash up. I am able to make good time if there is hot water. But, if the furnace has really cooled down, I have to heat up some water in the tea kettle on the kitchen stove. I try to clean up fast because I know that others will need to use the bathroom. Usually, the water that is stored in tanks by the furnace is hot enough if the fire has been kept going during the night.

7:15 A.M.   By this time, if I'm lucky, I am putting on my long underwear, heavy socks, dress pants, a dress shirt, and a sweater. After I get dressed I usually go down to see if the milkman has been here. He leaves us three bottles of milk every other day of the week -- Monday, Wednesday, and Friday. Before the war he came every day. But, because of gas and and rubber rationing, dairy companies had to limit their services.

7:30 A.M.   I eat breakfast. Grandma and Mom usually serve eggs, fried potatoes, toast with jelly if we have some left from the cellar where the home made canned goods are stored, and, of course, oatmeal. We eat a lot of that. Since sugar is rationed, we do not have pancakes, waffles, and sweet rolls very often These are reserved for Sundays or special occasions like a birthday breakfest. Sometimes we have orange juice or prune juice to go with this meal. Often we listen to the morning news on the small radio in the kitchen.

7:50 A.M.   I go back to my room to get my books and school supplies and then walk the two blocks to William McKinley High School. If I see Irene Phillips or Dave Patterson I walk with them; both live in the neighborhood. Carol and Buddy leave later for Willard because school starts later for them -- about 9:00. The high school complex is at the top of the 16th street hill; it is composed of two large dark red brick buildings that overlook the downtown area of Milltown. One goes back to the late 19th Century and has a lot of -- to use Grandma Mendell's word -- "character." It is noted for its imposing high square tower that can be seen from miles around. The other structure was built in 1915 and is very functional in its design. But, it does lack that Victorian splendor that Grandma so admires.

8:00 A.M.   After leaving my jacket, cap, gloves, and some of my books in my first floor locker, I go to my 1st period class. This semester I have Public Speaking with Miss Grant. The class is challenging but rewarding. Miss Grant has taught us the basic techniques of public speaking and now class members take turns giving speeches on topics suggested by Miss Grant. Some of the topics have been the following: "The Most Influencial Person in My Life;" "My favorite Hobby or Fun Activity and Why;" "Where I Would Like to be Ten Years From Now." She has restricted us to about five minutes on these speeches. She will assign more complicated topics later. She also talked about having some debates about the upcoming election or some other more involved topic. But, right now, she feels that we need to feel at home in front of an audience and learn how to project our voices and organize and present a short talk. She is a very fine teacher and has been at McKinley High for many years. She looks to be in her late 40s. She is rather plump and has grey hair that is short and curly. She projects her voice in a strong manner when she gives notes about the proper method of speaking. While she can become very angry with students who offend her, she has a wonderful sense of humor and a hearty laugh when she finds something to be very funny.

9:00 A.M.   By this time I'm in my second period class which is Chemistry. Today we were in the lab to work on an experiment. Jerry my lab partner wasn't too trilled with my lack of enthusiasm. If only I had a better background in math and science, I could feel more secure. Oh well, tomorrow we'll be back in the regular lecture room to take notes and to observe Mr. Howe present an experiment. I like that better than being in the lab. Poor Mr. Howe! I often sense that he is really trying to be patient with my dull brain. He is a young teacher; I guess he might be about 32. He is short (about 5'6'), has plenty of brown curly hair, and has a lot of enthusiasm for his subject. He is married and has two small children. I guess he got a draft deferment because he has two children and can teach chemistry. Someone has to be on the home front to teach kids about chemistry. He does a good job. I admire his patience and willingness to explain things again and again and again.

10:00 A.M. I am in my English Literature class taught by Miss Hennings. She is a very short lady -- about 5' in height -- with a full figure. She always wears taffeta dresses that probably have been custom made for her by a local seamstress. She has a round, friendly face that is framed with bangs and curls. By the way, despite her age (62) she doesn't have any grey or white hairs as yet. I guess she has her hair dyed at the beauty shop. Today Miss Hennings lead a discussion about Alexander Pope's "Rape of the Lock." I actually answered a few questions correctly. We also reviewed rules of footnoting for our research papers.

I really like Miss Hennings. I had her for American Literature last year and found her to be very nurturing. That's what I need sometimes. Besides, she really loves literature. She often says that she is giving us "something that will enrich our souls." She has her favorite authors. Last year it was Edgar Allan Poe. This year it is William Shakespeare. Despite being in her 60s, Miss Hennings has a youthful spirit and an engaging sense of humor. She has always made the study of English -- especially the literature part of it-- a joy. And, naturally, I also appreciate the fact that she has encouraged me to keep this diary and to stay on course with my desire to be a political journalist. She often tells us to have a dream -- a goal - and to pursue it and not give up.

11:00 A.M. I am in U.S. Government class. All seniors have to take this class for one semester. While a lot of students have mixed feelings about the class because it is a requirement, I am finding that I really enjoy it. Mr. May teaches the class. He is about 50 years old, 6'1" tall, and lean. He wears thick glasses. He usually has a very intense, serious expression. He is a very exciting teacher; he really knows his subject. He told us that he holds a M.A. in political science from the University of Chicago. Anyway, he certainly knows a lot of colorful stories about past politicians as well as being able to explain the political theories behind the federal system of government.

He starts the class by asking us about current events. Today, we talked about the war in Europe and the coming invasion of France by the Allied forces stationed in England. Also, we discussed whether F.D.R. should run again. I said, "Yes." Mr. May asked me to defend my position in detail. It was obvious to me that he doesn't believe that any man should have more than 2 terms as President and, of course, F.D.R. will be going for a 4th term. I defended his 4th try by saying that F.D.R. is the best one to work with other world leaders in making a lasting peace after the war is over. I argued that he has already worked with Churchill and Stalin and therefore knows what the situation is with regard to those two. "Besides," I continued, "F.D.R. has done a very good job directing the war effort by appointing able people to do the job and by trusting the wisdom of his generals." I argued that it doesn't make sense to "change horses in mid-stream, especially if that horse is doing a good job." I also argued that "F.D.R. is commited to the establishment of a United Nations organization to keep the peace after the war." I stressed that "some other candidate for the Presidency may not have the determination needed to make such a world organization a working reality."

Mr. May who I think is a Republican wasn't too impressed with my arguments. He argued that whoever is elected will have a difficult time. He stressed that "F.D.R. isn't indispensable." He reminded me and the entire class that it is "going to be difficult for any president to get capitalistic countries to work with a communist nation like the Soviet Union." "Besides," he continued," even the United States and Great Britain do not argee on everything." He reminded me that "Churchill is still in love with the idea of empire -- especially the British one." And, he ended by saying, "This idea of the United Nations preventing and resolving conflicts is still in the dream stage. How will it be organized? What will be the role of the great powers in it? Will small countries be willing to cooperate in an organization that will be dominated by the great powers?"

After that lengthy exchange, we discussed the homework about the federal system and how it works. Mr. May used diagrams on the chalkboard to illustrate the federal system and how it works. I took detailed notes. Since I would like to be a political journalist someday, I really find this course interesting and right up my alley sort of speak. A lot of other students in the class do not share my enthusiasm. They view U.S. Government as a requirement and therefore something that they must endure to graduate.

12:00 A.M. This semester I have my lunch break during the first lunch period. I usually go home since I live so close. Besides, the lunch room is usually very crowded, and I find I hate the noise. Dad usually comes home too unless he is really busy. Then, he has a working lunch at a nearby lunch counter. Buddy and Carol also come home. Mom and Grandma usually serve warm soup and sandwiches during the winter months. We usually eat in the kitchen. If the house is cold, Dad or I shovel in some more coal in the furnace. It is a nice time for everyone because we all get a break and are able to catch up on how our morning went.

1:00 P.M. By now I am in my German II class with Mr. Fogel. He is about 60 years old, bald, with heavy thick glasses. He is very precise in his manner and teaching. He explains things in great detail -- often repeating the sounds of words or rules of grammar. German II is a challenging class but Mr. Fogel makes it enjoyable. He has a dry wit and warm smile.

17

When he makes a humorous remark or tells a humorous story, he peers over his glasses to add to the moment. Besides that, being a musician he often sings a German rule of grammar in a loud bass voice so that we will not forget it. Believe me, I don't! Anyway, I think you get the idea -- Herr Fogel is full of surprises and is quite a character. Today, we did some translation from a mystery story and then we worked on irregular verbs. We also heard again Mr. Fogel's defense of the German language. He reminded us that just because there are a few bad Germans -- like Hilter -- doesn't mean that all Germans are bad or that the language is. He pointed out to us that during a war the peoples who are engaged in it often have wrong images of each other. Why? "Because," he said, "the leaders and the press tell their people that all the people on the other side are monsters -- animals only fit to be shot." Then, he told us that there were some people in Milltown who felt that the subject of German should not be taught at McKinley High School. "But," he proclaimed, "he hoped that the forces of good would continue to dominate the Board of Education and would resist such ideas."

2:00 P.M.   I'm off to the YMCA on 5th Avenue for swimming class. Since I'm good at swimming, this is one P.E. class that I really enjoy. I have the class three days a week. On the other days I have a study hall in the library on the second floor. The class is taught by Mr. Zarek. Despite the fact that he is in his late 40s, he looks like Tarzan -- only older. He is about 6 foot tall and very muscle bound; his upper arms and thighs are well developed and muscular. He has a deep, manly voice and presence. You know right away that you better behave or you will be in real trouble. He is a great teacher in terms of teaching swimming strokes and saving a person from drowning. We usually have warm up exercises and then participate in some team swimming relays using various strokes. We also play water polo on some days. [Code: This is all done in the nude which I find embarrassing. I don't care to have my bear ass and dangling circumcised pecker and balls on display. My pal Dave Patterson has told me that he feels the same way. Since he is one of the few Negoes in Milltown, the guys view his body as a curiosity. In my case my amble "fruit basket" dangling between my legs is enough to make me a curiosity too. I should mention that most of the guys in the class are not circumcised so when they are arroused, you can hardly see their "heads." In my case when I'm "in heat" sort of speak, it is fully evident.]

3:00 P.M.   After I shower, I leave the YMCA building to walk up the steep 17th Street hill to my neighborhood. When I get home I usually have a snack of some kind - usually cookies and Ovaltine. I take my books up to my room and set them aside to work on homework later.

4:00P.M.   Usually by this time Lennie Osgood our newspaper boy has delivered **The Daily Herald** so I'm able to glance over it before Dad gets home. While I'm doing that, Mom and Grandma are usually listening to soap operas. Their favorite is "Portia Faces Life." Carol and Buddy usually arrive home and play games in the living room or, if it isn't too cold, go outside to play. We are usually downstairs because the upstairs doesn't heat too well.

4:45P.M.   While Grandma and Mom are making supper, Buddy and Carol and I listen to "Dick Tracy."

5:00 P.M.   We all listen to the Associated Press News. Today, most of the news is about the fighting in Italy and in the Marshall Islands.

5:30 P.M.   Dad arrives home and relaxes by talking to Mom and the rest of us. Grandma is usually putting the finishing touches on supper. Buddy and Carol listen to "Jack Armstrong" on the radio.

6:00 P.M.   We have supper in the dining room. Supper usually consists of some meat -- again if ration stamps are available -- with baked potatoes and vegetables. Otherwise, we have things like spaghetti, stew, ham and navy beans. Some of the vegetables that we enjoy eating were canned last summer from what we produced in our Victory garden. We usually grow lettuce, green beans, tomatoes, and cabbage as well as the usual salad items. We seldom have a desert because, like I wrote before, sugar is rationed so much. A pie or cake is reserved for special events or Sunday dinner.

7:00 P.M. - 10:00 P.M.   I usually do my homework during this time. I try to spend at least 35 minutes on each solid subject. I have a radio in my room and I like to listen to some of the programs if I can spare the time. On Wednesday, I like "Suspense" at 7:00 and "Abbott and Costello" at 9:00. Tuesday is my favorite radio day because so many comedy shows are on. There is "Febber McKee and Molly" and then "The Bob Hope Show" and finally that crazy Red Skelton comes on.

10:00 P.M.   I go down to check on the furnace again if it is my turn. Also, I fill up the pans of water that we keep in the registers that cover the furnace pipe outlets so that there is enough moisture in the air.

10:20 P.M.   I'm in bed.

The Passing Parade

News Stories: "When Daddy Marches Off to War"
"As the Hour of the Great Invasion of Europe Approaches"

Song: "I'll Be Seeing You" by Jo Stafford

Movie: "Thank Your Lucky Stars" with Bette Davis and Errol Flynn

THE GREAT ESTATES

The Allied Forces have landed at Anzio. That's what we heard this morning on the radio. The Germans are fighting hard to maintain their positions and to push the Americans back into the sea. Dad said that he knows that casualties will be high. He feels a real closeness with the men doing the fighting. He told us that before some of the battles that he participated in during World War I, he would vomit and have to relieve himself out of fear.

While our men -- and Grandma Mendell would insist here that I include the women too -- are facing death in Italy and in the Gilbert Islands, some people in this country are going on strike. I'm talking about the steel workers especially. It was reported in the newspaper that a lot of service men are writing letters to protest the lack of support from the striking workers on the home front. One naval officer said, "If these strikers could see some of the bloody battles, they would see things differently." He referred to the case of nineteen year old Jack Stambough who was killed after trying to save his buddy. The marine killed three Japs before a Jap officer sneaked up behind him and killed him with a saber. Dad feels that the government should force striking workers back to work even if it has to use troops to do it.

I want to start describing most of the people who live in the neighborhood. I'll do it by reporting about what is going on within Hilltop in the next few entries in my diary. I have gotten to know the residents because so many of them have lived in the area for ten to twenty years -- in some cases more than that. I guess the Great Depression made it impossible for many to move. Others probably stayed because they liked the atmosphere of Hilltop Place. Then, of course, the war caused some to delay their plans to move until things were more certain again.

Just about everyone knows everybody else. The exception would be those of great wealth who rarely, if ever, have much to do with most of the rest of us Hilltop residents. Now, out of fairness, I will correct that general statement. The Bishop family does socialize a lot with us. They are all up in years and it could be that they see their common humanity with the rest of us. So, I stand corrected with regard to the Bishops. They do reach out to others -- especially since the Depression and the War. However, if we see the others who live on the great estates at all, it is either when they are being driven from and to their great mansions in their 4 door sedans -- mostly Buicks and Lincolns -- or when they go to visit some of their servants who live in their rental houses near by.

Of course, the other exceptions are the people who move in and out of the rental units. But, even there you find many people renting the same apartment for five to ten years. And, in the process of living there so long, they come to know others in the neighborhood.

In Hilltop Place the neighbors generally have gotten to depend on each other; they share their ups and downs, their views about the war and other neighbors, their hopes and dreams. Most feel responsible for all the children in the neighborhood. They do not hesitate to correct a child if he is doing something wrong -- especially something dangerous that might injure him or others. In a way I think that most of us know each other better than many of our own relatives who usually live in other cities and states.

As the map indicates there are many great estates in our neighborhood. The Standstadt estate is especially huge. The family's large three story frame victorian mansion with its many gables and chimneys sits on the very edge of a steep hill overlooking Milltown. A greenhouse, barn, swimming pool and club house are only a few of the buildings on the property. The Standstadt family helped establish the farm equipment industry in Milltown over 80 years ago. Mr. Harold Standstadt and his wife Florence have two grown children. Their gardener Mr. Olaf Hansen and his family are provided with a large home nearby the estate. Their house is on several acres of land that is used for growing flowers, vegetables and fruit trees for use by the Standstadt household. Mr. Standstadt's butler a Mr. Arvid Gustafson lives with his wife Caroline next to us in one of the rental homes owned by Mr. Standstadt. Caroline works at the mansion whenever her services are needed. During the winter months the couple accompany the Standstadts to their Palm Beach estate in Florida. There, they live in a small ocean front cottage that is located near the main house.

The Wellington estate is also quite impressive. Mr. and Mrs. Gordon Wellington live in a magnificent Tudor style mansion. He is connected with a wide assortment of banking, real estate, and borkerage enterprises in Milltown. Homes for their married children have been built adjacent to the main Wellington estate. Their daughter lives in a charming white Cape Cod home while her brother lives in a ground-hugging brick home designed in the style of a Frank Lloyd Wright home with simple lines, plenty of glass windows, and practical features like overhanging roofs. None of us know much about the Wellingtons. As I said before, many of the rich are only seen leaving from and returning to their private compounds. In this case it resembles a fortress because the entire Wellington property is surrounded by a high brick wall with iron gates.

The Wellingtons own two rental homes across the street from their estate. One is occupied by Mr. and Mrs. Theodore Patterson and their son Dave. They are Negroes. They have lived in the house for at least twenty years. Olivia Patterson is the Wellington's housekeeper. She grew up in Mississippi. She got to know Mrs. Wellington as a child because her mother was Mrs. Wellington's nanny. Mr. Patterson works as a janitor in one of the Henry Boone plants. Their son Dave is in my class and is very much interested in basketball and music. He has a rich baritone voice that has earned him roles in several musicals produced at the high school. Like his father, he is very tall -- 6'2" -- and has a face with striking African features. Unlike his father, he has a light brown complexion like his mother. We have gotten to know each other because we grew up together as children in the neighborhood.

Their other rental house is occupied by a Mexican family by the name of Montez. Mr. Jose Montez works as a machinist on the Arsenal. He and his wife Angela have three children -- Maria who is my age, Rose who is 15, and a 13 year old son by the name of Tony. He goes to Walt Whitman Junior High School. As far as anyone knows, they are American citizens. Mr. Montez came to live in our area after the war started; he had heard about the need for more workers at the Arsenal. I have really gotten to know Maria and Rose; they are both very attractive and have outgoing personalities. They are involved in a lot of school activities. Rose is a cheerleader while Maria plays the flute in the band.

Another estate belongs to attorney George Bishop. His mansion is a large, white frame two-story home featuring an impressive front portico with Ionic columns. Its dormers, chimneys, and railings are positioned in perfect balance with one another. Mr. Bishop is about 75 years old and looks very distinguished with his white hair and well-tailored suits. The only flaw in his image is his large red bulbous nose. He is an out-going, friendly man who usually waves at his neighbors from his '39 black Buick 4 door sedan and enjoys chatting with them when he takes his daily walk in good weather. When he was widowed for the second time about 13 years ago, he invited his two sisters -- Mrs. Moore and Mrs. Wells -- to live with him. Both are widows in their mid 60s. Then, when his brother Fred lost his wife, he came to live with his brother and sisters. While Mr. Bishop's sisters are genteel and aloof, Fred is about 72 and outgoing like his brother but more down to earth. Since he used to farm on the old family homestead outside nearby Red Bud, he has created a large garden-like farm opposite the large two story Bishop mansion on 12th Avenue. Fred dresses like a farmer too. I can't remember ever seeing him in a suit. He usually wears coveralls, plaid shirts, and work shoes. He has become a friend to many of us. He reminds me of Abe Lincoln. While Fred isn't as tall as good old Abe, he is lean and has a rustic face with a kind, friendly expression that has endeared him too all. He knows everyone who rents apartments from his brother. In the spring he goes around selling his home grown strawberries and cherries; in the fall he is selling home made apple cider and pumpkins. This gives him plenty of opportunity to talk with the his neighbors about the latest news and gossip. The kids especially like to see him come with his produce because they know that they will get a friendly pat and a warm smile from Fred.

Finally, there is the Harrington estate with its imposing Victorian mansion. It has two towers that overlook the neighborhood. One is Gothic and the other is Tuscan in design. Like the other mansions except the Bishop estate it is enclosed by a protective brick wall. Mr. Ronald Harrington heads one of the largest law firms in Milltown. He and his wife Catherine are very active socially. They make a handsome couple -- so well dressed and attractive. Both remind one of Hollywood stars -- Ronald Coleman and Katherine Hepburn types. Many feel that both are snobbish because they rarely condescend to speak to anyone in the neighborhood who they consider not of their social class. The Harringtons have two sons -- Edward and Paul. I know Ed very well because he is also in the 12th grade with me; he is good in sports -- especially baseball. Otherwise, Ed isn't the greatest student or for that matter human being in the world. [Code: He is very aggressive and loud, likes to bully other guys, and tells obscene jokes.] In my opinion he is a very obnoxious individual who is very spoiled. His younger brother Paul is in grade school and is shy, quiet, and studious. He is one of Buddy's good friends. He often plays with Buddy and Carol. Once in a while he goes to the movies with them. Recently, Mrs. Harrington's mother, a Mrs. Miller, came to live with them after the death of her husband.

The Passing Parade

News Stories: "Those WAC Hats Are Under Fire"
"Allies 12 Miles Inland Below Rome"

Song: "Moonlight Becomes You" by Bing Crosby

Movie: "Guadalcanal Diary" with William Bendix and Anthony Quinn

A Death March, Preparing Departure Bags, and A Boy Scout Meeting

The news programs and the newspapers are filled with stories about what happened to our men and, yes Grandma, our women too who were captured in the Philippines. The report stated that the Japs tortured and murdered U.S. prisoners. Some Americans were beheaded. Others were beaten to death after being forced on a long march which is being called a "Death March." It has been reported that the Americans and Filipinos would not have surrendered had they known the fate in store for them. President Roosevelt promised that those responsible would be punished after we win the war. People are really upset about this news. There is a real hatred for the Japs for their surprise attack on Pearl Harbor -- and now this. No wonder the kids in the neighborhood enjoy playing Americans and Japs. The kids get such a terrible image of the Jap anyway from movies, radio programs, and posters. Like Mr. Vogel said in German class, those engaged in a war make each other appear like animals that are only fit to be slaughtered. Did the average Japanese solider have this view of their American and Filippino prisoners of war? Does this explain their behavior? Are some of our military people doing the same against the Japanese and Germans?

Mom and Grandma spent two days this week working at the Red Cross Center. They worked with Mrs. Moore and Mrs. Wells and others. Mom and Grandma have really gotten to know "the Bishop girls" as the two women have been nicknamed at the center. When they first started working there, they showed up so well dressed that Grandma thought that there was going to be a tea party; they even had white gloves on. But, once they were told what they were going to do, they took off their gloves and got to work. The ladies have been preparing dressings and so-called "departure bags" for the war effort. The bags have to be packed with eleven essential items and are given to departing service men. Mom and Grandma are some of the few in the neighborhood who call "the Bishop girls" by their first names -- Opal (Mrs. Moore) and Hazel (Mrs. Wells).

One good thing about the war is that it does bring people from different backgrounds in contact so that they get to know each other better. My family thinks that is a real good outcome of the present war situation. Dad often refers to the Roosevelts as a rich family that has tried to reach out to people in all walks of life. He told me that they take a real interest in the people of their county --Dutchess county -- as well as people of all walks of life throughout the country. He feels that they set a good example. He wishes more people of wealth like the Bishops would become involved with the community. Of course, he agrees with Mom and Grandma that the middle class and those with limited resources

23

must also be willing to respond to the wealthy when they make an effort to work with others in the community. It is a two way street. If only people of various economic levels would be willing to reach out to each other, it would help end conflicts. Many times we have wrong images of each other. By working together, we get to know one another as individuals.

I went to Boy Scouts at Olaf Hansen's house across the street. He and his wife Christine are originally from Norway. They had first settled in Chicago until Mr. Hansen answered Mr. Standstadt's ad in the **Chicago Tribune** for a gardener. Two of his four sons belong to our troop of Scouts. I think that Mr. Hansen took on the job of being in charge of groups of Cub Scouts and Boy Scouts because he wanted to be accepted as an American. He and his wife never speak Norwegian in public and do a lot of volunteer work in the community in order to fit in better. Mrs. Hansen is the den mother to the troop of Cub Scouts. Most agree that they have been successful. Only the Harringtons have been overheard saying negative things about them and labeling them as "outsiders"; they use the same term when talking about the Montez and Patterson families. Of course, they look down on all the renters in the neighborhood; they consider them "poor white trash." Grandma Mendall especially admires the Hansens. She told me that she remembered stories told by her father about how difficult it was for the Goldmans to immigrate here from Germany and how much adjustment they had to make -- master a new language, learn about the operation of the U.S. government, and adapt to a lot of so-called American customs like Thanksgiving and 4th of July celebrations. "Nobody knows the difficulty of trying to be a citizen of another country until they have had to do it," declared Grandma with a lot of emphasis on "until they have had to do it." And, then she added her usual line, "Until you walk in their shoes, don't judge."

At the Boy Scout meeting this week we first went through inspection and then we worked on various projects and skills for our merit badges. The Hansens have fixed up a room in their basement for crafts and a lot of us go down there to work. On the way home there was the usual horsing around. It started with a snowball fight between Carl Winters and his pals and Mark Trotter and his gang. It ended with Trotter's gang forcing Winters and his buddies to make a run for it. Trotter's gang caught up with some of the slowpokes and pinned them to the cold snow covered ground and then filled up their pants with snow. You could hear the victims yelling all over the neighborhood.

Another yelling incident took place late Friday night when Jim Banister and Kelly Jackson came home drunk and started singing some of the tavern songs that they enjoy so much. It must have been 1:00 A.M. when this happened. Kelly had his dog Pal with him and it started barking. Kelly often gives his dog a beer at the tavern so that the poor dog gets as drunk as his master. Mrs. McCoy and other neighbors who live in Mr. Bishop's rental houses along 18th Street told the threesome to shut up and go home and go to bed. Their appeals were ignored and Kelly told them that nobody was going to tell him what to do. The two guys hang around together a lot. Jim works as a mechanic at the General Motors Garage in downtown Milltown while Kelly is a machinist at one of the Henry Boone Farm Equipment plants.

The yelling finally stopped when Dorothy Banister and Cora Jackson appeared and told their husbands to come home. Both women are church-going and have a hard time dealing with their husbands. Anyway, Dorothy led Jim up the stairs that lead to their apartment over the Gustafsons where they live with their two sons -- Henry who is my age and Timmy who is one year older than Buddy. Meantime Cora took Kelly and his dog Pal to their home on 12th Avenue. They live in the downstairs while Kelly's mother and his aunt live in the upstairs apartment.

Two more men in the neighborhood have been drafted. Bob Thompson who lives with his wife Ethel in an apartment on 12th Avenue told several neighbors that he had gotten his draft notice. He is taking it pretty well. He declared, "It is no more than right since I don't have any children to worry about." Ethel isn't so sure. She only married Bob four years ago and was looking forward to having children once they could afford a family. Bob works at Sears and she has a job as a clerk at the New York Store in downtown Milltown. People really warm up to her because she has such a beautiful warm smile and caring manner.

The other draftee is Glen Swedsen. He and his wife Anna also live in an apartment on 12th Avenue. He is a tall, handsome, friendly guy who works at **The Daily Herald** in the Circulation Department. Anna is taking the news hard. She is a small, shy, sickly lady who depends very much on her husband's support. She knows that it will be difficult to continue to rent their apartment on the small army salary. She may have to move in with Glen's parents who live in nearby Andersonville. Her own folks live in northern Iowa on a farm, and she would rather not move in with them because she would have to leave a lot of her friends in Milltown.

The Passing Parade

News Stories: "Nation Angered by Jap Atrocities"
"How Should Hitler Be Punished?"

Song: "My Devotion" by Vaughn Monroe

Movie: "The Cross of Lorraine" with Jean Pierre Aumont and Gene Kelly

180 8 11ᵗʰ Avenue

A R.R. Accident, Two Widows, A Coffee, "K.O. 1 Jap"

Two WACs [Women's Army Corps], and a Marine were killed today but not on some battlefield overseas but in Milltown. They were in a car that was hit by a Rock Island freight train at the railroad crossing near fifth avenue. Todd Wilkes who works for the railroad told Grandma that the three had met each other at a bar and had been drinking heavily. The driver, the Marine, drove around the guard rail in an attempt to beat the train and get across. Todd who lives with his wife Lily and his four year old son Danny in one of the Bishop apartments told Grandma that he was one of the first to reach the scene of the accident and that there were body parts in the car and on the tracks. He said it was the worst accident that he had ever seen. Grandma blames the war. She feels that young people tend to live for the moment and take chances for a little fun in wartime. They expect that the worse thing may happen once they get into thick of the fighting. In this case the worst happened right in Milltown, U.S.A.

Dad gave Aunt Rose a ride up the 16th Street hill. He couldn't miss the bent-over figure with her white hair and distinctive walk that is slow and seeming painful as she puts her weight on one side and then the other. She isn't really related to us; she is Kelly Jackson's aunt. However, she is called Aunt Rose by everyone in the neighborhood. It is a form of endearment. Dad saw her walking up the steep hill after completing her work cleaning offices in downtown Milltown. She often buys her groceries after working hours. Dad felt sorry for her because she was carrying two bags of groceries and obviously was having a hard time. When she goes to our local "mom and pop store" on 10th Avenue near our neighborhood, she puts her groceries in a cart with wheels so she can manage the load better. Aunt Rose is about 76 and is terribly crippled by arthritis which explains her difficulty in walking. Her legs and knees have been so affected by arthritis that she appears to be bowlegged. She lives with her sister Paula who is Kelly's mother. Paula is close to 80 years old. The two sisters came to this country together from Sweden as mail-ordered brides. They still often speak Swedish when they are together.

The women -- both widows now -- have a difficult time getting by. Rose makes a modest salary cleaning offices; Paula or Grandma Jackson as she is affectionately called makes a little money by braiding throw rugs out of scraps of cloth. She charges between $1.00 to $2.50 depending on the size of the rug. She wonders how long she will be able to make them because she has poor eyesight; also, like her sister Rose she has arthritis. Both women like to be independent but appreciate anything that is done for them. Some of the men in the neighborhood -- including Dad -- bring them fish to eat. They are especially fond of catfish. So, when Dad goes fishing, he always says that he hopes that he

27

will catch one for Aunt Rose and Grandma Jackson. Also, the ladies in neighborhood give Grandma Jackson plenty of scraps of cloth for her rugs and put in orders for them as often as they can. Also, they surprise Rose and Paula with homemade casseroles and soups to help them get by. Mom goes over to visit the two sisters often. She makes it a practice to especially visit them after Christmas so that she can read all the messages in the cards to them. Both women look forward to these visits. It is an excuse to make some tea and cookies and enjoy some small talk. Mom gets a lot out of the visits too. She says that it makes her feel good that she is bringing some happiness into their lives. Besides, she says, she learns a lot from the two women since they have lived a long time and have lessons to pass on to her about people and life in general.

Ed Harrington and I walked over to the REK [the Milltown Youth Center] at the high school the other night. We sat at a table drinking Cokes until I spotted Maria Montez at a side booth. I went over and asked if I could sit down with her. We talked about the classes we share while we watched couples dancing on the dance floor. Maria is a very attractive girl with long black hair, black eyes and a radiant smile. She is very petite and yet amble in the right places. Like the other girls she was wearing a simple blouse with a pleaded shirt. I finally got up the nerve to ask her to dance, and we joined together to dance slowly to a record by Tommy Dorsey's band. I don't even remember what the song was. Perhaps it was "I Think of You." I'm not sure. I only remember having my face close to Maria's and smelling her perfume and feeling her lovely hair. I felt my muscles tighten up in a pleasurable way as they came in close contact with her body. I sensed that she felt as I did. She didn't seemed to be surprised by my reaction to the closeness of our bodies. [Code: I felt my cob enlarge and push against my underwear. I hoped she wouldn't feel it pressing against her.] After the dance I asked her for a date to see "Jane Eyre" at the Illini theatre. She accepted. We are both fans of Orsen Wells, and he is supposed to be outstanding in the film. I walked back home with Ed and naturally he teased me about Maria and tried get my goat. He said that he was surprised that I wanted to go out with her since she was a Mexican. Then he asked point blank, "David, are you trying to get some pussy? I hear that Mexican women can really be something to fuck." At that point, I stopped him and told him that I wasn't interested in Maria for that -- that I simply liked her as a person. Ed just similed and said that he was happy to hear that because he didn't see how little Maria could handle that big pecker of mine anyway. Upon hearing that I lost my temper. In fact, I challenged him to a fight; I got my fists up and I was ready to hit him hard. At this point, Ed started backing off and told me that he was kidding me -- just trying to get my goat. That he did. Our "encounter" ended with me giving him the finger and yelling, "Fuck you Ed!" When I got home I remembered what Dad had told me about trying to solve problems in a reasonable manner. I thought to myself," Boy, is that hard to do sometimes."

During the week Professor Michael Olsen's wife Grace had a coffee for the ladies in the neighborhood. Her husband teaches history at St. Andrew College, a Lutheran college, in Andersonville. They are a very "down to earth" couple to use my Great Aunt Sadie's phrase. Both wear glasses and look studious. While the professor is lean, tall (over 6'3") with a long, rough looking face like Gary Cooper, Mrs. Olsen is short, somewhat plump with a round doll-like face that is transformed by her warm smile. They have three girls under the age of seven. Mom said that the coffee was well attended. Mom wasn't surprised by that because Grace has so much charm and genuine concern for everyone she meets. Besides, Grace is a young mother who reminds many women in the neighborhood of their own days caring for their small children. So, it was an interesting mixture of people. You had many ladies of various social groups there -- matrons with money like the Bishop ladies as well as some of the young ladies with children who are renting apartments in the area. Of course, Mrs. Harrington did not attend. I guess even being a professor's wife doesn't qualify one to be part of the Harrington's social circle.

Connie Phillips was there too. She lives in a large white frame house along 18th Street and is expecting another child in the near future. Her husband Bill is her second and works as an executive with a coal company. Her first husband died in the mid 1930s and left her with a little girl to raise by herself until she remarried. Her daughter's name is Irene and she is my age. We have been good friends since grade school. I often walk to the high school with her along with Dave Patterson. We are in some of the same classes. Irene is a tall, slender girl with long blond hair and blue eyes. She is quite intelligent, especially in math, science, and foreign languages. While she enjoys having a good time with other students, she can also become very serious. She can take on the most inquisitive expression when trying to solve a math problem or pronounce a French phrase properly.

May Taylor who lives down 11th Avenue in a large brick home with a Medieval-looking tower took time off from her volunteer work at St. Catherine's Catholic grade school to attend the coffee. She and her husband Charles have two sons and a daughter who all attend St. Mary's High School. Mr. Taylor spends most of his time operating his own filter company.

As I said above many of the women who live in the rental units along 18th Street were invited too. Mrs. McCoy along with her granddaughter Patty came. Nell McCoy and her husband Clyde rent an entire house from Mr. Bishop. He delivers coal to all Mr. Bishop's renters. Mr. McCoy also has a moving business on the side. The McCoys have four sons in service and proudly display four blue stars in their front window. George McCoy married before he was drafted and now his wife Laura lives with her in-laws. Patty is their one year old daughter. Laura wasn't at the coffee; she works in a doctor's office downtown. The McCoy's daughter Mary lives in Keyport and has a daughter named Joyce. She oftens visits her grandparents and plays with Buddy and Carol. Their other sons -- Charles, Thomas, Daniel -- are all overseas now. Charles is in the Marines while the other two are in the Army.

Pat Beck and Barb Powell attended too. Both have husbands in service. Pat's husband Rick is in the Army and is now in North Africa. Barb's husband Ken is in the Airforce and is at a training camp in Texas. Both women have small children to care for.

Another large billboard sign was set up the other day along busy 19th Street. It reads: "It takes 8 tons of freight to K.O. 1 Jap." The sign was put up by the Southern Pacific R.R. Throughout the area you see signs and posters either telling us about the war or urging us to continue our efforts for the fighting men. In front of the Post Office I saw another sign showing Uncle Sam stating, "Defend Your Children -- Enlist Now!" Another had a picture of a young mother holding a child's toy with the caption: "For All We Hold Dear -- Buy War Bonds." Some posters give us a view of the cruel enemy. The other day I saw one such poster in front of City Hall. It showed Nazis stabing the Holy Bible with a dagger. The caption was: "This is the enemy." I think that the best posters and signs are the ones featuring Norman Rockwell's paintings about the Four Freedoms -- freedom from want, worship, speech, and fear. They are positive statements about the objectives of the war rather than negative statements about the enemy. One wonders if it is really necessary to have such negative posters to arouse the people to action. Can't people read what is going on and make up their own minds without being barraged with images of a savage enemy?

The Passing Parade

News Stories: "Americans Take Kwajalein"
"Air Evacuation of Wounded"

Song: "Lili Marlene" by Perry Como

Movie: "Lifeboat" with William Bendix and Telullah Bankhead

ANZIO AND THE DEATH OF DOUG IRWIN

The fighting in the Anzio beachhead continues to be heavy. One news story told about Nazi shells hitting a U.S. hospital and killing two nurses. The nurses had refused to take cover because they did not want to desert their patients. A Lt. Rita Rourke was one of the lucky nurses. She refused to leave despite the fact that her patients told her to go to the foxholes. But, she survived the attack and quickly took charge to care for the wounded. Mom and Grandma thought that it was good that the newspapers were highlighting the heroic efforts of the nurses. Mom said, "We sometimes forget that women are out there too." Carol cut out the story about nurse Rourke (including her picture) in order to display it on the current events bulletin board at school.

Doug Irwin's body is scheduled to arrive in Milltown at the start of this coming week. He was killed somewhere in the Pacific in late December. His ship was attacked by Japanese airplanes and he was one of eight sailors killed. The Irwins who go to our church have two other sons in the service -- Kirk and Don. Both are stationed in Europe. Mom has been asked by Doug's mother Ruby to play the organ for the funeral that will be held next week at the the Riverside Presbyterian Church. Henry Banister has been asked to play taps at the funeral. Mom has known Ruby for about ten years and admires her commitment to the church and to her family. All of the Irwin's friends were shocked when they heard the news about Doug's death. Like Grandma pointed out at the time it doesn't seem right or natural when a young person dies. It is different if you have lived and are fairly old. By that time you see death as part of the natural cycle of life. Just as the seasons come and go, you begin to realize that you also have seasons -- and stages in your life that will eventually lead to death. But, when a young person dies, even if it was for a noble cause, it doesn't seem right somehow.

Poor Mr. George Bishop. He was driving his big, long '39 black Buick sudan the other day and as he turned to go into the alley behind his house to go to his garage, he lost control of it and ran over several trash cans and then plowed into the side of one of the garages that goes with his rental units. We think that he hit the gas pedal instead of the brake. Mrs. McCoy who has an opinion about everything, feels that, and I quote: "Mr. Bishop is just too old to drive." This time I think that she may be right. It would be a shame if he ran over somebody; a lot of children play in the streets and alleys in our neighborhood and it would be terrible if he hit one of them accidentally.

Maria and I went to see "Jane Eyre" and really liked it. It was nice to have a break from the war. So many movies are based on stories about the fighting going on in the Pacific or in Europe. It was relaxing to be transported back to 19th Century England and to be involved in a mysterious plot line

While we both like Joan Fontaine and Orson Wells, we found ourselves always looking for Margaret O'Brian. We both felt that she stoled a lot of the scenes from the other actors. Before the film there was a Disney short-- "Der Fuhrer's Face" which was really funny. Then came the newsreel with on the scene film footage of the war in Italy and on some of the islands in the Pacific. Finally, there was short ad urging everyone to buy more War Bonds. I have three bonds already -- each worth $25.00 at maturity. I received them as Christmas presents. Dad always attaches them to our Christmas tree. He rolls them up and puts a red or green bow around them. Buddy and Carol have received bonds too.

I treated Maria to a shake at White Castle before I took her home. While we were sitting there, I could sense that the other people around us didn't quite know what to think about seeing us together. In fact, some of them were probably thinking that it was wrong for the two us to be together. Most of Mexican-Americans are Roman Catholic and that doesn't make them popular with a lot of the Protestants in Milltown. But, I am sure our contrasting skin and hair colors probably had the most to do with the attention we were receiving. None of them probably considered the possibility that we might have grown up in the same neighborhood and had learned to simply like each other. Mr. and Mrs. Montez were waiting for us when we got to her house. I really like them, and I think they like me too. They always keep their home so clean and well-cared for. Like Maria, her parents seem like warm, out-going people. I have dated her a few times before and my parents have never told me not to ask her out. They know the Montez family and accept them.

I overheard more criticism of Miss Kline for sharing her home with her boarder -- a Miss Whitman. Mrs. McCoy and Mrs. Jackson were talking and and both feel that the relationship between the two women is "unnatural" to use their word. When I heard the term used in connection with the two women, I wasn't sure what they meant by it. I knew that they looked strange together. While the two ladies are both in their 40s, they look so different. While Miss Kline is short and fat, Miss Whitmore is tall and skinny. Some of the kids in the neighborhood even refer to them as "Stan Laurel and Oliver Hardy" [two Hollywood comics -- one skinny and the other fat] because of their comic appearance together.

Then, I remembered a conversation that Mom had with Mrs. Phillips about the women. She had a very different view of the situation. She knew Miss Kline as a high school student and always felt sorry for her. Miss Kline's father was an executive at the First National Bank of Milltown until his death. According to Mrs. Phillips, Miss Kline was not permitted to date. Her parents dominated her entire life and seemingly did not want her to ever leave their home and have a life of her own. So, after graduating from business college Miss Kline found herself working as a teller at her father's bank and living with her parents. After both of her parents died, Miss Kline put an ad in **The Daily Herald** indicating that she had a room to rent. Miss Whitman answered the ad and stayed. That was ten years ago. Mrs. Phillips feels that what the two women do is their own business. She, for one, is happy that Miss Kline has someone to share her life with.

[Code: I asked Dad about why some people consider that the relationship between the two women is "unnatural." He came out and told me that some people feel that the two women are sexually involved -- that they kiss and stimulate each other's sex organs. This really was something that I hadn't heard about or thought about before. Dad told me that not only do some women do this, but men often become involved sexually too. In fact, he had encountered a lot of men in the service who became involved sexually with other men. In some cases, the men also had sex with women too. They liked both sexes. Dad agreed with Mrs. Phillips that what the two women do is none of anybody's business. Besides, he feels that it may be what he calls "a platonic relationship." He explained that he meant that they have a romantic or spiritual sort of bond rather than one involving a physical sexual union. Could be. Nobody has ever seen them kiss or touch each other. After that conversation, I had a lot to think about -- a lot of new insight into relationships. One thing about Dad, he is direct about everything. If you ask him something, he will not put you off but will give you the information.]

Buddy came running with the newspaper to show me a special feature with several photographs of dogs who are helping to win the war. Most of the dogs are German Shepherds. The article highlighted five dogs that have made a difference in fighting the Germans and Japs. Naturally, Buddy, a true dog lover, cut out the entire page and put it up on the wall of his bedroom.

In the same paper was a sad story about an American soldier who had lost his life trying to save an Italian girl's dog. The dog had gone into a mine field and had been injured. The dog was whimpering pitifully from where it lay. An American soldier came upon the scene and tried to comfort the little girl but she continued to cry. He finally went to get the dog. He got to the dog, picked it up in his arms and then started back. It was then that his luck ran out; he stepped on a mine killing himself and the dog. When Buddy read this account, he could not forget it. He told me later that he had nightmares about the incident only in his dream the dog was Peggy and he was the soldier.

The Passing Parade

News Stories: "Dogs in War Make Good in Battle"
"Clark Promises March Into Rome"

Song: "My Prayer" by the Ink Spots

Movie: "Jane Eyre" with Orson Wells and Joan Fontaine

A FUNERAL AND A BIRTHDAY PARTY

This week started with a sad and moving funeral and ended with a happy celebration of a special 80th birthday. The funeral was for Doug Irwin. It was held at our church, the Riverside Presbyterian Church. The closed casket was covered by an American flag and was carried in by a military honor guard. Mom played "America the Beautiful" as the casket was brought down the center aisle and placed in front of the pulpit. Flowers in baskets and wreaths covered the front of the church which was packed with all of the friends of the Irwin family. Rev. Fritzgibbon waited until it was totally quiet before he lead the congregation in a prayer of thanksgiving "for the life of God's servant Douglas Paul Irwin." After that, Mom accompanied Ruth Winters as she sang "The Old Rugged Cross." Then, Rev. Fritzgibbon talked about Doug's life as a boy and later young man in Milltown. He expanded his talk by speaking about all of the young men and women in the service who are called to stand against the forces of darkness. He reminded his audience about how much we owe these young people for putting their lives on the line for our freedom and for the freedom of generations to come. At the close we all sang "Onward Christian Soldiers." There was a brief period of total silence and then we heard taps being played by Henry Banister. After that Rev. Fritzgibbon gave another prayer asking God to bless and care for Doug's family in its time of grief.

Despite the cold weather most of those who attended the funeral went out to Riverside Cemetery to see the internment in the Irwin family plot. There must have been 80 cars following the black hearse. The grave site was high up on one of the many hills located in the cemetery. The sky was a clear, radiant cold blue. As we stood there in the snow covered grounds, we could see the Mississippi River far off in the distance. The grave-side service was very moving -- especially when we heard the volley of rifle shots and taps being played again by Henry. Then, the naval officer offered the folded U.S. flag that had draped the casket to Doug's mother who now joined that ever expanding group of Gold Star Mothers. At that moment I couldn't help thinking about how uncertain life can be and how mysterious and how seemingly unfair are the ways of God.

Another sad thing that happened this week was Mrs. Walter's heart attack. Lois and Josh Walters live in a house on 12th Avenue. Both are in their early 70s. Josh retired from Henry Boone Co. about seven years ago. Mrs. Walters was stricken during the night. Josh told Ethel Thompson who lives upstairs that he awoke to find his wife in pain and having a difficult time breathing. He immediately called the hospital and an ambulance arrived promptly. Ethel and her husband Bob accompanied Josh to the Hospital. Lois is doing better now and should be home in about five days. Mom and Grandma have been going over to help Josh with the housework. Mom washed and ironed clothes while Grandma cleaned the house. Other ladies in the neighborhood like Mrs. McCoy and Mrs. Jackson have been supplying some hot meals for him until Lois is back and up to fixing their meals.

I took Irene Phillips to a basketball game this week at the Milltown Field House. We were playing our arch rival Andersonville High School. We won -- but only by four points. After the game Irene and I went to Mildred's for a hamburger and a milk shake. We both love their shakes -- really thick and creamy. We mainly talked about school and the classes we share. She also told me how worried she is about her mother's pregnancy. She has been feeling so weak and faint at times. Also, Irene said that she feels that her step father is too strict on her mother and on herself. He seems to want to control their every move. In fact, she had to do some fast talking to get him to allow her to go to the basketball game with me. Fortunately, because he knows my family, he was more receptive to her dating me. Irene told me that she often thinks about her own real father and how different things would have been if he hadn't died so young.

Feb. 14 was an important date in our household -- not only was it Valentine's Day but Mom's and Dad's wedding anniversary. This year it was their 18th. Dad took Mom out to the Plantation Club for dinner and dancing. Besides flowers he gave her a beautiful silver music box that plays "I Love You Truly." It was an important day for Carol and Buddy because that's when they exchange valentines with their school mates. They had been working on home-made valentines for at least two weeks. They got some of their ideas from Miss Murphy their art teacher. She comes to each class at Willard once a month. Anyway they used crayons, paints, and red and white construction paper to make their valentines. When Mom overheard Carol tell Buddy that she was only going to make them for her special friends, Mom told her that that wasn't the right thing to do. She told Carol to make one for each member of her class so that nobody would feel felt out. She said firmly, "Now, Carol, you don't have to feel that you must write a long greeting to everyone. Do that for your friends. For others, a simple 'Have a Happy Valentine's Day' will do. The important thing is that nobody feels left out."

Buddy and Carol had a good time the other day over at the McCoy house. Mrs. McCoy invited them over for a popcorn party with her two granddaughters -- Joyce and Patty. Buddy always says that Mrs. McCoy makes the best popcorn -- better than what you can get at the Roxy theatre. That is high praise coming from Buddy. We often have it too in the evening. We usually pop it in a pan with a thick bottom. However, Buddy claims that our popcorn can't compare with what he calls "the McCoy Specially Bended Popcorn." Buddy told us that Mrs. McCoy gets her popcorn from her brother's farm near Red Bud and uses real butter to flavor it. I guess her brother provides her with the butter; I have been told that he has about 10 cows that he keeps for milking. Inbetween eating popcorn, the kids played games. Mom always lets Buddy and Carol go to these parties despite the fact that she thinks that Mrs. McCoy gossips too much and tries to force others to conform to her way of thinking. She is a Southern Baptist and often gives the impression that if you are not one, you will go to hell. However, Mom often says that she feels "that down deep Nell (Mrs. McCoy) is basically a good soul who means well." And, everyone admits that the children in the neighborhood really like her -- for her popcorn and her good humor. When she is with children she jokes with them and enjoys whatever they are doing. She has a very distinctive laugh; it sounds a little like a high-pitched yodel. And, once she gets started, she has a hard time stopping. Anyway, the kids get a big kick out of her reactions to their play and her yodeling type of laugh.

On Saturday, the neighbors had a 80th birthday party for Grandma Jackson. "The Bishop girls" opened up their brother's large home for the event. They had an open house for Grandma Jackson from 3:00 to 6:00 P.M. so that everyone in the neighborhood could wish her a happy birthday. A lot of women who work were there besides the usual ladies. Marian Turner and her mother Mrs. Mario were there. Marian works at a defense plant on the Arsenal. Her mother takes care of her children and also colors black and white photo portraits for a local photographer at home. Pearl Helenkamp was there too. She works at a dry-cleaning establishment in Uptown on 15th Street. Her husband Pat is an auto mechanic with Miller Buick Garage. He also restores old cars for a hobby. His latest effort is a '26 Buick sudan. Even the controversial Miss Kline and her friend Miss Whitman attended. Mom said that everyone had managed to make it except Mrs. Harrington who declined the invitation; she said that she had some legal business to attend to. Her mother did not come either. Naturally, the Wellingtons did not attend since nobody has hardly seen them let alone know them. The Standstadts are still in Florida. They hardly know anybody in the neighborhood except their servants like the Hansens and the Gustafsons. Naturally, they have met George Bishop but do not consider him a close friend.

Mom said that every effort had been made to make the gathering a special one. Most of the people who attended had contributed ration stamps to make sure that the Bishop's cook Millie had enough sugar to make several sheet cakes and a special 9" round cake for Grandma Jackson. The cakes were all white and covered with white frosting and decorated with pink roses. "The Bishop girls" decided not to try to put 80 candles on the round cake but instead they placed 8 candles representing each decade in Grandma Jackson's life.

Grandma Jackson was really happy by all the attention -- and at times overcome with emotion by the kind words of congratulations. Everyone behaved themselves including her son Kelly although it just about killed him. Mom described how he was all dressed up in a suit and tie. She said that she could sense that he wished he was somewhere else -- like Betty's Tavern on 2nd Avenue with his dog Pal and Jim Banister. Kelly has been known to like a beer with a whiskey chaser. Also, he is well known for cracking an egg in a glass of beer and then downing it in one gulp. If he wasn't so opinionated, he would be simply a colorful character. However, he often verbally attacks Negroes, Catholics, Jews, and "big shots" in that order. This happens often and especially when he has had one too many.

Grandma Jackson received all kinds of gifts -- mostly practical things that she can use like a new frying pan, a heavy bathrobe, fleese-lined bedroom slippers, new bath towels, and a comforter for her bed.

Everyone who attended the event agreed that it had been one of the most memorable neighborhood parties in recent memory. The Bishops usually host a 4th of July Party and a Halloween Party for the neighborhood, but this special party for Grandma Jackson was a more sentimental occasion since so many people hold her in such high regard. Of course, I couldn't help thinking that here was Grandma Jackson celebrating her 80th birthday while poor Doug only lived to be 23. Where is the justice in that? How can one make any sense to it? Right now I feel confused and depressed about it.

It snowed again last night so we have an additional six inches of new snow. That, plus what was already on the ground makes for ten inches of the stuff. The snow plows are trying to clear the streets but our area still needs a lot of work. The alley behind the house is especially in need of shoveling. Dad is happy that he has chains on his tires so he can get around Milltown -- especially up and down the steep hills. We both got busy and shoveled the sidewalks and spread cinders where we saw slippery spots.

The Passing Parade

News Stories: "Churchill Promises Bombing Far Beyond Anything Imagined"
"Yanks Counter Attack At Anzio"

Song: "I Think Of You" by Frank Sinatra and Tommy Dorsey

Movie: "Destroyer" with Glen Ford and Edward G. Robinson

CONCERNS AROUND THE NEIGHBORHOOD

Sunday, Feb. 27, 1944

Druing the week I had a chance to talk with Rev. Fritzgibbon. I asked him how he would explain God allowing Doug to be killed at 23 and at the same time allowing Grandma Jackson to live to be 80. He told me, "We can't always understand what happens to people but we must have faith in God and accept His will." He said, "I must remember too that God gave mankind free will. Therefore, when some of our fellowmen use that free will in a selfish, destructive way, others become their innocent victims." Of course, in Doug's case, he was fighting against those individuals who were determined to get what they wanted at the expense of the greater good. Doug, of his own free will, had decided to join the Allied side to fight for the good of mankind. So, according to Rev. Fitzgibbon Doug was acting as God's agent for the forces of good.

I also talked with Professor Olsen about my thoughts concerning Doug and Grandma Jackson. He gave me a different interpretation. He confessed that he too often finds himself troubled trying to understand why things happen as they do. He said that it makes one wonder if God is really in control of things. I told him what Rev. Fitzgibbon had told me. Professor Olsen said that he often found the Hindu explanation helpful. He told me that in Hinduism one finds the concept that every soul is born again and again in order to learn from the experiences of life and that eventually through many rebirths one attains that mental and spiritual perfection that permits one to merge with God. "So," he explained, "in the process of living, the important thing is how we respond to challenges, how we learn from our life experiences so that we can be at a higher level of spiritual growth when we are reborn." He explained that a person could regress in spiritual development. For example, people like Heinrich Himmler [head of the German S.S. and the Gastapo] could be reborn but on a different spiritual level. He told me about the doctrine of Karma in Hinduism. One's future level of rebirth will be based on the good or bad works of one's present life. So, according to Hinduism Doug Irwin and Grandma Jackson will continue their spiritual growth in their next lives. Doug's dying for a just cause will help him be reborn on a higher spiritual level.

Professor Olsen also told me that many Hindus in meeting a person of great spiritual and ethical conduct often refer to them as "being old souls." Such individuals, like Gandhi, have been born many, many times and have in the process learned to live moral, ethical lives. I found what Professor Olsen told me to be very comforting despite the fact that it contradicted many of the teachings of Christianity. Professor Olsen, who teaches a class about world religions, told me to keep my mind open and receptive when it came to trying to figure out age-old questions. He pointed out that mankind since the dawn of history has tried to figure out the universe and human behavior. He urged me to check out books dealing with philosophy and religion if I wished to try to understand life. He said, "Many of the ancients came up with some valid ideas about the very concerns and problems that trouble us today. We can all learn a lot from them."

During the week we received a letter from Arvid and Caroline Gustafson. They are still in Florida with the Standstadts. They hope to return in late March. They sent Buddy and Carol coconuts. They had never seen one before so they took them to school to show them to their classmates. Later, Dad took a hammer and split them open so that we could taste the white milk or juice and eat the so-called "white meat" inside.

While Arvid and Caroline have been gone, their apartment has been occupied by their nephew Ron. He works as a car salesman with Packard. He is about 28 and is very good looking. He isn't in the service because of an irregular heart beat. So, he has been labeled 4-F by his draft board. Besides, he has two children to support from his first marriage. Despite his physical problem he has quite a social life and has a lot of girl friends. Arvid and Caroline hope that he will eventually find someone to marry and settle down; they feel that his first wife really didn't try very hard to keep the marriage together.

Ron entertained a lady overnight the other day. He does this quite often. I think it was Thursday when I saw a young attractive woman leave his apartment. Mrs. McCoy reported seeing whiskey bottles in Ron's trash. I don't know when she made this observation or how she got close enough to his trash. One thing for sure, you can't get away with much around this neighborhood -- especially with Nell McCoy around.

Dad had a chance to talk to Mr. Hansen the other day when he gave him a lift from the entrance to the Standstadt estate to the farm that Mr. Hansen manages. Dad learned that Mr. Hansen had heard from his relatives who recently escaped from Norway to neutral Sweden. Conditions in Norway became so bad that they felt as if they had little to lose. In the letter that he received he was told that they needed help and hoped that they would receive it from Hansen's family. They lost everything when they sought sanctuary in Sweden. While the Swedish government has been sympathetic to them, they really need clothing, bedding, and money for food. They expressed the desire to come to the United States after the war. Naturally, they asked the Hansens to sponsor them and help them get a new start.

Buddy's and Carol's grade school classes are busy filling up Red Cross boxes for refugees. After hearing what Mr. Hansen told Dad I'm glad that we can help the people over in Europe by filling boxes with things that they really need. The Red Cross gives teachers a list of the items (bars of soap, wash cloths, tooth brushes, etc.) that should be included in each box.

By the way, speaking of Carol, she received a letter from the White House about her request for controlling the price of horses. The matter has been discussed with the O.P.A. and it was determined that nothing can be done at the present time. Besides, the O.P.A. feels that Dad can buy a good horse for less than $200.00 if he would only do some comparative shopping. So much for getting a free horse.

Mom saw Mrs. Mario trying to shovel the sidewalk out to the street. Mom told her that she should let her son-in-law do that. Mrs. Mario only smiled at that suggestion and continued shoveling. Mom thinks the woman wants to be a martyr; she seems to feel that she must do everything for her daughter's family. Grandma Mendell expressed her opinion that Mrs. Mario has a deep seated need to be needed. Also, Grandma discussed the possibility that Mrs. Mario is trying to make up for something -- making amends for something in the past. Who knows?

During the week Mom and Grandma visited Grandma Jackson and her sister Rose. They often go over to chat and to check on them. This time Mom also needed to pick up several oval braided rugs that she had ordered. Mom had supplied the cloth scraps (blue, pink, tan prints) for the rugs. Mom was pleased with the rugs but concerned that the two sisters did not have enough to eat. Also, she thought that the apartment was too cold. She noticed that several storm windows had not been put up. Later during the day she made a meat pie from some of our left-overs and delivered it to the sisters. Mom and Grandma think that it is terrible that Kelly refuses to use more coal during the colder weather. Also, Mom sent Dad over to install the storm windows so that the sisters' apartment would be warmer. Kelly didn't seem to like it but didn't say anything while Dad was there doing the job.

Mom helped Dorothy Banister at church this Sunday. After playing the piano as the children sang "Jesus Loves Me" she had a chance to talk to Dorothy while the children heard the lesson about the death and resurrection of Jesus. The two have a very close friendship which is based on mutual trust. Mom often tells us that real friends are ones that can be trusted. If Dorothy ever tells Mom to keep a secret, she does. And if Mom tells Dorothy to keep a secret, Dorothy does. To do otherwise would show a lack of respect toward the other person. So, Mom tells us, and Dad concurs, that "if any of us wish to keep friends, we must remember to respect them and keep their confidence by keeping their secrets as if they were our own."

Mom told us (me, Dad and Grandma) that Dorothy was upset about what people will think when they read the police report in the newspaper. Jim had gotten drunk again and had been picked up and held in the lockup overnight. The judge had fined Jim $50.00 for the incident. Dorothy was ashamed of what he had done -- and worried about what people would think. Mom gave her a hug and tried to reassure her that her true friends would not hold her responsible. She reminded Dorothy that a lot of people don't even read the police reports anyway; many people may be totally in the dark about what happened. Poor Dorothy, she seems to be coming undone. She seems to be more nervous and withdrawn. Mom tries to help Dorothy by being there for her. She realizes that a person can't solve another person's problems. Only the individual can do that. But, a good friend can listen and can help with information and give advice if asked to do so. Mom commented that if she were married to Jim instead of Dad, that she would probably react as Dorothy is doing. Mom realizes that Jim's drinking and his being a loner would be difficult for anyone to take over a long period of time.

Grandma Mendell feels that many married couples grow apart over time. She pointed out that people change. Sometimes opposites attract and while they are fascinated with each other for awhile, over the long run they find it very difficult to live with each other. If they have children like Jim and Dorothy Banister, a couple often stays together. The only things they have in common are their children. Often, despite the fact that they may love one another, they can't really meet each other's needs. Grandma feels that one must work at relationships and realize that often you must permit someone else to meet the needs of the person you love. And, she said that one should not feel guilty if one can't meet the needs of another. Often, because of our nature and the way we were brought up, we can't supply what the other person needs. Also, she said that we should not condemn others if they can't meet our needs. She says that we should remember that they may be unable to do so. She explained that Jim may need what he finds in the people at the the travern. Perhaps he feels very insecure and out of place in the company of church-going people. And, Dorothy needs what church-going people can do for her. It would be nice if each could have their needs met by others and at the same time respect each other's choices. But, that is not easily done -- especially when Jim drinks to excess and infringes on Dorothy's life and the lives of their children. Their two boys have really suffered from not having a strong, dependable father. Henry skips school a lot and is content with average grades. He seems very headstrong at times and comes and goes when he wants. Dorothy can't control his behavior by herself. Timmy is a sweet kid but is very shy and insecure. Some of the neighbors feel that Dorothy has babied him too much. The kids like to tease him alot and he doesn't have anyone to help him stand up for himself and respond to the teasing. His father isn't there for him -- as a good example and guide.

Of course, in the case of the Banisters, Dorothy may have to seek a divorce if the situation affects her health. She is probably continuing the marriage because she is concerned about what would happen to her children. Really, the only things keeping the two together are their children -- Henry and Timmy. Dorothy feels insecure because she isn't able to make her own living. She certainly would not want her children placed in an orphanage or foster home. Grandma agrees with Mom that the only thing we can do for her is to be there for her -- to listen to her and to be caring, and yes to give advice if asked to do so.

Dad told me that both Grandma and Mom are worried about Great Uncle Aaron's son Joseph. He is a Marine and he is stationed somewhere in the Pacific. Uncle Aaron hasn't heard from Joseph for a month and it isn't like him to forget to write. Noah, his other son writes with regularity; he is stationed in England with the Intelligence Corps. He will most likely be part of the invasion force to liberate Europe. But, ever since our forces began "island hopping" in the Pacific, Great Uncle Aaron has been concerned about Joseph because battle casualties have been so high.

Again, Dad talked about his own war experience during the Great War. He said that before each battle he would be so tense that he could not eat or sleep. He said that the worst part of it was seeing guys slowly dying in agony from being gassed or being cut in scores of places by pieces of metal from bullets and bombs. Some cursed God as they were dying while others seemed to accept their fate. Others were in such a state of shock because of their injuries that they seemed to have no reaction. They laid where they had fallen and stared into space.

[Code: While I was talking to Dad, I was tempted to tell him about what happened in swimming class on Wednesday. The teacher was late and the nude guys began horsing around at the pool. Nick Temple and Todd Keller pretended like they were giving each other sex. As they hug from an exercise bar next to the pool, they used their legs to grab each other around their waists and buttocks. Then, they began to moan and breath hard like they were having sex. The other guys told them to knock it off since the teacher would be there shortly. I felt uncomfortable about the whole thing. I felt that Nick and Todd must really need to get attention. But, what a way to do it. I had never seen guys act that way before. I remembered what Dad had said about persons of the same sex pairing up and being sexual partners. Also, I wondered what other things Nick and Todd were up to. I had heard that a secret non-virginity club had been formed among some of the high school kids. I wondered if Nick and Todd were part of that.]

The Passing Parade

New Stories: "Dead Soldier's Effects"
"Nazis in Broad Retreat in Russia"

Song: "Marie" by Tommy Dorsey

Movie: "Hara Kiri" with Charles Boyer and Merle Oberon

Doug's Funeral

The Non-Virgin Club and The Purple Lady

One morning over breakfast we laughed about a news story that we heard on the radio. In the Pacific some of the Japs have been charging our lines with the cry "To hell with Babe Ruth." When "the Babe" was told about it, he commented, "I hope every Jap that mentions my name gets shot -- and to hell with all Japs anyway!"

I walked to school most of the week with Irene Phillips as usual. She told me that her step father told her that she could go to a movie with me on Saturday night if I brought her home by 10:00 P.M. We are planning to see "Whistling in Brooklyn" with Red Skelton. She complained again that her step father is very dictatorial and doesn't allow her -- or her mother for that matter -- to have much freedom. For example, her mother is given a certain allowance for the day to day expenses of the household and really gets yelled at if she needs some extra money. Also, Irene says that her step father isn't too excited about his wife having a baby; he wanted to wait to have children by her.

Irene and I met Dave Patterson while we were walking to McKinley High. He told us that he is working hard on the musical for this year. They are doing "Showboat" and he will be singing "Old Man River." He told us that things have been tense at home; his father has been threatened recently by some of the workers at the plant. They didn't like it when they heard that Mr. Patterson would be put on the assembly line. Up to now he has been a janitor. The federal government has ruled that all workers should be treated fairly -- that means Negroes too. This rule applies to any and all industries that are part of the war effort. If they are filling orders from the government, they must not discriminate. Dave hopes that his father can keep his new job because it pays so much better than being a janitor.

As we three reached 16th Street, we saw Miss Kline and Miss Whitman drive by in their '41 Ford Coupe. Dave said that he thought it was strange that two women live together -- especially when they aren't related. Irene took offense to this remark and told Dave that she knew for a fact that Miss Kline was a fine Christian woman and only agreed to allow Miss Whitman to live with her out of a kind heart. I didn't say anything. Of course, I remembered what Dad had told me about why some women live together. I wasn't sure that Irene would be receptive or for that matter ready to hear about same sex relationships. My only comment was to repeat what a lot of people have said about "staying out of other people's lives."

After Government class I walked with Maria up to the third floor to our Chemistry class. As we reached the area by the door of the Chemistry lab, we saw a fight break out between Tom Quick and Don Wilson. It got really bloody before Mr. Howe and Mr. Bolte, the Assistant Principal, broke it up and took the boys to the office. Both were later suspended. We later learned that the fight was over a girl -- Beth Larsen. Maria told me that both boys had dated Beth and had a very close relationship with her. (Code: In other words both had fucked her.) Maria also told me that the word around school was that the three were part of a secret club called "The Non-Virgins." I pretended that I had not heard about it. She told me that a lot of girls wanted to join and were asking boys to have sex with them so that they could qualify. Some of the girls involved were to use Maria's term "Khakiwacky." They were determined to date service men on leave. Why? Because they thought that they could contribute to the war effort by giving themselves to the men in uniform. She told me that some people call women who want to do this "Victory girls." Anyway, I guess some of the McKinley H.S. girls feel that having sexual experiences with some of their male classmates will prepare them for their "higher calling" at giving a serviceman a really good time.

The administration knows about the secret club and is trying to find out who is in it and what sort of activities they are engaged in. A few students have said that club members often meet at a house along the Mississippi River to engage in sex games -- like playing hide and seek and spin the bottle in the nude. "Special prizes" are given to the winners.

Dad told me that he ran into our neighbors Mr. and Mrs. Berry at the lunch counter at Woolworths on 5th Avenue. Mrs. Berry, as usual, was dressed to kill in a purple coat with a white fur collar. Naturally, she had a purple hat to go with the outfit. Dad hates to run into her because she is always talking so fast about so many unimportant things. Mr. Berry doesn't say much at all. Dad knows that as a bookkeeper he doesn't make that much money -- especially enough to keep his wife so well dressed. Dad figures that they are either in a lot of debt or else that the beauty shop business - called The Purple Lily Beauty Salon -- that Mrs. Berry operates is doing better than he imagines. Dad feels that the two are very mismatched. As I noted before, he feels every uncomfortable talking to her especially. He feels that she is firting with him. She always gets so close to him and always finds a way to touch him -- on his arm or shoulder.

In my opinion Mrs. Berry is an attractive lady. I have often called her "the purple lady" because of the way that she uses the color purple to bring attention to herself. It is so obvious that she loves being noticed and that secretly she would like to be a gorgeous movie star like Mae West. Of course, I think that most of us who go to movies a lot are not all unlike Mrs. Berry. We all want to be up there on the screen, playing the man or woman that we admire the most. But, getting back to the fact that she is attractive. She has long brunette hair, blue eyes, perfect white teeth, and an hour glass figure She has learned to enhance all of these good qualities by using mascara and long fake eyelashes, and wearing a lot of expensive clothes -- always in various shades of purple. One thing is for sure, everyone looks at her. In fact, everyone in Milltown knows about "the purple lady." I have always thought that there must be quite a story in her past. But, one thing for sure, she does make the neighborhood more interesting. Even Mom thinks so. She takes Mrs. Berry with a lot of humor. The Berrys rent an apartment along 12th Avenue. You can always tell that they are home because they always park their Packard (naturally painted purple) along the street in front of the house rather than in their garage.

On Monday, Miss Grant announced in Public Speaking class that she is going to direct a play by William Shakespeare entitled "The Taming of the Shrew." It will be presented sometime in late April. She told us that she decided to produce a comedy to help people get their minds off the war. According to her the play is one of Shakespeare's best comedies -- with a lot of rip-roaring physical humor. Then, she indicated that she would be happy to meet with anyone interested in appearing in the production. There are a lot of parts; also, there is a need for a lot of so-called extras for the banquet scene. On Thursday, she approached me and asked me to try out for the part of Grumeo. He is a servant to the leading man. She said that he provides the comic relief and that the part might be a lot of fun for me to do. I haven't been in a play since grade school. I asked about how much time it would take for rehearsals. She told me that she plans to have practice sessions three times a week for periods lasting no longer than two hours. Some of the sessions would be on Sunday afternoons. I told her that I would give it a try. I figure that since I like her class, I would probably enjoy being in a play directed by her too.

The Passing Parade

News Stories: "3,000 Japs Fall on Los Negros"
"Making Layettes for Enlisted Men's Babies"

Song: "Sleepy Time Gal" by Harry James

Movie: "The Story of Bernadette" with Jennifer Jones

Civil Defense and a Date with Irene

We have had a warm spell and a lot of the snow is melting. The large icicles that hang from the gables and gutters are dripping. Everyone in the neighborhood has responded to the clear skys and the bright sunshine. We all hope that winter is coming to an early end. But, since this is Milltown, we all know in our hearts that we are probably not out of the woods yet.

The thaw helped Buddy with his job of putting out the tins for the scrap metal drive. He takes off both ends of the cans and then flattens them out after removing the labels. It's a lot of work, but he does a good job. He then puts the flattened tins in a cardboard box to be picked up once a week by the trash men.

Mr. McCoy, our Air Raid Warden, came over to our house to report that he saw a light coming from one of our upstairs windows during a recent mock air raid. He told us to remember that when we hear the siren to turn off all lights or else draw thick draps over the windows. When we have drills, airplanes from the Milltown Airport fly over and drop small bags of flour. Buddy and Carol and their pals love to see if any have fallen in our neighborhood. One time they did find evidence of a broken bag of flour on top of a garage in the alley behind our house. While it seems farfetched to think that we could have a Jap or German air attack, it makes us feel that we are part of the war. However, it seems to me that it makes more sense to have these drills along the coastal areas of the U.S. It has been reported that German subs have been sinking ships -- usually oil tankers -- sailing out of the Gulf of Mexico into the Atlantic. Nevertheless, many of our neighbors like Mr. Wilkes defends the air raids because we live so close to the Arsenal.

Some of our neighbors make fun of Mr. McCoy. They feel that he looks ridiculous in his white helmet and that he takes his job too seriously. In truth, he does carry a lot of flesh on his frame; his fat face seems to overpower the relatively small helmet. A few like to say that he looks like a fat Charlie Chaplin. I agree with those who say that he takes his job as warden too seriously. He certainly takes great pride in wearing his helmet and armband and in blowing his whistle when he wants to get our attention. Most of us go along with whatever he tells us to do; we do not want to seem to be unpatriotic and uncooperative. We also remember that he has sons fighting for us overseas.

Mrs. Powell's husband Ken is home on leave. He has finished his training in the Airforce and now has a week home before he reports to active duty. He believes that he will be assigned to help fly B-29 Bombers in Europe. He will be serving as a radio technican. His wife was very happy to have him home. This fact was brought home to me when I looked out of my bedroom window around 8:00 P.M. and saw them together. My window faces the Powell apartment. Anyway, I saw him getting out of the tub. He had forgotten to pull down the shade. There are some curtains at the window but you can see right through them. The guy really had a "heart" on as he stood up to dry himself. At that point, I saw Barb, his wife, enter the bathroom with an extra towel. She proceeded to help him dry off and in doing so gave him a loving pat on his buttocks.

The administration's attempt to investigate The Non-Virgins Club continued throughout the week. Many students have been called to the office for questioning. The kids are getting a big kick out of the frustrations of our principal Mr. Milton. A code of silence seems to be operating; nobody has talked yet. He seems to be calling in students who have been in trouble with the administration before. Believe it or not, some students consider being called to the office as a way of gaining status. Since I know very little about the club, I don't think that I am in any danger of being called to the office. Of course, Mr. Milton may want to talk to a wide variety of students just to see what they have heard. I'm not sure what I will do if I find myself before Mr. Milton. I have some suspicions but no hard evidence.

I took Irene to see "Whistling in Brooklyn" at the Illini theatre. It was a really funny movie with Red Skelton playing a radio sleuth by the name of "the fox" who gets mixed up in a murder and impersonates the pitcher of a bearded baseball team playing the Dodgers. During the movie I lightly glided my fingers up and down Irene's arm and finally placed my arm around her. She smiled and snuggled up to me. I felt my heart beating rapidly as I enjoyed feeling the closeness of her body. I was tempted to gently touch her breasts but resisted the temptation. As we walked home I stopped her under the street light and leaned over and gave her a kiss. She responded with a playful laugh. I laughted too and then we kissed some more. We tried different kinds of kisses -- some on the lips and some with our mouths open. As promised I had her home by 10:00 P.M. Irene's parents were waiting for us. Mrs. Phillips asked us about the movie while Mr. Phillips only nodded at us and continued to read his newspaper.

[Code: I had a wet dream last night and frankly I'm not surprised I haven't husked my "cob" for seven days. I guess it was brought on by my date with Irene and also seeing Mrs. Powell's reaction to seeing her husband's big pecker. Anyway, in my dream I found myself with Irene who seemed as anxious as I was to have sex. She opened her legs and revealed what I call "her hole of creation." I then felt my "cob" fully expand and enter Irene. After pumping away I felt the head of my "corncob" get that longed for great feeling and then spurt out my "creation juice." At that moment I awoke and found my pajama bottoms wet. I got up slowly and removed them and I took the dry part and wiped my upper inner thighs and my "cob" which responded by getting stiff again. I decided that it needed more release so I wetted my hand with my saliva and then husked my "cob" until it came a second time. I closed my eyes while I did this and imagined the Powells together. After I came a second time, I found my body completely relaxed. Of course, the next thing I had to do was to find something dry to wear. I got up and went to my drawer and got a fresh pair of underpants and then laid out my pajama bottoms to dry. I hoped that they would dry by morning so that nobody would ask questions. I thought that if they were not dry, I would hide them under the bed until they were dry enough to put in the hamper.]

I'm finding memorizing the lines for the play difficult. Miss Grant says I'll master the part in time. Cole Stewart who plays the male lead Petruchio is doing very well. He has been in other productions and hopes to major in drama at college. Also, Judy Wells who plays Katherine has a good command of her lines. The rest of us are stumbling along; most of us are new at being in a play. But, Miss Grant's love of Shakespeare and her constant encouragement keeps us going. I still think that she has a a lot of courage to put on a play by William Shakespeare in a factory river town like Milltown, Illinois.

I saw Professor Olson out with his two little girls during the week. One of his daughters named Sarah had a baby carriage with a doll in it. His other daughter Clara had a small red wagon filled with bears and dolls. I told the professor that I was thinking of going to St. Andrew College in the fall and that I was planning to major in English with minors in Political Science and History. I told him that I wanted to be a journalist. He assured me that he would be happy to welcome me to campus and that I would find the atmoshere of the college very friendly.

Mom told me that she had heard that both Bob Thompson and Glen Swedson will be stationed in England and will probably be part of the invasion force. For some time now we have been aware that an invasion will take place in the near future. Naturally, their wives are tense about the situation. Anna Swedsen seems more upset than Ethel Thompson. We all know that the casualty rate will be high because the Nazis have had so much time to fortify the coast of France with guns and mines.

The Passing Parade

News Stories: "Hell's Angels Now on Its Forty-Ninth Mission"
"Ditching a B-17"

Song: "Doin' What Comes Naturally" by Dinah Shore

Movie: "Whistling in Brooklyn" with Red Skelton

Church Pews, Dad's Gift,
and Grandma Nebling

The crew of a Flying Fortress was highlighted in a two page feature in the newspaper. The crew which calls itself Hell's Angels has just completed 48 missions. That's a record. All of their photographs were included in the story. Anyway, the crew will go on tour of the U.S. to visit war plants and lecture other ground crew members on how the jobs should be performed when the game is played for keeps.

The thaw continued all this week and many of the neighbors took down their storm windows and put up screens. It is quite a job especially on the second floor windows. Dad and I joined in with the neighborhood "fun" and took care of seven downstairs windows. We plan to finish up the job next week. After we take down each storm window, we clean it and store it in the basement. Then we bring up a screen. There is a cellar door at the side of the house. This saves us some time. We also wash the inner window before we put up the screen which we also have to clean. To do the 2nd story is a bit tricky since we will have to use a ladder.

As we were doing the job, Mom came out to watch and talk to some of the neighbors. Toward the end of the job Mom swore that she heard a cry for help. Dad and I thought that she was hearing things but I went with her to try to find the source of the cry. Mom went across the alley to check out the houses facing 12th Avenue. As we approached the house owned by the Walters, even I heard someone yelling for help. We both looked up to the side window on the second floor and saw Ethel Thompson's face. Fear and pain could be read from her agonizing expression. Mom immediately knew what had happened. Ethel had been cleaning the window when the robe broke in the casing resulting in the window dropping on both of her hands. If she had been lucky, it would have only dropped on one hand, so that she could have used the other to lift the window. But, with both hands held in place, it was impossible for her to free herself. Mom and I found Ethel's front door unlocked, so we went up the stairs and into her side bedroom. We raised the window in order to release her hands. Mom washed Ethel's hands and put a home-made bandage around three of her fingers that had cuts on them. She used a wash cloth and some iodine that she found in the bathroom to make the bandage. We both felt sorry for Ethel because her husband who is now overseas would normally be cleaning the windows and putting up the screens. So ended the "fun day" of taking down storm windows and putting up screens.

George Bishop was the topic of conversation among the neighbors this week. It seems that he had gone to his church and accidently sat in the wrong pew. I guess at the Episcopal Church parishioners purchase their own pews to sit in. Anyway, poor Mr. Bishop who is getting more and more forgetful sat in the wrong place. The people who own the pew complained to the minister. So, Rev. Hammond sent

49

a letter to Mr. Bishop requesting that he sit in his proper pew the next time that he attends services. Well, Mr. Bishop was very upset and offended by the request and wrote a letter to the good Rev. Hammond in which he posed the following question: "Would you have sent such a letter to Jesus if he had made a surprise visit to your church and sat in the wrong pew?" Mr. Bishop then went on to express his opinion that the true loving spirit of Christian charity is no longer present at the Episcopal Church and therefore he would not attend in the future. His sisters told neighbors about what was in the letter. All the neighbors who heard about what had happend agreed with Mr. Bishop and said that they would not feel welcome in such a church either. It is a shame that the situation was handled so badly. I'm not sure why the people who owned the pew and Rev. Hammond thought that sending such a letter was the right way to deal with such a minor problem. They should have considered Mr. Bishop's age and the fact that his family had supported the church for many years. When Dad heard about it, he told me, "Holy Cow! What a good example of what not to do."

Grandma Mendell talked to Dorothy Banister yesterday. She wondered how the hospital work was going. Dorothy does volunteer work at the Milltown Public Hospital two days a week as a way of helping the war effort. More nurses are needed in the military so civilians have been trained to take over some of their routine duties. Dorothy says that she enjoys the work despite having to remove bed pans and prepare bodies for funeral homes. She told Grandma that the hospital work has helped her feel better about herself and keep busy. She said that she doesn't worry as much about what to do with Jim's drinking problem when she is busy at the hospital.

Carol has decided that she wants to be a nurse. She heard on the radio about a Pvt. Otto Hutteness who was severly injured by a land mind in Italy. He was blinded in both eyes, lost his left hand, and the index finger of his other hand. During the first few weeks in a hospital in England, he was so depressed about his condition that he refused to eat. I guess he wanted to end it all. Then that all changed when a nurse came into his room and told him that she was there to help him -- that she and the other hospital staff members were concerned about his progress. She started going to his room to read to him and to have long talks about his life before the war. Finally, he began to respond. He eventually allowed her to guide him down to the dining room for tea. Now, he has learned to read Braille and to use a typewriter with his remaining fingers. So, now Carol wants to do the same -- become a nurse and help people. She has already asked Dorothy Banister if she could visit the hospital when she works there on a Saturday. She also asked Mom and Dad to buy her a toy medicine kit with a lot of the instruments to play nurse with. Buddy has been recruited to help her operate an infirmery, and she has asked a lot of her playmates to be patients. Of course, I was thinking that if she becomes a real nurse, she will probably be the only one to make house calls on horse back. I'm sure that she will find a way to include horses into her chosen career.

Irene and I talked with Ed Harrington as we walked home for lunch. He was really on top of the world. He is ready for the baseball season. Practice starts next week. He told us that he wants to try out for the pros after graduation. He told us that a lot of teams have summer try outs for guys with a lot of talent. He said that he intented to be part of one of the summer "round-ups" after graduation. His coaches have been encouraging him to go to college first and major in P.E. He isn't too receptive to the idea. Ed isn't very good in a lot of subjects. Besides, he really doesn't want to teach P.E.; he wants to be in professional baseball. He told us that he feels that he is good enough for the big leagues now. I mentioned to him that Uncle Sam may have other plans for him. Ed thinks that he will be able to get a deferment if the big leagues offer him a contract. When I heard him mention this, I wondered to myself if Ed was living in a dream world. In my case I will be lucky to finish a year of college without being drafted. I'll have to take my chances. I don't have any physical problem that would make me a 4-F. Right now 18 year olds are required to register for the draft. While they are taking older men, you never know. It depends on how the war goes and what the U.S. military needs.

The play is coming along. Miss Grant got a bit disgusted with some of us for not being prepared and knowing our lines. Several of the students admitted that they had not memorized their parts yet. Upon hearing that she told us to go off by ourselves in the auditorium and find a quiet place to memorize our parts for Act 1. We did that for about 30 minutes and then we continued the rehearsal. Things went very well after that. I always come prepared. Of course, I'll admit that I sometimes become confused and have trouble with my lines. My major problem is projecting my voice and trying to say my lines with the proper timing and feeling. Also, I'll admit that I feel a bit intimidated by Cole; he seems to hog all of the scenes. He has quite an ego. Oh well, that is show business I guess.

[Code: I had a long talk with Dad the other night and received "a gift" from him. He came into my room late Thursday night to hear about my college plans and to find out how things were going at school and with my social life. He told me that he was happy that I had so many friends. However, he told me to go slowly with dating and not to get too serious about anyone -- that I had plenty of time in terms of getting married. Then, he told me about his own urges as a teenager. He talked about the need to masturbate -- that it was alright to do it. He told me that when he was around 14, he had discovered from his buddies how enjoyable it was to play with his pecker. He asked me if I had started the practice and I told him that I had -- and that I had learned about doing it from my cousin Philip Johnson who lives on a farm near Iowa City. I had spent about a month up there and being the same age we had become pals -- and eventually shared a lot of information about girls and sex. We even created our own terms for things sexual: "cob", "husking", "hole of creation", and "creation juice."]

[Code: Dad told me that if I ever had the desire to have sex with a girl to use a "rubber" or to use the proper term "prophylactic." He told me that he hadn't had sex with a woman until he was in the army. Then, it was with prostitutes in France. But, he told me that he had not worn a rubber and it was a miracle that he had not gotten gonorrhea or syphilis. Then, he took out of his pocket packages of rubbers. He said he wanted me to have them just in case I'm overcome with temptation to engage in sexual intercourse. He pointed to the instructions about using a rubber that were printed on the package. He said that he found that one's own saliva works best as a lubricant on a rubber. He told me he would be happy to supply more to me if I needed some. But, the one thing he wanted me to do was to confide in him -- to ask any questions that I might have about relationships with girls. I took the rubbers. I wondered if he had been reading my mind. Did he sense that I was anxious to have a sexual experience with a woman? Did he know what I had a wet dream the other night? I thanked him for being willing to answer my questions and then I told him that I had a question about size. I came out and said that one thing that I worried about was hurting a woman because of the size of my pecker. Can a woman accommodate different sizes of peckers? Dad smiled and said, "Yes, if the guy takes his time and uses plenty of saliva." He said that as I knew he was as big as I was and that he found the vagina expands if the woman is arroused too and if he took his time entering and used plenty of saliva. He said he produced plenty of saliva by having a glass of water and then retaining some of it to mix with the saliva that he produced by motions of his tongue and cheek muscles.]

Mrs. McCoy had a baby shower for Mrs. Phillips. The usual ladies who don't work during the day attended. Mom reported that Mrs. Phillips got all sorts of things for the baby. The baby is expected to arrive sometime next week. Irene seems to be excited about the prospect of a baby sister or brother.

Pat Helenkamp was the subject of a lot of talk among us all. He came home drunk the other night and drove his car through the garage door. Pearl was so embarrassed about it. Pat is usually not into the bottle. It goes to show that anyone can fall off the wagon. Some of the neighbors are saying that he was upset by not being able to be in the service. He had enlisted but failed the physical. For some men being 4-F is a sign that they aren't really men. Pat may have felt that way. Naturally, he had to pay Mr. Bishop to have the garage door repaired.

Neighbors are really worried about Grandma Nebling. That's what we all call her despite the fact that she is not related to any of us. But, to get to the point, Grandma Nebling seems to be so confused at times. Of course, she is in her late 70s and seems to have lost her footing since her husband died and she had to come to live with her son's family in their small downstairs apartment on 18th Street. Yesterday, she took their dog Patsy for a walk and failed to return. The police had to be called. They finally located her -- still walking the dog -- at Riverside Park. She told police that she was fine and had simply wanted to visit her husband's grave which is at the nearby Riverside Cemetery.

Well, the police drove her home. Once Patsy got home, she drank up to three bowls of water and ate a whole can of dogfood. The poor dog was really hungry. Patsy is about twelve years old and needs all the energy she can get. We aren't sure what the Neblings will do with grandma. They do not have enough money for a nursing home. Her daughter-in-law asked the neighbors to keep an eye out for grandma as she walks the dog. We all said we would. We realize that the woman can't be kept in that small apartment all the time; getting out is good for her -- and for Patsy too. Patsy really enjoys being taken for a walk. It is rather touching seeing the two together. Both are at the end of their lives. They are a great comfort to one another. Ever since grandma came to live with her son, Patsy has insisted on sleeping at the foot of her bed.

The Passing Parade

News Stories: "Victory Fashions"
"16 From This Vicinity Listed as Recent Casualties in War"

Song: "My Buddy" by Sammy Kaye

Movie: "Sherlock Holmes Faces Death" with Basil Rathbone

Spring, the Buildup, and School Activities

Spring is here! Some of the trees and scrubs are budding and the daffodils are coming up. Children have taken to the sidewalks with their roller skates, bikes, scooters, and jumping ropes. A few are playing hop-scotch. Many are flying kites. Buddy has one that looks like an American flag with red, white, and blue stripes and gold stars in a field of blue. Unhappily for Buddy his kite got entangled high up in a tree -- too high for anyone to untangle it.

Carol is talking about going horseback riding again and has asked Dad for the 20th time to buy a horse for her -- one that looks like Roy Roger's horse Trigger. Dad says that she can have one if she can find a place to bed it down at night. Also, it will need a fenced grazing area. Up to now she hasn't found either. But, for now she is content to go out to Fargo's Stable near Red Bud and ride their horses.

As the big build up continues in England, those of us who know someone over there are getting more tense. Neighbors are wondering when the invasion take place and where. We are also concerned about how many will have to give their lives for a successful landing. Dad said that he learned a lot from Colonel William Templeton a friend of his from the Arsenal. The Colonel told him that the invasions of North Africa and later Italy had not gone as smoothly as the news reels and the newspapers told us. This did not surprise Dad because he always suspected that a lot of the horrible realities of the war were being kept from the public.

Dad's view about how the government is not telling us everything was reflected in a news story about Thomas Dewey who will probably be the Republican candidate for president. In a recent speech Dewey charged that the Roosevelt administration is suppressing war news at home. Dewey says it is a "deliberate and dangerous policy of the administration aimed to make it look good." We talked about this issue in government class. We considered the following questions: How much disclosure should there be in wartime? How much freedom of speech and press can be tolerated? We all agreed that anything that would endanger the safety of our fighting forces can be legally suppressed. The problem is trying to decide if the information once released would effect the safety of our troops.

A lot of touching stories concerning the war are constantly being reported to us. Recently, there was one very sad one about Lt. Raymond S. Weck a flyer missing over Germany. The story centered around a letter that he sent to his little girl along with a gift. In the letter he told Jeannie Rae how to conduct herself. It will be kept by her mother until she is old enough to understand it. Basically, his advice was "to be honest with yourself." Lt. Weck said that the letter and gift carry "my great love for the dearest daughter a father can have."

There was another story about rationing and how some people are getting around it through the Black Market of a lot of essential goods (tires, gas, oil, meat, etc.) and using counterfeit rations. Some claim that organized criminals are behind the counterfeiting. Who knows. The only thing that I know for sure is that people really resent those who resort to these tactics.

Mrs. Phillips had her baby on Wednesday. It was a six pound baby girl. Things did not go well and Mrs. Phillips was put on the critical list. She will have to stay in the hospital until she gets her strength back. Dorothy Banister said that she heard that there was some internal bleeding after the delivery. The baby is seemingly healthy. Irene dearly loves her. She is very worried about her mother and goes to the hospital every day after school. She said that they plan to name the baby Betty Elizabeth. Mom, Grandma, Mrs. McCoy and other ladies have been to the hospital to see Mrs. Phillips. They all came away thinking that she was having a difficult time bouncing back. Meanwhile, Mrs. Phillips sister Elizabeth and her husband Greg are here to help. They plan to stay as long as it takes to get Mrs. Phillips back home and on her feet.

Arvid and Caroline Gustafson have returned. They drove the Standstadt's cars from Florida to Milltown. Their nephew has moved out of their apartment. Caroline talked to Mom and told her that she received an anonymous letter telling her that her nephew was allowing women to stay overnight. Caroline felt that her nephew's activities were nobody's business. She wanted him to have a social life and eventually meet someone to marry. She thought that whoever sent her the letter should have signed it or not sent it at all. She told Mom that she suspected Mrs. McCoy was the one who sent the letter.

The P.T.A. at Willard Grade School is organizing the annual fair to help raise money for projects and equipment at the school. Mom thought that she would help organize the fish pond booth. She enjoyed doing it last year. Also, she promised to bring some items for the bake sale. Grandma Mendell is working on some embroidery blocks for a quilt to raffle off. She is hoping that some of the ladies in the neighborhood will help her do the quilting.

Miss Grant told us that the costumes for "Taming of the Shrew" will come from a place in New York City. The art department is finishing making several colorful sets for the production as well as posters and programs. Miss Grant came up with the idea of having some of the members of the orchestra and choir play and sing some Elizabethan music. The teachers in the Music Department liked the idea and have created several short programs to present before the play and inbetween the acts. It should add a lot of atmosphere to the production.

"Showboat" was presented at the high school auditorium to full houses at each performance. While the sets and costumes were imaginative and colorful, the thing that stopped the show was Dave singing "Old Man River." The audience stood up and demanded that he take extra bows at the end of the song and at the end of the production. Of course, at the time I couldn't help thinking about the fact that hardly any white students want to have much to do with Dave outside of school activities. The girls especially shy away from being seen with him alone. I guess Irene and Maria are the only ones who seem not to mind but that is because they have known him and his family since childhood. Perhaps things will change now since he has shown what he can do with his voice in a production like "Showboat." By the way he told me recently that his dad will keep his new job on the assembly line despite protests by other workers. Dave is happy about it because he would like to go to college and his parents have indicated that they will help him if they can afford it.

On Saturday, Mrs. McCoy and her married daughter planned a special birthday party for Joyce. They decided to treat all her friends to a Saturday double feature at the Roxy Theatre followed by ice cream treats at Mildred's up on 15th Street. They asked Mom to help with the children. Mom says that there must have been at least 15 in the birthday party. Mrs. McCoy not only paid their admission but also treated them to bags of popcorn. The kids saw two westerns -- one staring Gene Audry and the other staring the ever popular Roy Rogers and Dale Evans. Mom had never attended a Saturday matinee and so she was completely unprepared for the yelling and screaming by the kids at every dramatic or scary part. She said that it was especially bad during the serial -- particularly when the villain who was dressed in a black robe with a skeleton mask threatened to kill the heroine who had been tied to some railroad tracks. Anyway, she was very happy to leave the Roxy and go to Mildred's (an ice cream parlor) for some ice cream treats.

The Passing Parade

News Stories: "Blood Transfusion on an Italian Beach"
"Europe's Children are Hungry"

Song: "Linda" by Buddy Clark

Movie: "Rationing" with Wallace Berry and Marjorie Main

Mr. Mc Coy

The Purple
Lady

WAR JOKES, EASTER, AND APRIL FOOL'S DAY

According to a newspaper story jokes about Hitler are told even in German held territory despite the efforts of the Gestapo. Two of the jokes appeared in the paper and gave us all a laugh. One joke involved Goebbels dying and accidently being sent to heaven where he was bored to death with all the praying and singing. An angel let Goebbels use a telescope to see what his pals were doing in hell. He saw them enjoying wine, women, and song so he asked to be transferred. It was a mistake; he found himself in hot coals with a devil poking him with a fork. When he asked about what he had seen through the telescope, he was told that that was just propaganda for foreign consumption.

The other joke was about all the important leaders dying and being sent to a lake of mud by St. Peter. F.D.R. was up to his chest in mud. Churchill was up to his chest, and Stalin up to his neck. However, Hitler was only up to his ankles in mud. "I say Adolf," demands Stalin, "how did you wangle that soft spot?" "Don't breath a word," answered Hitler, "I'm standing on Mussolini!" We agreed that that joke was one of the best of the war so far.

The ladies in the neighborhood are hanging out their Monday wash. Naturally, the ones with money like the Bishops don't have to do this personally; they have maids that tend to it. The whole washing operation takes most of the day. Most of the wash machines which are located in basements are like Maytag with a tub and a wringer. Most women usually have other tubs for starching some of the clothes like dress shirts and for rinsing. Wooden clothes pins are used to fasten the clothes on the rope or wire clothes lines. Before the ladies hang the clothes they take a wet cloth and clean the line if it is permanently installed between the garage and the back of the house. In order to make sure the clothes dry all over, the ladies find out what parts need drying and hang the clothes then from a different side or corner. Naturally, if it rains there is a mad rush to take the wash down. It is then hung in the kitchen or basement or attic or in rooms throughout the house. Usually clothes take twice as long to dry under those conditions. Tuesday and Wednesday are usually ironing days. While a few women have several irons of various sizes, most rely on one. All use the sprinking system. A soda bottle capped with a stopper with small holes is used to sprinkle the clothes. The clothes then are rolled up for awhile before they are ironed. Dress shirts are the hardest item to iron. Even the most experienced ironers sometimes scorch a shirt collar.

Most of our neighbors who have children are planning to buy new clothes for them to celebrate Easter. Mom has already told Dad that she wants Buddy to have a new suit and Carol a new dress with a straw bonnet. Some of the children also get new shoes to wear. Before the war the children used to get chocolate easter eggs but because most of the chocolate is going to our service men, this isn't a common practice anymore. I guess we all would love to have a Hersey candy bar again. Most of the kids will have to be content with coloring eggs for Easter. There is an Easter Egg Hunt planned by the city of Milltown; it usually draws quite a crowd. Also, many of the children will get baby chicks and real bunny rabbits. Grandma Mendell disapproves of the practice; she feels that many children do not know how to treat such "new borns." Mom and Dad are planning to take us to the Sunrise Services at the Milltown Field House. Mom is scheduled to play the organ for the services and she has been practicing for a week on all the old favorite hymns for the event. I'm sure that Grandma will not go with us. She rarely goes to our church; she says that she prefers to read the Bible (usually the Old Testament) and pray in the quiet of her room. She plans to have an early "luncheon" as she calls it ready when we return. She plans to make a fancy stollen and then serve a stand-up rib roast with baked potatoes and various vegetables. Instead of roast a lot of people serve ham but Grandma and Mom always complain that they can't stand the smell of it.

Grandma has invited all the ladies from the neighborhood to help her with the quilt to raffle off at Willard's fair. She has set up her quilting frame off to the side of our large dining room. She is donating the embroidered squares for the quilt. She worked most of the winter on them. Each has several spring flowers done in yellow, blue, and pink. She plans to use solid blue, pink and yellow squares along with the embroidered flowers. Already, Mrs. Hansen, Mrs. Banister, Mrs. Thompson, the Bishop sisters, and Mrs. McCoy have indicated that they will be over to help. Grandma has told them to either come in the morning between 9 to 11 or in the afternoons between 2 to 4. She told me that people are selling raffle tickets for the quilt at 25 cents apiece.

Grandma asked Mrs. McCoy if her daughter-in-law will be helping with the quilt. Mrs. McCoy said that would not be possible. Besides working full time as a receptionist for a doctor, Laura never did learn how to quilt and doesn't seem very interested in doing so. Laura often goes away on weekends to visit her girl friend in Peoria. So, this prevents her from helping with the quilt on weekends even if she had an interest in learning the craft.

Tony Montez has been arrested by the police for burglary. Maria told me that he is now in the custody of the juvenile authorities. The family hopes to have him freed before his hearing. Tony is charged with stealing things from the Wellington mansion and trying to sell them. Many of the neighbors aren't surprised by his arrest because Tony has been a handful most of his life. I feel sorry for Maria and her sister. I overheard the kids at school talking about her brother and making a lot of unfair remarks about Mexicans.

Mrs. Phillips finally came home from the hospital. She is still very weak. Irene helps to take care of her mother and her new sister. Mrs. Phillips' sister Elizabeth has stayed on to help out. She and Mr. Phillips do not seem to get along according to Irene.

At school I had a hard test in U.S. Government class. All of us -- including the very brightest -- worked most of the period on the test. At the end of the period, Mr. May told us to print the following letters at the top of our test papers:

THIS IS A PRE-TEST- APRIL FOOL

The whole thing was a joke! While Mr. May laughed and some of the students joined in, I found his "joke" not to my liking. Besides, it was the last day of March -- not April 1. He defended his "joke" by saying it was a good way for us to review the material. I still didn't like it. I considered it mean. Don't get me wrong, I like the man and I think he is very bright and more like a college teacher, but I find his humor to be mean and downright painful.

Before I leave the subject of school, I should like to note that Mr. Milton's investigation of The Non-Virgin Club is at an end. That's the word around school. I'm not surprised because the code of silence became like a tribal loyalty oath among the students.

The Passing Parade

News Stories: "First Negro Ensigns Welcome to Britain"
"4,261 Yank Airmen Lost in Europe"

Song: "Deep Purple" by Larry Clinton and Bea Wain

Movie: "Purple Heart" with Dana Andrews

A Sunrise Service, Two Deaths, and the 14th Amendment

Mom, Dad, and I managed to get out of bed to drive to the Field House for the interdenominational Sunrise Service. Buddy and Carol stayed home with Grandma; I must admit that I envied them. Getting up at 5:00A.M. is not my idea of fun. Mom played the organ while the audience sang such hymns as "On An Old Rugged Cross." She also played while a Miss Taylor sang "I Know My Redeemer Liveth" from the **Messiah.** The large choir under the direction of Professor Hugo Vetter who teaches music at St. Andrew College sang other selections from George Frederick Handel's **Messiah** including the dramantic and stirring "Hallelujah" Chorus. The sermon was delivered by Pastor Andrew Holstrum from the First Lutheran Church of Milltown. It was entitled "The Promise of the Resurrection." He especially pointed out that Christ's resurrection gives hope and comfort to those who have lost loved ones in the war. The pastor also related Christ's resurrection to mankind's resurrection that will come as a result of the forces of light (Allied powers) winning over the forces of darkness (the Fascist powers). He expressed the hope that after the war mankind would find itself uplifted to new heights of spiritual growth. He predicted a more just and fair world resulting from the conflict. He felt that it was part of God's plan.

After the service we talked to some of our neighbors who were there. The Bishop sisters were there. They were dressed in matching light blue taffeta dresses with bonnets made of straw and decorated with cloth flowers in various shades of blue. As always, they wore their white gloves. We also spoke to "the purple lady." She was dressed in a light purple outfit with a hat to match. She even had on purple gloves. Where she found them is anyone's guess. Perhaps she dyed a white pair. After paying our respects to others, we returned home for an early lunch.

As the weather warms up, more neighbors are sitting out on their porches. A lot of the porches have swings hanging from chains attached to the ceilings. Since most porches are large and curve around the corners of the house, there is plenty of room for chairs and small tables. Many have plants and ferns nesting on the porches too. The setting provides a great place to escape the heat of the house especially after a meal. As people sit on the porches, they talk to their neighbors who are walking about the neighborhood or sitting on nearby porches. The talk ranges from the weather to the war to other neighbors. The children have started to play hide and seek, kick-the-can, and kick ball in the streets during the early evening hours. Since we are on day-light savings time because of the war, it doesn't get really dark until 8:00 P.M. Some play kick-the-can even after it is dark outside; they would rather do that than go into their homes which still haven't cooled down.

One of the topics that the ladies are discussing is spring cleaning. All plan to wash walls, clean wallpaper, and shampo rugs and carpets, and clean appliances. Because coal is used in most the houses for heating, the wallpaper and woodwork get very dirty. Even in the homes heated with oil, like the Harrington and Bishop houses, there is a build-up of dirt. While some will send their rugs to be professionally cleaned at a dry-cleaning establishment, others will do the job themselves by spreading the rugs on the grass in their back yards and then shampooing them. Others will use a rug beater first and then apply the soap. Throw rugs are often hung on the clothes lines after being washed. Curtains are a special challenge. Lace curtains have to be placed on curtain stretchers and allowed to dry outside. Again, the weather and insect population play a part in the process. Sometimes a small child will topple a curtain stretcher over and earn the anger of its owner.

Some women plan to do some painting and wallpapering in order to make their homes or apartments more attractive. Mr. Bishop who owns most of the rental property in the area is agreeable to his renters doing their own redecorating. He even gives them a credit toward their monthly rent payments. Of course, he hasn't been very happy with rent control that came in with the war. At times he often feels that he isn't making much money from his rental units. However, at his age friendship with his renters seems to be more important to him than earning extra dollars. Of course, he has owned the rental houses outright for years.

Kelly Jackson told Jim Banister that he is afraid that Aunt Rose may have cancer. She has had stomach problems for weeks; she is having a hard time keeping food down. Kelly refuses to pay for any visits to doctors. Kelly called Rose's son Earl Palmer in California and told him about his mother's illness. He told Kelly that he would pay for any office visits or hospitalization that his mother needs and that he would take a train to Milltown as soon as possible to see his mother. Kelly told Jim that he feels that Earl should take his mother back with him to live with his family in Los Angeles. Kelly hasn't told Rose or his mother about this. For years, they have resisted such an idea. They treasure their togetherness and have tried to support themselves. They certainly haven't asked Kelly for much over the years. Earl should arrive sometime next week.

Death has claimed two of our neighbors. Grandma Nebling had a stroke and later died in the Lutheran Hospital. She was 79. Her son seems to be relieved because his mother seemed so helpless and confused at times. It was really sad for him to have to see her decline on a daily basis. So, death was a blessing. The neighbors contributed money toward a lovely flower arrangement for the funeral. She now lies next to her husband at Riverside Cemetery.

We have also lost Patsy. The Neblings had to put her to sleep after she developed a tumor on her side. We will miss seeing the two "old ladies" taking their stroll together down the street toward the woods.

In Government class we had a lively discussion about the rights of minorities. We discussed what has happened to Negroes, Jews, and others in the past and whether or not the U.S. Constitution has really protected them. Mr. May expressed the opinion that the record isn't too good. He pointed out that the Supreme Court has changed its opinion about enforcing parts of the Bill of Rights and other important admendments like the 14th. We also discussed the internment of the Japanese-Americans. Only Steve Graham argued that it was wrong to put them into camps. The rest of us told him he was naive and that it had to be done to preserve national security because some of them may be potential saboteurs. Even if most are innocent, it was best that they are in a secure place; otherwise they may be attacked by other Americans who are losing sons in the war. Mr. May informed us that some

Japanese-Americans were now serving in the American army in Italy and that it is entirely possible that most of those interned are really loyal to the United States. He asked us how their treatment was different from how the Nazis have treated Jews and others in Germany. That really opened up the discussion; everyone had to state an opinion. It turned out to be the most memorable and exciting day in Government since the "joke" about the pre-test.

Of course, the news of the war continues to occupy our minds. The newspapers have run several stories about Sgt. Charles E. Kelly. He was awarded the Congressional Medal of Honor in Italy for killing sixty Germans in rear guard action. He has six brothers who are also in the service. Because of his heroic deed, Sgt. Kelly has been called "one-man Blitz Kelly." Another story was about Kelly's mother Irene who is going blind. She had her sixteen year-old son write a letter to President Roosevelt requesting that he give her son a furlough for a few days. She wants to see him again while she still has her sight. Mrs. Kelly's son wrote: "Mom said she was going to offer up another prayer that you will make a lonely mother's heart light and happy by letting her see Charles soon." In the paper the next day was a follow-up story entitled, "One-Man Blitz Sgt. Kelly Coming Home for Visit." President Roosevelt had granted her request.

The Passing Parade

News Story: "One-Man Blitz Sgt. Kelly Coming Home for visit."

Song: "The Gypsy" by the Ink Spots

Movie:: "Passage to Marseilles" with Humprey Bogart

School Activities, a Fist Fight, and Aunt Rose

One of the issues of **The Daily Herald** featured a photo of a Nazi Beetle Tank which is being used in Italy to counter the Allied invasion. It is only five feet long and three feet wide. It looks like a toy tank. It is a device controlled by an electric cable and loaded with a 150 pound explosive charge. Fortunately, it hasn't been very effective. It is propelled by a two-cylinder gasoline engine and upsets easily.

Another story that Buddy found fascinating was about Sgt. James A. Raley who fell 19,000 feet in a tail of a B-17 and survived. The tail landed in a tree and Raley was only slightly injured. Buddy cut out Raley's picture and put it on his bedroom wall.

We had another air-raid Wednesday night. We heard the Victory siren around 8:00 and so we all rushed around the house turning off all the lights and then gathered in the informal living room until the raid was over. Mom considered making blackout curtains to cover the windows but then dropped the idea as being too expensive in a house like ours with so many windows. In a way Carol and Buddy enjoy the sense of impending danger that the blackout conveys. We usually light a candle or two just to be able to see each other. Often Dad entertains us by using his hands to make flickering shadow figures (a swan, rabbit, etc.) on the wall.

At school the annual, **The Mc K,** was put to rest. The final pages were prepared and mailed to the publisher in Chicago. I helped with the layout for the class photos. The editor Mark Stern has done a brilliant job directing the staff in putting together what we think is an outstanding yearbook. We all hope that it will be well received in late May when it will be distributed to students and teachers. Mark and the business editors Bill Watson and Teresa Wilcox sold more ads than ever before in order to pay for better quality paper and more pages. The theme of the yearbook is very different this year. We decided to try the idea of the shadows that we have left behind during the year. The divider pages show usually one or more students doing something (playing a trumpet, studying at a desk, holding a football, etc,) that is imprinted in a shadow on the wall behind them. The photographer had to work for hours on the special shots for the divider pages, but they all turned out great.

I submitted a story to the school paper **The McKinley News** for the next issue. It was about the baseball team and their hopes for the season. I interviewed Coach Hagen and several players including Ed Harrington. I included their assessment of the tough teams to beat in the conference. I even reported some heated words about our old rival team from Andersonville High School. None of this mattered; my story was rejected. Why? "Lack of school spirit" was what I was told. Holy Cow! (to use Dad's favorite phrase). What an excuse! Naturally, I do not agree with this criticism. I also submitted some poetry for **The Mc K Spirit** and again met with rejection. This time no reason was given. Perhaps my efforts to use Walt Whitman's free verse style in describing wartime America did not meet with much enthusiasm by the editors. Who knows? So much for my writing career. I wonder if Hemingway had these same problems at my age?

Boy, do I hurt all over. Why? Because of a fist fight that I got into. It was with Edward "Red" Shapleigh. We call him "Red" because of his red hair. Where? When? In the locker room after swimming class. "Red" is six foot two and built like a bull. He came over to me with only a towel around his ass and told me to stay away from Maria. He has been dating her and apparently feels that my walking and talking with her is a threat to him. He then pushed me against the locker and took his towel off to whip me with it. He yelled, "I'm going to whip your ass until you give up the idea of getting your big pecker into Maria." I responded with anger and came out fighting. I thought to myself, "I'm not going to take this shit." Anyway I slugged him in the jaw and in his ribs. Then, I felt his powerful fist hit my mouth and nose -- and felt blood running slowly down my chin. By that time other guys had gotten between us while still others grabbed both of us from behind to stop the fight. They also told us that the teacher was coming. Since neither one of us wanted to be suspended, we both backed off. Dave Patterson asked me how I felt and was nice enough to get some toilet paper to put up my nose to stop the bleeding. When that didn't work, he pressed several of his fingers against my upper nose until the bleeding stopped. Right now I really ache all over. But, I'm sure "Red" does too; I hit him hard and scored some good punches.

Dad noticed that I had bruises on my face when I sat down to dinner. I couldn't bring myself to tell him the truth. I told him that I accidently bumped into a kid during swimming relays. He didn't accept the explanation and he told me that he would talk to me after we ate. So, we went into the formal living room and closed the sliding doors. I finally told him what happened. I was surprised when he indicated that he could understand my anger and my reaction to being attacked by "Red" and said that he probably would have done the same thing

I asked him what I should do, and he said that it was important to make it clear to "Red" that I am only interested in Maria as a friend and to tell him that we have known each since we were children. He even offered to go to "Red" and his parents and tell him that for me. However, he looked at me and said that before he does that he wanted me to tell him if I had any other intentions with regard to Maria. I told him that I did find her attractive and that I had thought about dating her more. Dad then told me that since that was the case, that it would be difficult to reassure "Red" that my relationship with Maria was only one based on friendship. Therefore, he suggested that I give "Red" and Maria plenty of room. If their relationship cooled later on, then it might be the right time for me to consider dating her. He also told me to defend myself if "Red" came at me again but not to deliberately start a fight with him. He also told me that if "Red" brings up the subject of Maria again that I should tell him that I do not wish to come between them -- and that I respect Maria's right to go out with whomever she wants.

Of course, I feel bad about Maria. However, I'm going to following Dad's advice and give Maria and "Red" plenty of room. Besides, I'm dating Irene anyway. So, if Maria brings up the subject about not walking and talking with her so much, I'll tell her that I have to spend more time with Irene -- and that I realize that "Red" is her steady for now. And it is true; I should spend more time with Irene. I hope that Maria buys my story without pressing me for details. I don't care to have her find out about the fight.

[Code: You can sure tell it is spring because young lovers are everywhere and doing crazy things. I saw one boy chasing a girl down the sidewalk on 16th Street and then catching her, embracing her as they both fell into the grass and started rolling on the ground. He gave her a kiss at the end of the "wrestling match." Also, more used "rubbers" are showing up along the sides of the streets surrounding the high school. Some of the kids go to their cars for lunch and do more than eat. Of course, some guys use "rubbers" to masturbate in. Also, in the shower rooms the nameless ones are displaying unrolled "rubbers." I saw six of them the other day forming the word "FUCK" on the shower floor. Nick Temple and some of his buddies like to do this to get a rise out of the other guys. Naturally, Ed Harrington is part of that group. He is desperate for attention. Every once in awhile when he is drying himself in the locker room he yells, "I sure need some pussy." Or, he will say, "Pussy, pussy, pussy come to papa" while he points or grabs his pecker. Or, even more disgusting he might ask one of the guys, "Hey, Fred (or whoever) did you get some pussy lately?" Well, the point I'm trying to make is that the "juices of creation" are really flowing.]

We had another assembly on Friday to support the baseball and track teams. The coaches introduced all the players. Ed Harrington was in all his glory dressed in his white and maroon sweater. He waved to all of his fans. The cheerleaders took us through the usual cheer -- "Give me an M -- a C -- an I -- a N -- a L -- an E -- and -- a Y." We had the usual yelling contest between the various classes. The seniors won as usual. The noise was incredible. In a way I will not miss this scene. I'm looking forward to college where more serious academic pursuits are honored too. Perhaps, if I was better at team sports like football and basket ball, I would probably feel different.

We had a dress rehearsal for "Taming of the Shrew." Everything seemed to be going well until Bruce Talbot got carried away in a sword fight and accidently found his weapon flying into the air and landing on one of the empty (fortunately) seats in the center section of the auditorium. Miss. Grant stopped the production immediately and yelled for Bruce to keep a firm grip on his sword. She yelled, "We want to entertain our audience, not kill it!" Naturally, the entire cast, including Bruce, laughed at this remark.

Earl Palmer arrived by train during the week to see his mother. Before he arrived Rose had gone to a doctor and was told that she did not have cancer but ulcers. The doctor gave her some pills and put her on a special diet. Earl agreed to take his mother back to California with him. Kelly felt that the next time Rose became ill, it would be cancer or something worse. Rose and her sister are very upset about the decision; Mom says that a lot of tears have been shed over the situation. Both Mom and Grandma Mendell wish that there could be another solution to the problem. But, what is one to do when you are dealing with someone like Kelly Jackson who will not compromise. Rose will be going back with her son next week.

Grandma Mendell told me that often our lives are in the hands of others. We must accept the situation bravely. She said that many now in the war feel that same way. They are in the power of forces beyond their control. The only thing that one can do is face the situation bravely and play out the hand life has given you. We discussed why most of us experience unhappiness in life. I asked Grandma, "Why can't we be happy all of the time?" She responded, "Mark, how can a person learn about life if he only experiences good things? We learn through dealing with adversities. We need challenges so that our character and values can be tested and grow." One thing about Grandma, she always comes up with profound understandings of relationships and life situations. One time I asked her where she had gotten her "gift" of insight. She smiled and said that a lot of these so-called "insights" had come from her grandparents and parents and from simply observing and listening to others over a long life. At the end, she looked at me and said, "Mark, you will find as I did that you learn by living -- by experiencing both the bad and the good and reflecting on both." [Code: I wonder, however, if too much adversity can result in making many so bitter and angry, that they lash out or commit suicide.]

I heard by the grape vine in the neighborhood that Tony Martinez had his court hearing and that he was placed on probation in the care of his parents. He got off with a light sentence because he had never been in trouble with the law before. Next time it will be different; he will be sent to reform school.

Mrs. Phillip's sister finally went back to her home in Rockford. She found Mr. Phillips hard to get along with. Now the entire care for Connie and her baby has been left to Irene. She continues to go to school and also cares for her mother and sister. She told me that it has been hard. The doctor still makes house calls to see her mother. I suggested that she ask her step father to hire someone to come during the day. Some of the neighbors like Mrs. McCoy are helping her when they can.

The Passing Parade

News Story: "How to Make a Victory Garden Grow"

Song: "Embraceable You" by Jimmy Dorsey and Helen O'Connell

Movie: "4 Jills in a Jeep" with Martha Raye

Hitler's Birthday, a Car Crash, Victory Gardens, and War Games

Hitler turned 55 on or about April 19th. The news on the radio said that Herman Goering led the nation in congratulating him on his birthday. Goering asserted that an oath not to lay down arms should be Hitler's birthday gift. Of course, I wish someone would kill him. Too bad the invasion force isn't ready -- that would have been a great birthday present -- an Allied invasion of France.

A story that touched a lot of us was about Mrs. Roosevelt helping a mother visit her son who was dying in a California hospital. Pfc. Robert d'Angelillo was injured somewhere on an island in the Pacific when a tank rolled over his leg and chest. He met Mrs. Roosevelt when she visited the Pacific. Anyway, when he was transferred to a hospital in California, it looked like he wouldn't make it. His mother was told to fly out as soon as possible but she was unable to book a flight. She called Mrs. Roosevelt asking for help. Mrs. Roosevelt came through and got her a seat on a plane. As a result of the use of penicillin, Mrs. d'Angelillo's son awoke from a coma and the first thing he saw was his mother who he hadn't seen for three years., Now he is on the road to recovery. Grandma Mendell really liked the story and said, "Mrs. Roosevelt is someone that I would like to have on my side if I ever needed help. She is the the real thing when it comes to caring about people. She says that she cares, and she really does."

Well, "Red" and I seem to have truce going on. During swimming class we eyed each other but that was about it. I could see a few bruise marks on his upper body where I hit him. I'll admit that I was happy to see them. It gives me more reason to work out and keep in shape just in case I have to defend myself. I think that he knows that I will come out fighting if he tries to attack me again.

The big news in the neighborhood is that Mrs. Turner had an auto accident late Thursday night. She had stopped at a tavern with some of the people she works with at the Arsenal and then was driving home when her car was broadsided. We don't know whose fault it was. Mrs. McCoy and Mrs. Helenkamp think that she may have been drunk. Both women have had long discussions about Mrs. Turner's morals -- or lack of them -- and the fact that she imposes too much on her mother. They even speculated that she may be having an affair with some of the service men from the Arsenal or some of the men who work with her at the plant.-- that she is one of those to quote Mrs. McCoy "Victory girls." Mom has a different view. She thinks that Mrs. Mario has a real need to be needed and to make her "child" dependent upon her. And, she dismisses all the talk about Mrs. Turner being a "Victory girl" as being completely untrue. Well, whatever the case may be, Mrs. Turner was taken to Milltown Public Hospital with a broken leg and internal bleeding. Mrs. Mario asked Dad to take her to the hospital. She is really worried that her daughter will die. The doctors have tried to reassure her but she doesn't seem to be convinced. Her son-in-law took off from work to care for the children until things are better.

Mom and other ladies from the neighborhood went over to the Jackson house to say goodbye to Aunt Rose before she left for California. Mom dreaded going over because she knew how the two sisters wanted to stay together until the end. However, after she arrived over there, she found that the two ladies were making the best of it. Their acceptance helped everyone else think of the good times that all have shared with both sisters. Earl said that he would be willing to pay for long distance phone calls so that his mother can talk to her sister at least once a week. He also said that he would try to bring his mother back to Milltown to visit her sister at Christmas or some other holiday. That helped the two women feel better about their situation.

The play is now past history. It was presented two evenings before large audiences. It was well received thanks to the strong leads -- yes, especially Cole --, lots of action, and the colorful sets and costumes. Oh, yes, I should mention the biggest factor -- Miss Grant whose enthusiasm for Shakespeare was transmitted to us and then to the audience. Without her inspired direction, the response wouldn't have been so positive. If I do say so myself, I played the part of Grumeo with good effect; I especially stressed the physical comedy of the character to the delight of the audience. The family saw me perform on the first night. Grandma especially felt that I added a lot of humor to the play. Fortunately, my fame was further enhanced by my outstanding interpretation of the role on the second night. Cole could not stand sharing the spotlight and told me backstage before we went on that I should not upstage him -- or that he would "beat the shit out of me." I simply looked at him and told him that I didn't think he could do that and that if he tried I would bloody his pretty face. So, I went on and deliberately upstaged him with glee. I wasn't the only person that he had it in for that night. The leading lady was also one of his targets. He had not liked being upstaged by her either. His revenge took place toward the end of the play. He rinsed out his mouth with Listerine before kissing Kate during the last act. Needless to say, the leading lady did not appreciate it. Well, I think that I have had enough of Cole to last me the rest of my life. Hollywood can have him.

During the week we surprised Dad with a birthday party. Instead of eggs and oatmeal for breakfast, Mom and Grandma surprised Dad with home made Belgian waffles with whipped cream. After we had our fill Dad was given several birthday gifts -- a tool box, a new pipe, a fishing pole, and a photograph of all of us to put on his desk at work. Naturally, we sang "Happy Birthday" to him. Dad's reaction was simply to smile and to then to quietly look over each of his gift. Mom told us all that Dad's favorite dishes (pot roast, baked potatoes, and apple pie) would be served at other meals during the day.

Many of the men in the neighborhood are planning their Victory gardens. They are busy plowing up the ground. Mr. Hansen told them to use plenty of fertilizer. He suggested horse or cow manure. He buys his from a farmer near the village of Cambridge which is about ten miles outside of Red Bud in the next county. Most of the Victory farmers plan to plant tomatoes, lettuce, radishes, potatoes, green beans, and cabbage. Fred Bishop also grows a lot of fruit like strawberries, grapes, peaches, and apples. He has a small shed with an attached greenhouse on the grounds of the Bishop farm. A lot of the produce in the Victory gardens will be canned and stored in cellars or in the case of the Jacksons in a fruit cellar near their house. Dad and I usually plow up our Victory garden (located on Bishop land on 12th Avenue) and then mix the soil with manure. We let Carol and Buddy help with planting the seeds by first making sure that the rows are straight by tying string to pegs stationed at the start and end of each row. They also help us plant the tomato plants that we get from Fred Bishop. Later, we all do our bit to weed and water the garden.

The kids in the neighborhood are playing "Germans and Americans" and "Japs and Americans." Both war games are favorite past times for the young soliders. The girls usually join in to be field nurses. Most have fake guns and rifles that they got for Christmas or for their birthdays. The Taylor kids have built an elaborate camp or what they call "battle headquarters" in the woods. Buddy and Carol and their pals have "army tents" for their headquarters and field hospitals. They are made with old and discarded bed sheets and blankets. Sometimes they use the clothes line to create their tents. The kids form separate armies and think out their battle strategy. They argue who will be in which army. They also argue over who got shot. Some "soldiers" keep on fighting despite the fact that they are shot again and again. Some of the kids pretend that they are famous generals like Patton, Eisenhower, and Rommel. They know the great military men by heart because they collect pictures of them from packets of bubble gum. A few of the kids even like spending the night out in their "military camps" with flashlights and sleeping bags.

It isn't surprising that the kids in the neighborhood play war games because they are reminded of the war all the time. Most, like Buddy, collect tin cans for the scrap drives. They also collect newspapers for the war effort. At school they read stories in their readers about fictional characters experiencing the war. They participate in mock air raid drills too. They are told to get under their desks and away from windows during the fake air attacks. All of the grades prepare Red Cross boxes for refugees. At home many prepare packages for loved ones fighting overseas. This is especially true at Christmas time. At church they hear sermons and prayers that often include references to the war such as "preserve and protect our troops fighting in the war against the forces of the evil." Sometimes, a serviceman's body like in the case of Doug Irwin is shipped back for burial and the funeral is conducted at one of the local churches. When they go to the movies, they often see war pictures like "Thirty Seconds Over Tokyo" or "Life Boat." The radio shows like "One Man's Family," "Captain Mindnight," "The Thin Man," and "Cavalcade of America" often feature war plots. So, it isn't a mystery why the kids play war games.

News Stories: "Women Fight for Freedom"
"An Illinois Farmer Goes to War"

Song: "Where Or When" by Guy Lombardo

Movie: "Uncertain Glory" with Errol Flynn

A Telegram, A Maypole Dance, and A B-29

While a lot of men are being injuried or killed in battle, some people in Washington D.C. are only interested in going to parties and having a good time. Republican Representative Buffet of Nebraska gave a speech about it the other day. He feels that the situation is deplorable. One party had as many as 1500 in attendance. I asked dad about this and he said that war is a crazy thing -- you have people dying in terrible battles and meantime others are living it up or are bored to death. He feels that it is due to people feeling that they better enjoy themselves while they can. He told me that humans can't be serious all the time -- that you need a release -- especially if a war is going on. He admitted that he did the same thing in World War I. When he was on leave in Paris, he visited the night spots, drank and had women. He felt at that time that he might only have a few days to live. One never knew. Besides, there was a atmosphere of excitement about the war and living dangerously and doing what your buddies were doing. In his opinion the Washington parties don't necessary mean that people have forgotten the horrors of war or the serious goals of the war. The parties simply reflect what human nature does under pressure.

Telegrams from the War Department are something everyone fears to get during wartime. This week Mrs. Beck received one. She was informed that her husband Rick had been wounded at Anzio. She hadn't been aware that he was even part of the invading force. The last time she heard from him, he was in North Africa. Rick is now in a hospital back in North Africa. She told her children about what had happened to their daddy. She doesn't have any details-- how it happened and what is exactly wrong with him. The children are so young -- two and four -- that they hardly understand what has happened. Mrs. Powell who lives in the downstairs in the same rental house with Mrs. Beck and other ladies in the neighborhood have voluntered to help her during this terrible time. She is hoping to learn more about her husband's condition in the next few days.

Mrs. Turner is finally out of the hospital and resting at home. Naturally, Mrs. Mario is delighted. But, she is now left to do for the entire family. Her son-in-law has gone back to work since the emergency is over. While her daughter hasn't been charged with any traffic violation, she has been having a difficult time getting her car repaired. The other driver's insurance company is not being very cooperative. The company's lawyers are trying to prove that Mrs. Turner was drunk at the time of the accident and is responsible. According to the grape vine around the neighborhood, she had been seen drinking heavily with several men at the the tavern in Andersonville. Of course, Mrs. McCoy has been doing most of the gossiping; according to her Mrs. Turner was having an affair.

Carol's 4th grade class has been selected to participate in a Maypole dance at the Field House. Each grade school in Milltown will be represented. Ten Maypoles will be on the gym floor. Willard's colors will be pink and green. At a given signal all the Maypole dancers will start to interweave the colored streamers. Instead of doing regular P.E., Carol's class has been out on the school grounds practicing doing the Maypole dance correctly. Carol says it is very simple; you only have to remember when to duck and when to go to the right and to the left at the proper time. Of course, you can't drop your streamer; that would be a disaster. The big event takes place next week and the entire family intends to see it. Besides the Maypoles, there will be singing groups as well as a band and orchestra composed of grade school students.

The plans for Willard's Fair are well underway. Students and parents are selling chances for the quilt that Grandma Mendell and others are making. Other fund-raising activities are being planned. Some Disney cartoons will be shown in a large classroom. There will be a Gypy fortune teller in another room. The "fish pond" that Mom is in charge of is in one of the rooms in the basement. Mom and others have collected various prizes to put on the hooks of the "fishermen." The auditorium which is on the third floor will feature several acts -- a male singer who sings like Frank Sinatra, two tap dancers, a magic show, a ventriloquist with a Charlie McCarthy look-alike, and a couple who will perform ballroom dancing like Fred Astaire and Ginger Rogers. Cost - 15 cents for admission. Popcorn and candy as well as slices of pie and cake will be sold at several booths.

In speech class, Miss Grant asked us to divide into groups and write scripts for radio shows. I was assigned to a group with four other students -- Joe Schmidt, Debbie Hill, Benny Hogan, and Lisa Forman. We wrote a script for "Mystery Theatre." The story line is about an English woman who is a secret agent who has been sent to Nazi Germany to try to find out about the development of secret weapons -- especially rockets. She is arrested by the police, questioned, and tortured. However, when she begins to tell about herself the German officer in charge discovers to his horror that she is his long lost sister. He then decides to help her escape by killing his commanding officer and giving her a disguise along with false papers. At the end as she is leaving she asks him why he helped her. At that point he calls her by a nickname that only her family would have known and tells her that he is her brother. Since I am studying German, they asked me to be the S.S. officer who questions her. They said, "You look like a German S.S. officer -- you have blond hair and a good build." They told me to work on having a German accent. I am also in charge of sound effects which include a vicious barking dog, footsteps that sound like they are coming from military boots, and the sound of a whip lashing the spy during the torture segment. We will present our program next week. Debbie Hill is our director and we plan to meet at her house over the weekend to finish the scrip and practice our parts.

I walked home with Irene the other day and asked her to go to the prom with me. She said that she would love to but she would have to ask her step father if she could accept. She knows that her mother would like her to go to the prom. She hopes that her step father will not insist that she stay home to care for her mother and sister. I told her that I was sure that Mom and Grandma Mendell would be willing to stay with her mother and baby sister on the night of the prom if I asked them. I told her that I would ask them when I got home and phone her.

Buddy's class is studying transportation and his teacher Miss Lang asked them if they would like to build a model of some form of transportation -- a car, a train, etc. She told them that there is an empty classroom that they could use. Hank Tower suggested that they build an airplane. The other kids liked the idea and after considerable discussion decided to build a B-29 Bomber. Now, Buddy is trying to get enough cardboard and paint to build it. The kids have already voted to name the bomber -- "The George Patton." See what I mean, the kids are all involved in the war. Poor Miss Lang. I hope that she is up to it. Of course, it may not matter. She is scheduled to be married after the end of the school term and she will have to give up teaching. Those are the rules. The students in her class are really going to miss her. Mom and Grandma think that the rule is out-of-date. They feel that good teachers should be encouraged to stay on. Besides, her future husband may be drafted so she may need the job.

The Passing Parade

News Story: "Heart of Berlin Set Afire in Raid by 2000 U.S. Planes, Yanks Lose 63 Bombers"

Songs: "Love Letters" by Dick Haymes

"Shoo-Fly Pie and Apple Pan Dowdy" by Dinah Shore

Movie: "Snow White and the Seven Dwarfs" (a re-release)

Willard Grade
School

Good Old M.H.S.

Axis Sally, May Flowers, Maypoles, and Land Mines

During the week I read an article by Ernie Pyle about Axis Sally. He claims that her radio program has good American music but "pathetically corny jokes." Sally comes on five to six times a day from 6 A.M. to 2 P.M. The program opens by playing "Lili Marlene" and then Sally reads off names of the recent prisoners of war. This is followed by "I'll Walk Alone" and "Moonlight Becomes You." She plays a lot of Bring Crosby records. Inbetween the records she tells corny jokes. I guess Tokyo Rose does something like it over Japanese radio. I have heard though that she is more cruel -- often talking about the girlfriend or wife back home dating a guy who managed to get a draft deferment.

Buddy and Carol have been busy hanging May baskets of flowers on the doors of the homes of their favorite friends. They use construction paper to make the baskets and then fill them with violets, buttercups and other flowers that they pick in the nearby woods. They usually include a love poem in the basket.

The musical program at the Field House was quite a spectacular event. Several choral groups sang songs from the musical Oklahoma. While the songs were being sung, some students in costumes acted out the lyrics. The most applause came when the choral group sang "The Surrey With the Fringe On Top" while students acted it out with a real surrey. After that the combined grade school bands presented a medley of Sousa marches, and then the grade school orchestra strugged through several light classical numbers. After that the spectacular Maypole event took place. All the schools did a great job. One youngster from Grant school dropped his streamer but fortunately picked it up quickly. The band played while this was going on. However, there were so many children involved that the stamping of shoes on the gym floor could be heard echoing throughout the field house. Carol seemed to be relieved when it was over because she was so concerned that she or someone in her class would make a mistake and disgrace Willard -- and her beloved teacher Miss Masson.

In public speaking class we presented our radio shows. The best jobs were done by those groups who did comedy shows like "Fibber McGee 'n Molly" and "Amos and Andy." My group did a good job too -- got a B. Some students thought that Lisa who played the lead (the British spy) overacted -- was too dramatic. However, they found my protrayal of the sinister S.S. officer very convincing. And, they loved the sound effects too. But, in general, they found the plot too unrealistic. Another group did a script for "The Thin Man" show that seemed to be better all the way around. I guess we learned that it is difficult to write a script for a radio program and that an audience needs actors with plenty of talent to help them visualize the characters that you have created.

Miss Lang has planned a great field trip to end the study of transportation for Buddy's class. The students will walk down to the train station near 5ᵗʰ Avenue in downtown Milltown, board a train there and ride it across the river to Keyport. From there they will walk from the railroad station to the river front to board a steamboat called The President. They will then go across the river and land at the main dock at Andersonville. Then they will board a public bus to go up the hill to uptown in Andersonville on 17ᵗʰ Avenue. Then, they will walk from there back to Willard in Milltown. That will be quite a walk; it is about ten blocks from the bus stop to Willard. Miss Lang never ceases to amaze Mom. She thinks that the lady is a very caring and creative teacher with the patience of Job.

Irene's step father reluctantly agreed to let her go to the prom with me. He agreed because Mom and Grandmother told him that they would be willing to stay with Connie (Mrs. Phillips) and Betty. I promised him that we would be home by 12:30 P.M.

The prom will take place next Saturday at the ballroom of the Biltmore Hotel in downtown Milltown. It will consist of a sit down meal and dancing afterwards. The cost is high -- each couple will pay $25.00 for the evening. I have a lot to do before then -- rent a tuxedo and order a corsage for Irene. She has told me that her dress will be a light blue. I've ordered a corsage of white and pink carnations. Dad has agreed to let me use the car and has given me an advance on my allowance so that I will have the money to pay for everything.

Mrs. McCoy told Mom that Mrs. Beck's husband stepped on a land mine; it blew one leg off. He is supposed to be sent to the States in a few weeks. The insurance company finally agreed to repair Mrs. Turner's car. After investigating the accident, they felt that it could not prove that she was guilty of reckless driving. Finally, Dorothy Banister reports that Grandma Jackson is really lonely since Rose left. Kelly has suggested that she have all her meals with them downstairs and only use the upstairs apartment for sleeping and making rugs. She has reluctantly gone along with the idea. She realizes now even more than before how much Rose did for her -- especially in the tasks of buying groceries and preparing meals. The men in the neighborhood still remember to bring her fish which she now shares with Kelly and his wife.

While I was walking to Chemistry class, I found Maria walking next to me and wanting to talk. I hesitated at first because I didn't want "Red" to get angry. We stopped in the hall and she told me that she had found out about the fight in the locker room and was sorry that "Red" had attacked me. She said that she was going to go with "Red" to the prom but that she was going to drop him after that because he was so possessive. Also, she said that her father found "Red" arrogant. She smiled at me and told me that she wished she was going with me to the prom. I told her I was going with Irene but that I was happy that our relationship would continue in the future. Secretly, I was more than happy. I had always been attracted to her -- especially to her dark eyes and beautiful smile and outgoing personality.

The Passing Parade

News Story: "Pattern of Bombing Offensive in Europe"

Song: "I Can't Begin To Tell You" with Harry James and Betty Grable

Movie: "Song of Russia" with Robert Taylor

D - Day, the Prom, and College Plans

The newspapers and new magazines have been filled with stories about the coming invasion. A lot have photos of troops training. All refer to the invasion as "D-Day." The "D" stands for "Day." An invasion prayer has already been written by Bishop Henry St. George Tucker. Even the Germans are awaiting it. One story was all about German propaganda presenting a skit on radio about the invasion. Of course, they made fun of the effort to challenge their domination of Europe. They are very confident that the fortress that they have created will hold against any invasion attempt. We'll see. It won't be long now.

Irene and I had a lot of fun at the prom. Despite the war, the staff at the Biltmore Hotel gave the class of '44 a memorable evening. The ballroom was decorated all in pink. Pink streamers flowed down from the large crystal ball suspended from the center of the ceiling to the walls. The lights had been turned low and rose spot lights were used to create a romantic atmosphere. The dance floor was encircled by large round tables that can accommodate six couples. Each table had a floral display featuring pink and white carnations with green ferns set in gold containers. A small lamp with a pink shade was on each table. Even the table cloths and napkins were pink -- but in different shades of it. We were served dinner first and then the rest of the evening was for dancing and taking photographs. There was a side room where a professional photographer took our pictures.

We danced to the music of The Ted Collins Band. He and the band imitated the Benny Goodman sound. A soloist by the name of Betty LaVern sang "Green Eyes," "My Heart Cries for You," and "Baby It's Cold Outside." Also, a male vocalist by the name of Ron Morris sang several numbers associated with Dick Haymes -- "It Had to be You," and "Love Letters." Irene and I saw Maria dancing with "Red." Ed Harrington had brought one of the cheerleaders by the name of Judy Woods to the dance. I noticed that every once in awhile Ed would take Judy off to a dark corner in the ballroom where he not only kissed her but took a drink out of his flask. He was one of several students who were getting a bit drunk as the evening wore on. Liquor is not supposed to be brought to the prom but every year some people do it anyway. Several teachers were there besides the chaperons. I was suprised to see Miss Grant looking very elegant in a black gown dancing with Mr. Herbert the business teacher. I noted that she went to one of the chaperons to tell them to check on Ed and I later I overheard her say to Mr. Herbert, "Can't these young teachers see what is going on?"

When Irene and I arrived at her house, it was 12:20. Everyone wanted to hear about our evening. Irene's mother who had been sleeping got up to hear our account of the prom; she seemed to be anxious to hear about every detail of the prom. We told about the dinner, the decorations, the music, and about seeing Miss Grant Naturally, we did not mention seeing Ed and others getting drunk. I guess it was close to 1:00 A.M before I left with Mom and Grandma to go back home. On the way back I thanked them again for staying with Mrs. Phillips and Betty so that Irene could go to the prom with me.

During the week the seniors who had ordered yearbook pictures and graduation announcements and name cards received them. I immediately started sending them to my relatives. Most of my dad's people live in Iowa -- especially around Iowa City and Des Moines -- while my mother's people live in the Chicago area.

I had a long talk with dad about what college I should attend next year. Dad graduated from the University of Iowa back in 1925. It wasn't too expensive for him because his family lived on a farm outside Iowa City and he stayed with them while he completed his degree in Business Administration. I indicated that I would like to go to a state college like he did -- either the University of Illinois or the University of Iowa. Dad's brother John still lives on a farm near Iowa City; I threw out the idea to Dad that perhaps I could stay with my Uncle John and Aunt Virginia while I attended the University. Besides, their son Phillip will be attending the University of Iowa next year too in the hope of earning a degree in agriculture. Phillip and I have become real buddies and could help each other get through basic freshman courses. Also, I told Dad about my conversation with Professor Olsen about possibly going to St. Andrew College.

Dad asked me if I was really sure about what I wanted to be and what I wanted to major in. I admitted that while I tended to think in terms of journalism that I still was open to other ideas. He felt that it might be best for me to go to St. Andrew for two years and then decide after that. I would have completed a general academic program by that time, and I would have a better idea of what I really wanted to do. He also said that it would be less expensive that way. He felt that if I stayed with my aunt and uncle that I should pay them room and board. Also, he said that he knew that Phillip and I got along but that we might spend too much time socializing and not studying. Also, he felt that at a small college like St. Andrew that I would get more individual attention. At the University of Iowa he said that he often felt like just a number and that was about twenty years ago. Also, he is hoping that the war will end in another year so I will not be called up. He thinks that I can get a scholarship if I earn high grades the first year. He admitted that a large university has several big advantages over a small liberal arts college. In his opinion at a state university a person can meet a wider cross section of people there. Also, at a public university more diverse views are usually expressed in the classroom. At St. Andrew the Christian view is naturally going to be presented and encouraged. And naturally, the Lutheran view of Christianity is going to be presented as the correct interpretation. He told me that I needed to keep my mind open about religion, politics and people of different backgrounds. He told me that he felt that he got that chance to broaden his outlook when he was in the service and later when he attended the University of Iowa with its large and more diverse group of students.

The Passing Parade

News Story: "Allies Launch All Out Drive in Italy"

Song: "As Time Goes By" by Dooley Wilson

Movie: "Shine on Harvest Moon" with Dennis Morgan and Ann Sheridan

A Going-Away Gift for Miss Lang and Mrs. Roosevelt's Visit

Sunday, May 21, 1944

Mom and Grandma read with interest a newspaper story telling women how nylon is being used in the Armed Forces. Like a lot of women, Mom and Grandma Mendell have to be content with leg make up, the so-called "bottled stockings," that with luck and no baths will last for 3 days. The article lists 12 ways in which nylon is helping the troops. It is used for foxhold covers, netting, shoe laces, and moisture-proof bedding rolls. Both women are looking forward to the day when the war will be over and they can buy stockings that really do the job -- yes I am talking about nylon stockings.

Another article was about the first time that a large number of wounded vets were transferred from hospitals on the east coast to hospitals in the mid-West. Around 640 patients have been moved to hositals in Indianapolis, Cleveland, and Battle Creek. Dad feels that this information is more evidence of the approach of D-Day,. The "higher ups" as he calls them want to make sure that there will be beds available for new causalities from the invasion.

Willard's fair is over and netted around $800.00. Miss Wheellock the principal thanked everyone for working so hard to make it a success. Well, according to Mom and Grandma it was a lot of work setting it up and taking it down. The janitor helped with the cleanup but it was still quite a job. A lot of people disappeared when it came to the dirty job of picking up paper and putting away things in order again. But, at least it is over for another year. The money will be used to buy needed supplies (crayons, pencils, etc.), classroom furniture (desks and tables), and equipment for the nurse's office.

The McK was distributed on Tuesday after school and got a fine reception. The students really thought it was something special. The theme about how we left our shadows was a success. The divider pages were handsomely done. On the padded maroon and white cover were two students in caps and gowns. Students signed yearbooks throughout the week at lunch time, and at REK in Tower Hall after school. Also, a few teachers allowed us to do it in class during part of the period. I asked all my teachers to sign my yearbook. Naturally, my class buddies got a chance to sign it too. Most wrote funny, crazy things. All wished me luck in the future at college.

Also, the McK Spirit came out on Wednesday to those who had paid for one. It contained poetry, short stories and essays. When I got mine, I remembered the large number of items that I had submitted. Only one short epigram written by me appeared. However, I could understand why when I read the pieces that had been selected. I was up against a lot of tough competition. There were several essays and poems about the war. The one entitled "G.I. Joe" was very touching. It was written by Maggie Hall about her reaction to losing her older brother in the war.

Swingout (the going away senior skit) was also presented during the week. To be exact it was presented on Friday during an all school assembly. It lived up to the tradition of Swingouts. They usually are very funny and this one was. Sharen Brooks and her committee put it together. It included the history of the Class of '44, wills, and prophecies. The setting was Heaven with St. Peter and his angels hearing about the members of the Class of '44. Angels talked about the history of the class and what happened to many of the members. Actors played the parts of some of the seniors who had supposedly spent their lives doing all sorts of interesting things -- operating a night club, being a movie star, managing a dating service, performing as a clown in a circus, etc. It was all done in good fun.

After school on Friday seniors received their caps and gowns. Our class decided by a vote to have the girls wear white gowns and the boys wear maroon ones. I didn't like the idea. I wanted the traditional black. Be as it may, we have the caps and gowns until we graduate. Seniors will not take finals with the other students unless they need to do so to pass a course. We will have a few extra days off until baccalaureate and graduation.

The students in Buddy's class decided to buy a going-away gift for Miss Lang since she will be leaving teaching to get married. They collected about $4.50 and set out to find something to buy after school let out. They walked over to the Uptown on 15th Street to try to find something. When they did not have any luck, they decided to trek down to the 5th Avenue shopping area. They went into the New York Store and saw several things that they thought would make a nice gift -- white gloves, a linen corsage of white roses, and a bottle of perfume called "Moonlight Magic." Then, the next problem they had was trying to agree on which gift to buy. They finally split up into two groups -- one buying the corsage and the other a small bottle of perfume. Well, to make a long story short, they presented both gifts to Miss Lang who seemed deeply touched that the students had gone to so much trouble to buy her going-away gifts.

Despite the fact that the week was filled with a lot of end-of-school activities, the family did get to see and hear Mrs. Eleanor Roosevelt when she visited Andersonville for a Victory War Bond Drive at the Armory. The place was packed with people but we found a place to sit. Mrs. Roosevelt had already arrived and was seated with other dignitaries on the stage that was decorated with red, white, and blue bunting. She was dressed in a tan Red Cross uniform with the distinctive billed cap that goes with it. Mayor Richard Harmon of Andersonville welcomed the crowd and asked us to stand while the flag was brought to the stage by the two M.P.s from the Arsenal. Then we all said the Pledge of Allegiance to the Flag. That was followed by soprano Florence Taylor singing the national anthem. After that the drill team stepped forward to perform some fast-moving drills with their rifles. Finally, the person that we all had been waiting for -- Mrs. Roosevelt -- spoke.

The mayor introduced her as "a woman who gives hope to other mothers who have sent their sons to war" and "a woman who works tirelessly for the war effort" and finally "our own brave First Lady -- Eleanor Roosevelt." As she quickly got up and went to the podium, she received a standing ovation. She smiled and waved until the crowd sat down to listen to her. She waited for several minutes until everyone was quiet. Then, she started her talk in a serious tone. She talked about recently visiting wounded soliders in military hospitals in the Pacific, and of the suffering that she had seen among our men and among civilians. She reminded us that "our soldiers have a long tough road ahead before victory will be won." She told us that "they need our support in every way." On a personal note she said that she had accepted the fact that her own sons might not be coming back -- that they might be killed on some battlefield. "But," she said, "they are fighting for what they believe in -- a world in which all can be free." Then, she asked us to continue to buy war bonds so that our men will get the weapons they need to win the great fight. She ended by saying, "It will be a tough fight but if we set our minds to do it, we can and will win. But, we must make the effort -- again and again until the job is done." At that, the audience stood up and gave her a standing ovation that lasted for at least five minutes. Then, before we left the mayor asked us to remain standing while we listened to a recording of Kate Smith singing "God Bless America." That was followed by a prayer for victory and for the safety of our Armed Forces given by Rev. Roger Collins of the First Methodist Church of Andersonville.

As we drove home, we talked about what a great and moving speech Mrs. Roosevelt had made. Despite her high-pitched voice, Mrs. Roosevelt's sincerity and earnestness came through. You could not help but feel that she cared and knew what others were going through. Also, she made us believe that despite the hardships, Victory would be ours if we only stayed united together. I will always remember seeing her and hearing her message.

The Passing parage

News Story: "Supreme Allied Invasion Chief and His Staff"

Song: "To Each His Own" by Eddy Howard

Movie: "Tender Comrade" with Ginger Rogers and Robert Ryan

MEMORIAL DAY AND EISENHOWER'S LETTER

Sunday, May 28, 1944

Memorial Day was celebrated by a large parade that started in downtown Milltown and marched to Riverside Park. The high school band participated along with other bands from various civic groups. Soldiers from the Arsenal marched in the parade along with a lot of military vehicles -- tanks, trucks, and jeeps. Groups like the Boy Scouts and the Gold Star Mothers also participated. There were even a few patriotic floats sponsored by such groups as the Kiwanis Club in the parade. The one with a large flag made of flowers was especially beautiful. It also had a large likeness of the Statue of Liberty with an enlarged copy of the Declaration of Independence behind it. Finally, veterans from other wars also were in the parade. The older vets from the Spanish American War and World War I road in decorated cars.

Dad and I took Buddy and Carol to see the parade. We decided to sit in the park near the Biltmore Hotel so we could see everything. In the middle of the park is a large bronz memorial to the dead of World War I from Milltown. It is round with various military figures on it. Each figure represents a branch of the Armed Services. The names of the war dead are engraved at the base of the monument. As I watched the parade I also turned to look at the W.W.I. Memorial and thought about the men who would stortly die in the planned invasion of Hitler's Europe. As a child I had been brought to the park by Mom. I had often stepped up upon the edge of the granite base of the memorial to try to look into the metal eyes of the soldiers. Now, it seemed I could feel the ghosts of the past war dead near me as I watched the parade.

I sent out my graduation announcements last week and this week I received some gifts. Dad's sister, my Aunt Maude, sent me a nice pen. From Aunt Emma I received a camera and from dad's brother John a dress shirt. My Great Uncle Ira and Great Aunt Sadie sent me a check for $25.00 to apply toward my college tuition. From my mother's sister Ruth I received a brief case. Also, I received a dictionary from Grandma Mendell's brother Aaron (he would be my great uncle). All of the gifts came with cards and notes of congratulations. They were all happy that I wanted to go to college and wished me good luck and smooth sailing. Dad took several pictures of me with my cap and gown on. In one photo I had my gifts displayed on a table. Mom was so excited about my graduating that she insisted on wearing my cap and grown. I guess this made her feel that she had accomplished something too in seeing one of her children finally graduate. Anyway, Dad took her picture wearing my cap and gown.

In honor of my graduation Dad took the family out to eat at the Plantation restaurant located way out on 21ˢᵗ Avenue in Milltown. It is a really fancy place. It looks something like Twelve Oaks in **Gone With The Wind.** It used to be the mansion of a prominent family that owned acres of land in and around Milltown during the mid-19ᵗʰ Century. We were seated at an elegant table set with blue Wedgwood china and long-stemmed blue crystal glasswear to match. It made my graduation very special because we seldom eat out. We had roast beef with side orders of baked potatoes and two vegetables. Desert was a selection of cookies and small cakes with chocolate ice cream. Dad had his flash camera and took a lot of pictures. Before the meal I was presented with the family's graduation gift to me -- a gold Elgin watch with my name engraved on the back with the date. During the meal Dad and Mon insisted that everyone have some wine and drink a toast to the graduate. Even Carol and Buddy had small classes of wine. What an evening!

The last issue of **The McKinley Herald** came out and it was mostly about the graduating seniors leaving. The class will was published and what each member of the class expected to do next year. I was surprised by the number of students going into the service. All the men in the class have to register with the draft board when they turn 18 and then wait to be drafted. However, some of the guys want to join up right away and get it over with. Besides many are very patriotic and want to do their part to end the war. I was surprised by that. I thought some would try to finish at least one or two years of college or a vocational school. Most of the guys want to join the navy or airforce. Some girls are also planning to enlist in Armed Forces -- a lot want to join the WAVES. Others are planning to get married right away -- most to someone who is already in the service.

Irene and I got our prom pictures back and they were pretty good. I wished I had combed my hair better but you can't have everything perfect. I thought that Irene looked especially lovely in the pictures; she seemed so radiant. While she wasn't entirely happy with them, I thought that she resembled a tall June Alison. When my mother saw the pictures, she really liked them and said again that she was happy that things worked out so that Irene could go to the prom with me.

At Willard Buddy's and Carol's classes heard about General Eisenhower's letter to a 6th grade class indicating what kids could do to help win the war. He asked them to do the following: say the Pledge to the Flag together, pray for the safety and welfare of the fighting men of the United Nations, earn extra money so that they could buy war bonds, urge adults to support the Red Cross, write letters to service men, and study U.S. history and our rights. The teachers at Willard are urging the students to follow Eisenhower's suggestions.

The Passing Parade

News Story: "Time Out for Weary Yanks in Italy"

Song: "Miss You" by Dinah Shore

Movies: "Up in Arms" with Danny Kay

"Pin Up Girl" with Betty Grable

Mrs. Roosevelt

D - DAY

During the early hours of June 6 I was awakened by factories sounding their whistles. It was only about 5:00 A.M. I came out into the hall and met Dad coming out of his room. He told me to turn on the radio in my room to see if we could find out what happened. On the NBC station the announcer was saying that the invasion of France had begun; it was specifically in Normandy. While casualties were very high, a beach head had been established. Later as the family ate breakfast, we heard church bells tolling too. We ate breakfast with a certain anxiety and fear for the invasion effort. We also remembered our neighbors -- Ken Powell, Bob Thompson, and Glen Swedsen -- who were probably part of the invading force. We kept the radio on in the living room while we ate so we would not miss any of the news.

We heard Eisenhower's Orders of the Day for June 5. They were later published in **The Daily Herald.** Here are some of what he had to say:

"Soldiers, Sailors and Airmen of the Allied Expeditionary Force!

"You are to embark upon the Great Crusade, toward which we have stiven these many months. The eyes of the world are upon you. The hopes and prayers of all liberty- loving people everywhere march with you. In company with our brave Allies and brothers-in - arms on other Fronts, you will bring about the destruction of the German war machine, the elimination of Nazi tyranny over the oppressed peoples of Europe, and security for ourselves in a free world.

"Your task will not be an easy one. Your enemy is well trained, well equipped and battle-hardened. He will fight savagely.

"But this is the year 1944! Much has happened since the Nazi triumphs of 1940-41. The United Nations have inflicted upon the Germans great defeats, in open battle, man-to-man . . . . . The tide has turned! The free men of the world are marching together to Victory!

"I have full confidence in your courage, devotion to duty and skill in battle. We will accept nothing less than full Victory!

"Good Luck! And let us all beseech the blessing of Almighty God upon this great and noble undertaking."

Before Dad left for work he felt we should all pray for the safety of the landing forces. He told me to turn off the small radio in the kitchen while he went into the living room and turned off the large set. He returned to the kitchen, sat down at the table, and asked us to join hands while he prayed for the success of the D- Day operation and for the souls of those who were giving up their lives so that the rest of us could live in a more peaceful and democratic world.

Throughout the day all one could think about was the invasion. At school some teachers took the time to discuss the invasion and the hopes that we all have for its success. Buddy told us later that Miss Lang had asked the class to pause for a moment of silent prayer for the Allied Forces.

Later during the day we heard that the beachhead had been secured on Omaha Beach and that the Allied Forces were pushing the Nazis back. Then at 2:00 Eastern War Time the President prayed while Americans across the country joined him. I tried to copy down what he said and I got some of it. This is what he prayed for:

"Almighty God: Our sons, pride of our nation, this day have set upon a mighty endeavor . . .

"Lead them straight and true; give strength to their arms, stoutness to their hearts, steadfastness in their faith . . .

"These men are lately drawn from the ways of peace. They fight not for the lust of conquest. They fight to end conquest. They fight to liberate . . . . They yearn but for the end of battle, for their return to the haven of home.

"Some will never return. Embrace these, Father, and receive them, Thy heroic servants, into Thy Kingdom . . . .

"And, O Lord, give us faith. Give us faith in Thee; faith in our sons; faith in each other . . . . Thy will be done, Almighty God. Amen."

The newspapers have been filled with maps showing the English Channel and landings in Normandy. Also, there have been some photographs of landing craft and tanks. While the Germans were expecting the landing at or near Calais, they fortified the entire coastal area with mines and gun placements. Causalities have been very high and our neighbors Anna, Barb, and Ethel have been very worried about their husbands. There has been a black out on the specific names of the dead and wounded.

The Passing Parade

News Stories: "Allies Invade Northern France -- 4,000 Ships"
"The Ruins of Cassino"

Song: "Auf Wiedersehn, Sweetheart" by Vera Lynn

Movies: "Lady in the Dark" with Ginger Rogers and Ray Milland

Baccalaureate, Working at The Daily Herald and Fishing

The Rev. Charles Bergman, President of St. Andrew College in Andersonville, was the main speaker at Baccalaureate. His speech was entitled, "Our Democratic Faith." He spoke about our commitment to liberate Europe and to restore basic liberties. He stressed the need for people to recognize and respect the importance of everyone to have freedom of worship. He proclaimed that "no matter what a person's religion may be -- Catholic, Judaism, Hinduism, Buddhism -- no one should have the power to prevent a person from worshiping."

The atmosphere in the auditorium was serious and emotional. The presence of several service men in wheelchairs and on crutches made the occasion even more of a reminder of our concern for the men fighting on the beaches of Normandy. They were all past graduates of William McKinley High School. They were introduced to the audience at the start of the program, and we were told where they had been fighting before they were wounded. After the flag had been brought in, they lead us in saying the Pledge of Alligence and singing the National Anthem.

Graduation took place two days after Baccalaureate admist the mood of national concern over D-Day. It took place at the Field House. After the class marched in to "Pomp and Circumstance" all joined in singing "Onward Christian Soldiers." The Rev. Thomas Bailey of the First Christian Church gave the opening prayer in which he echoed President Roosevelt's request for the safe return or our fighting men and also for their admittance into Heaven if they were killed in the battle for freedom. The address was given by the Lieutenant Governor of Illinois Roger B. Goodwin. His talk was entitled simply "Courage." He talked about the need for courage on the battlefield and in life in dealing with daily problems. He referred to those brave and courageous men and women engaged in the invasion of Normandy to rid the world of the evil, totalitarian power that Hitler's Germany represents. He told us that thoughout our lives we would be asked to deal with many problems that would require great courage. Some of us, he said, may be drafted into the service and be required to be part of the present great struggle against Germany and Japan. He indicated that we still had a long road ahead in defeating the totalitarian powers -- and that sadly many more lives would be required to finish the job. It was a very moving speech and one that was made all the more so because of the D-Day invasion of France.

The newspapers continue to tell the story of the D-Day Invasion. There have been more articles about it in **Life** too, and I have been reading them very closely. Another big event that happened last week but was overshadowed by the D- Day invasion was the capture of Rome. Also, yesterday I heard on the radio that the invasion of Saipan and the Mariana Islands was launched. So, big offensives against both Germany and Japan are well underway.

Rumors about the high causality count continue despite optimistic accounts coming from the government. Like Dad told us, every major military target is going to cost a high price in terms of American lives. This was brought home to me by a political cartoon that appeared on June 8th. It contained a cross with the number of American lives it cost to take Rome -- 9,689. Underneath the illustration was the caption: "Least We Forget the Road to Rome."

I started working part time at **The Daily Herald**. My hours are between 1:00 to 5:00 and 7:00 to 8:00 P.M. I'm looking at it as only a summer job. However, my boss Ed Mayberry has thrown out the idea of the job continuing after I start college; however, I think, and Dad agrees, that my grades may suffer if I take a part time job. I have several jobs at the newspaper. I post the scores of the baseball games in the front window. A lot of people -- especially retired men -- stop by to keep up with the scores. Many of them sit outside of the Milltown Public Library most of the day. Periodically, they walk up to the newspaper office which is only about half a block away to check up on the scores. Also, a lot of people going by to their work or during their lunch break check on the scores too. I get the scores from the wire service machine in the news room on the second floor. The scores come in and I copy them down and later place them on large score sheets in the windows.

The other job involves helping Roy Cook with the "morgue." In this "morgue" we do not deal with dead bodies but with dead stories. I cut out important stories and photographs and then they are put in brown envelopes along with the lead plates used to print them. We label the envelopes and make a card for each one to place in the file. Both jobs are interesting. I like to see the reaction of people to the scores and I enjoy getting into envelopes in the morgue that include stories about crimes, trials, and controversial persons in Milltown's past. In the evening when I am usually down there by myself, I have plenty of opportunity to dig into the "morgue."

I have seen but have not been introduced to some of the local columnists. Besides their daily columns, they all write regular stories too. Ted Turner writes the sports column. He is a very short man with a tire of fat around his middle. His wife Violet sometimes comes with him when he comes in late after a local game to write his column. She is a blonde -- probably a dyed one -- with blue eyes and a very attractive figure. She is always nicely dressed with lots of jewelry and gloves and purses that are coordinated colorwise with her dresses. She uses a lot of make-up. She spends her time smoking and reading fashion and romance magazines. Then, there is Lloyd Young who has an off-beat column. Instead of his photograph appearing at the top of his column he has created a humorous sketch of himself. He has stressed his thick glasses, messed up hair, and heavy beard. His sketch of himself presents a man who is under a lot of stress. Now, the real Lloyd Young seems to be very much in control.

Another columnist is Jennifer Quick who writes the society column. She is about 54 and is heavy set with a "grand dame" manner about her. She is usually dressed in conservative colors -- black, brown, dark purple -- with a simple pearl necklace and matching earrings. When she comes in to type her column, she removes her gloves and puts them over her purse. Finally, there is Ken Corbet who writes a column about local history topics and local personalities. He is about 60 and drinks a lot; I often smell whiskey on his breath. With his white hair and beard he could look very distinguished. But, that is impossible since he looks like he sleeps all night in his clothes and smokes a cigarette every ten minutes. The thing I want to stress however is that they all write well -- all of them produce very interesting columns. [Code: Also, they all -- except Jennifer Quick -- cuss a lot. Since I have been here, I certainly have expanded my four letter vocabulary. In fact, I'm wondering if I want to be a columnist if one of the requirements is to cuss so that I will fit in. So instead of using Dad's "Holy Cow!" I will have to use "Hot Damn!" or "Holy Shit!" to really get a job as a serious newspaper man and win some respect.]

The Daily Herald building is noisy and hot. You can hear the press machines working away on the second floor. While the newsroom on the second floor is airconditioned by one large unit, the rest of the building only has some large stationary fans to circulate the hot air. There are a lot of large windows that are kept open; this is especially true where the presses are located. Anyway, in the summer the building in which **The Daily Herald** is published reminds me of a room in hell.

Dad took the entire family-- including Peggy -- fishing on Saturday. As usual, we went deep into the wooded ravine to dig for worms while Mom and Grandma prepared a picnic lunch of fried chicken, potato salad, and iced tea. Dad decided to drive to our usual fishing spot along the Mississippi River that we call "the sand pile." It is off 1st Avenue that is lined with many factories. The river front is accessible so that barges can load and unload cargo. Next to one of the landing docks is an area where huge piles of sand and gravel have been desposited for use by some of the factories. This has become our so-called "sand pile" where we have been fishing for the last five years or so. Buddy and Carol like it because they love to climb up to the top of the sand pile. And, most important the fishing is good. In addition, sometimes there is a barge roped to the landing that people can board for fishing and for having a picnic.

We all threw our lines in and then began the long wait. Grandma and Mom used the time to work on some neddlework and talk to some of the other ladies who had come with their husbands. Meanwhile, Carol and Buddy secured their lines to the barge and then headed for the sand pile. They spent most of the afternoon climbing to the top of the pile and then sliding down again and again to the bottom. Peggy joined them in this activity; she especially enjoyed running after them as they slid down. Also, Carol and Buddy made elaborate sand cities at various levels of the sand pile. Eventually, even I fell under the spell of the great sand pile and decided to secure my pole to the barge and climb up to the top. The view of the Mississippi and the boats and the suspension bridge to Bennington is really beautiful from up there.

We had some good luck fishing. Dad caught a large carp and a medium size catfish. While I only caught three small catfish, Grandma landed a six pound one. We all decided right there that it would be given to Grandma Jackson when we got home. Even Mom, Buddy, and Carol managed to catch some small perch.

As it got darker, lights began to appear along the river and on the suspension bridge. We all enjoy this part of fishing at this spot -- it is so beautiful at dusk. Also, Carol and Buddy like to see the lightning bugs blinking on and off. They have a great time catching them and putting them in jars. Usually, we all enjoy this early evening scene for about an hour and then Dad asks Mom if she feels that it is time "to head for home." Before we leave Dad and I usually help Buddy and Carol shovel sand into a box or burlap bag to take home with us for their sandbox that is in our back yard. As usual before Dad drove up the steep and winding 15 th Street hill, he stopped at White Castle so we could all have cold root beers served in a frosty mugs. The place is famous for putting their mugs in a large refrigerator before they are filled with root beer. The drinks were so good that most of us ordered another one of their specialities-- chocolate malt shakes. They make them so thick that you have to have an extra wide straw to drink them. Anyway, the stop at White Castle was the perfect way to end our finishing trip to the sand pile.

The Passing Parade

News Stories: "London Meets Its Second Blitz"
"Rome Taken, Battle Moves to North"
"Pyle Says It Was A Miracle That Americans Landed At All"

Song: "Five Minutes More" with Tex Beneke

Movie: "Two Girls And A Sailor" with Van Johnson and June Allyson

War Casualties, Why Bad Things Happen, and Carol's Request

The war suddenly has become more real to us because some of our own neighbors have become casualties of the war. Barb Powell received a telegram telling her that her husband Ken was killed in action. She later learned from his commanding officer that he died when the B-17 that he was in was making an emergency landing in England. It had lost its wheels along with other damage. Ken was a gunner in the lower compartment of the plane and was unable to get out of it as the bomber made a belly landing. He was crushed to death as the plane hit the runway.

Ethel Thompson's husband Bob made it through the D-Day invasion without any injury. He was one of the lucky infrantrymen who had been transported to Normany in gliders. Most were killed or injuried severely. The gliders had been towed across the channel behind DC-35s. The Germans had planted long poles in the ground ten feet apart in every empty field that might have been a landing ground. Many of the gliders were impaled on these poles when they came down and if they weren't, they had their wings sheared off by others as they bumped and skidded to their violent stops.

Anna Swedsen received a telegram that informed her that her husband Glen had been wounded at Utah Beach in Normandy and was now in a hospital in England. He along with thousands of other soldiers had been transported by landing craft to Normandy and as they came close to the beachhead, they were confronted by heavy fire from the enemy. Glen was hit by some of the flying shrapnel as he ran from the landing craft to the beach. Several pieces had hit his back and one had severed his spinal cord; he has lost the use of his lower body.

Mrs. McCoy, Mrs. Banister, "the Bishop girls", Mom and Grandma are only a few of the women in the neighborhood who have offered to help Mrs. Swedsen and Mrs. Powell. They are preparing meals, sitting with the children and helping with the daily chores like washing clothes and ironing. Anna Swedsen hopes that Glen will be transferred to a veteran's hospital in the U.S. in the near future so that she can see him on a daily basis and help with his recovery.

The horror of the invasion was highlighted in an article entitled, "Yank Dead Lie On Blasted Beach Awaiting burial in Common Grave." The article reported that enemy snipers even shot and killed some of the men collecting the dead.

One night over supper the family talked about the events of the last few days and why so many have to die and be injured and in some cases disabled for the rest of their lives. Mom wondered why terrible things happen to good people. We all agreed that it is a mystery why God permits these things to happen. Dad pointed out that according to Christian doctrine God created man with a free will -- to choose to do good or evil. That in itself helps us understand why bad things happen to innocent and good people. A lot of individuals, like Hilter, choose to do evil and his decisions backed by great power has affected a lot of people -- those who are willing to be his active supporters, those who find themselves innocent victims of the evil forces that have been set in motion, and those who know he is wrong but do nothing.

Grandma Mendell voiced the belief that there is such a thing as collective guilt. She observed, "By many people going along with a inhumane policy, they become responsible for it and eventually pay dearly for their silent acceptance of it. People must learn to speak out against acts of wrong doing or be prepared to take the responsibility and consequences of their inaction." Dad agreed and pointed out that our treatment of Germany after World War I was too severe. Placing all the guilt of starting that war on Germany wasn't fair; other powers like Russia, the Austro-Hungrian Empire, and France had a hand in it too. This "war guilt" resulted in a desire on the part of many Germans to get revenge and created an environment in Germany that helped the Fascists come to power. Now, the average German is paying for going along with Hitler; they are seeing their cities reduced to rubble and their sons dying on the battlefields. However, other Europeans must bear some of the blame because they were so harsh toward Germany after the war.

But, still it is difficult to understand why so many good, innocent people have to suffer so much. It makes one wonder about God and his power and justice. We all agreed that if the present war ends with the defeat of Fascism and the creation of a more peaceful and just world, that the suffering of the innocent will make more sense. At least we will feel that the forces of good eventually win and that mankind is progressively moving toward a better and hopefully a more just and democratic future in which individual freedoms are safeguarded.

Not only has the war heated up but here it is early June and it is already very hot. The temperatures have been in the 90s and the humidity has been high too. We are trying all the usual ways to keep cool. We wear light colored clothes -- lots of white; even the boys are wearing white wash pants. Most of us have several old electric fans operating in our houses. However, the most they can do is circulate the hot air. A few of us have window fans that draw the cool air in during the evenings. Some of the ladies spend the hot afternoons on front porches where they drink iced tea or lemonade. They often have basins of cool water at convenient locations so that they can bathe their faces. A few houses have screen porches -- either in the back of the house or on the side. In the case of a few houses a part of the large front porch has been screened in. Our house is that way.

Many of the children and teenagers spend a lot of time at the Milltown Public Swimming Pool at Riverside Park. Others go swimming in the Mississippi River. Cold sodas are favorite drinks among the kids. They especially like Coke. Of course, there is also Dr. Pepper. Many of us obey the Dr. Pepper ad and drink one three times a day: 10:00 A.M., 2 P.M., and 4 P.M. Then, there are always the movie theatres that advertise that they are "Air Conditioned." The only problem is that there are only a few movie theatres in town and the features do not change all that often. In the evenings some families take long car rides and later come home to sleep on porches -- especially screened in ones -- or outside on the lawns.

Poor Carol, she wants a horse so much. She asked me if I thought that the Standstadts would be willing to let her rent a place to keep a horse. She feels that they have plenty of grazing land for an additional horse. She also feels that they probably have enough room for another horse in one of the several barns or stables on the estate. I told her that I couldn't predict what Mr. Standstadt's reaction would be but that it would not do any harm to ask him. So, she dressed up in one of her best dresses and asked me to walk over with her to the Standstadt mansion. She rang the door bell and Arvid Gustafson answered the door. He was surprised to see us. Carol told him why she was there. Arvid told us to stand in the vestibule while he inquired if the "master" would see us. As we waited we noticed the beautiful inlaid parquet floor and the magnificent wooden staircase that led up to the second and third floors. Even in the vestibule there were stained glass windows and paintings on the walls.

Arvid finally came down and told us that the "master" would see us. We followed him up to the second floor with some hesitation. I could feel Carol getting nervous. When we finally were admitted to the study where Mr. Standstadt was seated, we both felt a bit intimidated. Mr. Standstadt was dressed in an elegant smoking jacket; it was made of a rich dark blue velvet. He was striking with his tall, lean body, white hair and commanding blue eyes. He smiled and asked us to sit down and then asked Carol what she wanted. Carol got right to the point. While her voice seemed a bit shaky at first, she gained confidence as she told about her desire to own a horse and how she loved horses and how Dad had told her that he was prepared to buy her one if she had a place for the horse to stay. Then she asked Mr., Standstadt if he would be willing to rent out a parcel of grazing land and a stall for a horse if she got one. Mr. Standstadt hesitated. I could tell that he wasn't prepared for the idea. Finally, he said that he would think about it and let her know in a week or two. He added that he could understand Carol's love of horses because that is how he felt as a young man. Indeed, his love of those animals had caused him to build a stable and to buy six horses at one time. Now, he told us, there were only three on the estate.

As we walked home I could sense that Carol wasn't too hopeful. I tried to comfort her by telling her that perhaps Dad would still buy her a horse and let her keep it out in a stable near Red Bud. This didn't seem to make Carol feel much better. She was hoping for an immediate "yes" answer. I have to admire Carol's courage for going to the Standstadt mansion and making her request. I'm sure that I would not have done that at her age. But, then again, I do not have a great passion for horses. Later, Carol told Dad about what she had done. He seemed proud of her and promised to get her a horse if Mr. Standstadt came through with a place to keep it.

The Passing Parade

News Stories: "Yank Dead Lie On Blasted Beach Awaiting Burial in Common Grave"

Song: "Now Is The Hour" by Bing Crosby

Movie: "See Here Private Hargrove" with Donna Reed and Robert Walker

Politics, the G.I. Bill of Rights, and a Neighborhood Circus

The Republicans meeting in Chicago have selected Thomas E. Dewey, the Governor of New York, as their presidential candidate. The vice -presidential spot went to John W. Bricker of Ohio. Both are capable men. They are saying that it's time for new blood to take over the Federal Government -- that F.D.R. and his cabinet are tired, old men -- and women too since Francis Perkins is head of the Department of Labor. They say that the Democrats have dominated the government since 1932 and that that is long enough. The campaign promises to be a heated one as usual. There are news stories that say Roosevelt is not well enough to run again. Naturally, the Democrats deny this. They say that he is tired because of the weight of the job but that he can continue if he paces himself better and guards his health.

Life magazine has noted that it is a tribute to our democracy that we can have an election during a war. It's something like the situation back in 1864 when Lincoln ran for reelection. Of course, in a sense that situation was worse because the country wasn't united; instead, you even found some people in the North wondering if it would not be best if the South was allowed to go its own way.

As a Democrat and an elected member of the Milltown City Council Dad loves politics. He has asked to be a delegate or at least an alternate at the Democratic Convention that will meet in Chicago during the last week in July. He hopes that Roosevelt will run again for the Presidency. Dad feels that F.D.R. has the vision to create a better world after the war. Also, Dad points out that F.D.R. has worked with Churchill and Stalin and a new personality might upset the alliance or make mistakes in setting policies that will be the basis of a new world order.

Dad feels that after the war the Soviet Union and the United States will have to work together in order to achieve a stable peaceful world. That will be difficult because the Soviet Union is basically operating under another form of totalitarianism. Only one political party rules there; also, great power has been given to Stalin even before the war. Also, Dad explained to me that not only do our respective systems of government differ but also our respective economic systems. In the United States we have basically a capitalistic economic system with plenty of governmental checks but in the Soviet Union you have a socialistic system that is supposed to gradually move toward pure communism. Besides the differences between the United States and the Soviet Union, Dad told me that you also have differences between the British Empire and the United States. Dad said that Churchill still seems to want to cling to the idea of colonialism whereas Roosevelt strongly feels that imperialism is a thing of the past and that independence should be granted to those peoples who desire it. Also, it is well known that Churchill fears the expanse of the Soviet Union in Europe and might therefore tend to use the wrong means to deal with the Russians. Dad concluded by saying, "At this point in time only F.D.R. has the vision, personality, and the ability to bring about a peaceful world based on the principles set down in the Atlantic Charter." Dad hopes that the United Nations will be able to operate more successfully than the old League of Nations. He feels that Roosevelt is more committed to the concept of the U.N. and has the ability to make sure that it is set up properly.

Another important news story was about the G.I. Bill of Rights. It was passed by Congress on June 22. It provides benefits to G.I.s. Dad is really excited about the program. He wished that they had had such a program for American soldiers after World War I. He is especially happy about the provision that encourages G.I.s to get more education. He told me that the legislation had come about because many people in Washington -- both Democrats and Republicans -- recognized that the G.I.s needed to be assured that they would be rewarded for fighting by being given an opportunity to better their lot after the war was over. Dad told me that many feel that Mrs. Roosevelt was especially instrumental in influencing her husband and others to consider the kind of peace that the fighting men and women could look forward to after the war. Dad felt that her insight into the feelings of the ordinary people in the Armed Forces was very perceptive. He said, "It is one thing to talk about the U.N. and establishing a more peaceful world. It is quite another to talk especially about the opportunities that service men and women will have by continuing the struggle against the Fascists. They can relate to specifics like being able to go to college and getting loans for housing and businesses."

Maria and I managed to go to the Milltown Swimming Pool after work during the week. Maria works part time at the A&P Store in downtown. It was so hot that we thought that a good swim would be a way to cool off. Unfortunately, everyone else had the same idea. We managed to get in though and had a good time. She looked beautiful in her one piece white bathing suit. Her dark skin helped to highlight the suit and her figure. However, we found that we weren't able to do much real swimming because we kept bumping into other swimmers. Henry Banister was there too. He was hired as a life guard for the summer. He looked great in his trunks. They weren't the boxer type. They were made of elastic material that fits snuggly to his body revealing at times -- especially when wet -- the outline of his amble "fruit basket." I think it was Dave who told me that Henry took the lower part of a woman's bathing suit to fashion these revealing swim trucks for himself. One thing that Henry does well besides playing the trumpet is diving. He is quite an example of ideal manhood when he climbs up the ladder to the high diving board, pauses and then with confidence takes deliberate jumping steps to the end of the board to enable him to spring up high in the air to perform a double somersault drive. Everyone in the pool seems to stop what they are doing to see him do this and then to applaud as he hits the water and then comes up slowly to the surface. Then, he swims to the side of the pool, gets out slowly, smiles, and waves to the crowd. The girls love to see him dive. [Code: Of course, I often wonder if they are applauding his dive or his "amble fruit basket" that is highlighted by his tightly fitted swim suit.]

Buddy and Carol along with about seven other children put on a circus to raise money for veteran hospitals. This is the third summer that they have done this. As usual it was held on the grounds of the Hansen's "farm." They had it under a lot of shade trees behind the house where the Hansens live. They had several tents set up. One was for a fortune teller. For 5 cents Madame Carol would tell you all about your future. Another was for an exhibit for model planes. Buddy had asked a lot of kids to share their best model planes at the circus. Cost of admission was 10 cents. The kids decided to include "the best decorated bike contest" in the circus. Blue, red, and white ribbons (1st, 2nd, 3rd place) were given as prizes plus free admission to see the stage show. Grandma Mendell, Mrs. Banister, and Mrs. Jackson were the judges. The contest was a real crowd getter. About 15 kids brought their decorated bikes. They used colored crape paper to design various colorful images in the wheels and to make streamers to attach to the handlebars and back fenders of their bikes. First prize went to a kid by the name of Chuck Williams for his red, white, and blue patriotic design. He even had attached small American flags on various parts of his bike.

They had some food stands too. In one you could get a glass of strawberry or orange coolaid with crushed ice. At another you could have your choice of various types of cookies and or a bag of popcorn. By the way, I should mention that the mothers had cooperated in making the coolaid and cookies. They had pooled their sugar to sweeten the coolaid and make the cookies. Mrs. McCoy had popped the corn for the circus and as usual everyone thought it was the best that they had ever tasted.

The stage show was really good this year. Buddy and his acting pals had created a stage with a curtain. Lawn chairs and two glider swings were used to seat the audience of about 35 people. Most were kids from the neighborhood or nearby neighborhoods. You had to buy a ticket for 5 cents to get into the circus. Then, if you wanted to see the stage show you had to pay an additional 10 cents. Otherwise you were prevented from going into the area in which the stage had been erected. The acts included a magician, tap dancer, clown, dog trainer, and singer. Everyone seemed to really enjoy themselves; there was plenty of laughter and applause from the audience. The most popular act was Randy Larson's dog act. The kids loved to see Randy's Chihuahuas jump through hoops and perform other tricks. Buddy and Carol counted up the profits at the end of the afternoon and were please to find that they had made an astonishing $7.87. Someone from **The Daily Herald** found out about the circus (Dad had called the paper.) and sent out a photographer at the end of the day to take a picture of the performers. The next day they were all delighted to see a photo of themselves in the local news section of the paper.

On Saturday, Buddy had his birthday. I guess his best gift was the photograph about the circus in the newspaper. He was really proud about being the "producer and director" of the circus and the fact that it had raised so much money. Mom and Grandma planned a nice birthday party for him in the afternoon. They served not only cake but Buddy's favorite desert -- peach cobbler -- with ice cream. Naturally, the family joined in to help eat it up. The kids played the usual games -- pin-the-tail-on-the-donkey, spin-the- bottle, and musical chairs. Buddy received a lot of presents. He must have received five new model airplanes. Dad and Mom presented him with a set of airplane hangers produced by the Coca-Cola Co. The cardboard signs or posters show American war planes winning the war. He also got a new kick ball, a ballbat, and a catcher's glove. Of course, we all sang "Happy Birthday" to him while he stood there with that loveable grin on his face. After the kids had left, Mom tried to give him a kiss. His response, "Holy Cow! Mom, I'm too old for that!"

The Passing Parade

News Story: "Red Armies Closing Circle Around Vitebsk"

Song: "Something To Remember You By" by Dinah Shore

Movie: "The White Cliffs of Dover" with Irene Dunne

Fishing Near The Sand Pile

CELEBRATING THE 4TH OF JULY AND DISTURBING LETTERS FROM CHICAGO

Wednesday, July 5, 1944

The Allied Forces continue their invasion of France. One report that I read claims that six Nazi divisions were killed or captured during the invasion so far. Some of the young Germans who were captured complained that the Allied bombing was inhumane. When the American soliders pointed out how the Germans had devastated Warsaw, Rotterdam, and London, they were told that that was different. The excuse was that the Germans were only defending themselves because the other side had started it.

Hitler gave a major address on July 2. It was his first since January 30th. In an attempt to boaster morale, he claimed that "National fanaticism will bring victory for Germany." To me he sounds desperate. And he has cause to be. The Russians have the Germans on the run in the east while the Americans are pushing them out of Italy and France. I wish he would surrender; it would save so many lives. Dad feels that this will not happen because Hitler is such an insane fanatic. Besides, Hitler would have to surrender unconditionally. This Dad feels he will never do. However, if there could be an internal revolt against Hitler and new leaders take over, a surrender may be a possibility.

Meanwhile, back in Hilltop Place we have our own worries. All week long the neighbors have been concerned about Miss Kline. She is now in the Milltown Public Hospital suffering from cancer. She had not felt well for some time -- always tired and dragged out -- and finally had gone to a doctor. He found lumps in her breasts. She is going to have surgery and then radiation treatments after that. The situation doesn't sound good. Miss Whitman is trying to be strong and courageous for her friend, but it is obvious to everyone that she is having a hard time coping with the situation.

The 4th of July parade was really something. We saw it all from the entrance of the Milltown Public Library. We stood on the top steps of the Greek styled library that is located on the corner of 5th Avenue and 17th Street. It gave us all more height and also some shade provided by the portico. The usual bands and marching groups passed by. Carol especially liked the equestrians. There were about twenty in the group. They were dressed in colorful western cowboy and cowgril outfits. Carol pointed out the fancy saddles and bridles that the horses wore. She proudly announced the proper name for each type of horse and gave her evaluation of its fitness in order to display her knowledge of fine horse flesh to the rest of us.

Buddy liked the Shriner crowns that appeared in their small cars. Another feature that attracted a lot of attention was the appearance of antique cars. A Stanley Steamer was among them. Out next door neighbor Pat Helenkamp drove his restored '29 Buick in the parade. Also, there was a group of children who had decorated their bikes with colored crape paper. They had placed red, white, and blue crape paper through the spokes in the wheels of their bikes. There were quite a lot of floats with patriotic themes. The one with the sogan "Beat the Japs" got the most applause. It showed two marines bayonetting an effigy of Hirohito. Toward the end of the parade came Miss Milltown riding in a Lincoln convertible. She was dressed in a light blue formal and held a bouquet of red roses. She waved and smiled at the thousands of people who lined the streets.

The neighborhood had its traditional 4th of July celebration on the grounds of the Bishop estate. It makes a great setting for a party because you have some tall shade trees and also flower beds in the sunnier areas. "The Bishop girls" are especially proud of their beautiful roses this year. The high white trellis that runs along the east side of their property was filled with gorgeous red, pink and white roses. They get the full sun during the day and that along with Fred making sure that they receive plenty of fertilizer ensures a magnificent floral display. Most of the yards in the neighborhood have flowers -- especially iris and tulips in the spring and roses and petunias in the summer. Our yard has all of those plus lavender and white lilacs and pink and red peonies. Of course, hollyhocks of various colors -- especially red and white -- grow in abundance in the alleys behind the houses in the neighborhood.

Everyone who decided to come brought a covered dish to add to the basic meal of hot dogs, potato salad, and watermellon supplied by the Bishops. Before we sat down to eat, Dad was asked to read parts of **The Declaration of Independence.** Ever since he was elected to the City Council he has been asked to do this. After that, George Bishop gave the blessing which included a prayer for our fighting forces overseas. As we were eating Mrs. McCoy said that she felt that we were probably having the same thing as the Roosevelts at Hyde Park. She reminded us that Mrs. Roosevelt had served the King and Queen of England hot dogs back in 1939 when they visited the U.S.

The entertainment for the celebration came at night when Buddy helped by Carol put on his display of fireworks. He had saved his allowance and had sent away for a whole box of fireworks for $4.75. He and his friend Timmy Banister had enjoyed the "bulldogs" and other types of fire crackers during the days prior to the 4th. I'm not sure all the neighbors appreciated the noise but none complained. Every once in a while the neighborhood would be rocked by the sound of an explosion. Uusally they came from the wooded hallow. The sound was made all the more threatening because of the echo produced by the "bulldog" being set off in the ravine. Needless to say Buddy and his pal Timmy really enjoyed being the source of such loud bangs. At night Buddy set off Roman candles, fountains, and the spectacular Wheel of Fire. The latter was attached to a post and as it spun around the brilliant colors of the exploding powders made everyone gasp, and oh and ah. Everyone agreed that Buddy had out done himself. Of course, he loves to put on a show. In his mind it was just another show business production -- like the successful circus that had earned him so much fame as a local showman.

Dad received a letter from his sister Maude who lives in Iowa City. She wanted to set a date for the annual family reunion for late July or early August. We usually have it at a park in Iowa City. It is the only family reunion that we attend. Dad's mother's people -- the Kelleys -- were small in numbers (his mother Roberta was an only child) and so never did have reunions. When Aunt Maude wrote her letter, she hadn't received the news that Dad had been selected to be one of the alternates for the Illinois delegation at the Democratic National Convention. The convention is scheduled to meet in late July. So, dad phoned her to tell her about the the good news and to suggest that the reunion be held on a weekend in mid August.

Speaking of family reunions reminds me that Grandma Mendell is talking about going to Chicago to visit her brother Aaron and daughter Ruth. She has been receiving letters from both of them lately. She got two letters yesterday. Todd Miller our postman delivered one at the morning delivery and another at the late afternoon delivery. Apparently some of the letters have contained some very disturbing news because Grandma seems to be deep in thought and rather down. When I finally got up the nerve to ask her what was the matter, she told me things that I had never heard about before. The information really surprised me. She started out by telling me that she had learned from my Aunt Ruth and my Great Uncle Aaron that many of our relatives on the Goldman side who live in occupied Europe have not been heard from for over two years. However, Aaron told her that recently one branch of the family had been helped to flee from Denmark to England. Then, came the real surprise. She lowered her voice and whispered, "I feel that I must tell you Mark that the Goldmans are Jewish. My maiden name was Goldman. I married into the Mendell family; it is also Jewish. Of course, your mother knows this. Your father found out before he married her. I think that it is time you and Buddy and Carol know the truth about your Jewish heritage. We must do something to help our relatives who have been persecuted by the Nazis. And, we can't very well do it if some members of the family do not know what is going on."

Then, she elaborated on the plight of our Jewish kin. She told me that Aaron had learned from his son Noah who is in U.S. Intelligence that Hitler set up concentration camps throughout Europe for the purpose of killing Jews in mass. [The two of them must have worked out their own secret code because V-mail was censored.] Aaron feels that many of our relatives may have been placed in such camps and murdered. That would explain why we haven't heard anything from so many them. Grandma indicated that she would like to go to Chicago to visit Aaron in order to read Noah's letters and those of the Goldmans who are now refugees living in England. Hopefully, she and Aaron could agree on how they might help them. She told me that she had asked Dad to drive to Chicago but he had suggested taking a train because of the gas and tire shortage. She would like some company on the trip and she asked me if I would go with her if I could get off from work for a few days. Right now our plans are up in the air.

Of course, Grandma Mendell had already told Dad and Mom about the contents of the letters. After supper when Carol and Buddy were outside playing, we had a long discussion about Aaron's letter. Toward the end Grandma expressed the view that we should not tell anyone outside the family about our Jewish heritage for awhile. She explained that she had really tried to fit in and be part of the neighborhood. She did not want that to change. She felt that we could celebrate our heritage among ourselves. She ended by saying, "There are some things -- private family things -- that don't have to be shared with others. This is all the more true in this case because discrimination toward Jews is a fact of life." Mom and Dad agreed with this. However, Dad expressed the view that sooner or later it would come out and that we would have to deal with the way people react to it. "Hopefully," he said, "people in our neighborhood will understand and judge us as the individuals that they have gotten to know and like."

The Passing Parade

News Stories: "War Comes to the People of Normandy"
"War and Civil Liberties"

Song: ""You'd Be So Nice To Come Home To" by Dinah Shore

Movie: "Follow the Boys" with Marlene Dietrich and George Raft

Planning a Trip, Polio, Insanity, Carol's Request, and a Paper Drive

Sunday, July 9, 1944

I'm going to be able to go with Grandma Mendell. I talked to my boss at **The Daily Herald** and he said it would be fine as long as I trained a replacement. I had to make a lot of phone calls before I found that Cole Stewart would be willing to fill in for me. Mom would like to go too but feels that she needs to stay home to take care of Carol and Buddy. Grandma and I will take the Rock Island rocket to Chicago where we will be met by Aaron at the train station.

Mom and Dad still seem a bit uneasy about the trip; they had a long discussion with Grandma yesterday in her room. I'm not sure what they discussed. Later that night Dad came into my room, closed the door, and had a long talk with me. We covered the usual topics: college, working at **The Daily Herald,** and yes girls -- and then he told me that he thought that it was good that I was going with Grandma. He said that he felt she would be safer if someone went with her and besides I could get to know Mom's relatives better. He told me that he had never said much about Mom's family because he felt it wasn't his place to do so. He said that he had been waiting for Mom or Grandma to find the right time to tell me more about the Mendells and Goldmans. I asked him if he had told his family about Mom's background. He said that over the years he had told a few close family members -- his sisters and brother and his Aunt Sadie and Uncle Ira. They promised to keep it a secret until Mom wanted to share the information with others. They all realized how hostile many people feel about Jews -- that many feel that Jews are "Christ killers" and are only interested in money. He told me that when people find out about it -- as they were bound to do-- some of them may turn their backs against the family -- and even perhaps be openly hostile.

Miss Kline is still in the hospital; she seems to be getting weaker. Dorothy Banister told Mom that she had tried to see her everyday before or after her volunteer work. Dorothy said that Miss Kline seems to be resigned to dying. She seems to be comforted by the thought that she will soon join her parents in heaven. She told one of her visitors that she is looking forward "to waking up in heaven and looking into Christ's face."

Another real concern among the neighbors this summer is the number of polio cases that have occurred in our area. There have been 22 cases reported up to now; most of those who got it are children. 4 children have died of it so far. Polio strikes so suddenly and there isn't much one can do but take the person to a hospital and put him in an iron lung machine and wait for the illness to take its path -- which may be complete paralysis or death. The March of Dimes provides some money to help families pay for hospital bills. Of course, you might be lucky like President Roosevelt and get it and then recover the use of most of your muscles. [Like most people at that time Mark was under the impression that F.D.R. was more mobile than he was.] I think the worst part of a polio epidemic is that everyone is so scared. I guess it is the uncertainty that gets to everyone. What causes it? Who will get it? Is there anything a person can do to prevent getting it? If someone gets it, what will be the result? Can you be close to anyone who is suffering from the early stages of polio?

Right now some parents have told their children not to go to movies, to the swimming pool, or any place where they may come in contact with someone who has the germ or infection or whatever causes it. It's scary. I guess, like I mentioned before, we are fearful because we don't know what causes it let alone how to cure it.

Mom heard from Mrs. McCoy that the Harringtons are having problems with Ed. As I understand it Ed decided to try out for the St. Louis Browns and failed. He came home and went into a deep depression. His behavior became more and more irrational. He woke up one morning and asked for 2 eggs for breakfast. After he finished, he demanded 2 more -- and after that 2 more. This strange behavior went on for 3 hours. When they ran out of eggs, he began yelling and being abusive to his parents. Finally, the family had him institutionalized at the Milltown State Mental Hospital on the advice of their family doctor. He will remain there for as long as it takes to bring him out of his depression. It has been reported that shock treatments have already been started.

The entire Harrington family is having a difficult time dealing with the situation. Mrs. Harrington is especially depressed about it. She always thought that they -- and especially her children -- were so much better than everyone else. Well, mental illness -- like polio -- can strike anyone at anytime. Mrs. McCoy and the Bishop sisters have talked to the family and told them that they are available to help in anyway. But, up to now they have declined any help.

On a happier note Carol finally heard from Mr. Standstadt about her request to board a horse on his estate. It came by way of Arvid. Mr. Standstadt told him that he would give the idea a six month trial. However, Mr. Standstadt wants Carol to wait until after Mr. Standstadt's daughter's wedding which takes place during the last week of July before she brings her horse to the estate. I guess the reception will take place on the estate and there are over 1,000 guests invited to the wedding. Of course, Carol was trilled to find out that Mr. Standstadt would give the idea a trial and didn't mind waiting a bit. It will probably take most of the summer to find a horse that Carol likes and that fits Dad's budget. But, right now, Carol is one happy cowgirl.

The local Cub Scout troops have been collecting paper for the war effort. Buddy really got carried away with the project. He was told that if he collected 10,000 lbs. of paper, he would receive an Eisenhower Medal. Well, he did it. He collected every piece of paper he could get his hands on. This included not only newspaper but wall paper, shelf paper, and notebook paper. He received his metal which was made even more impressive by a red, white and blue bar above the round mental image of Eisenhower. Dad took a photograph of Buddy with his medal. He wears it all the time now. He pins it on his suit when he goes to church. He wears it when he goes out to play. And, yes, he pins it on his pajamas at night.

The Passing Parade

News Stories: "Refugees Arrive From Europe"
"Red Cross Workers Speed Production"

Song: "Peg O'My Heart" by the Harmonicats

Movie: "Home In Indiana" with Walter Brennan

An Attempt To Kill Hitler, F.D.R.'s Letter, Trip to Chicago

It's been quite a week in terms of news about the war, the up-coming presidential election, and our own family.

First, let me write about the war. There was a report that there was an attempt to kill Hitler. Someone planted a bomb in his headquarters and it exploded injuring but not killing him. Too bad -- getting rid of him probably would shorten the war. Another big story was about London being bombed by Robot Bombs. They are small rockets launched from Europe; they are designated to strike at cities in England. They have inflicted a lot of damage because they come in unexpectedly and are difficult to stop. There has been some reports that Germany will eventually have the ability to send rockets to the eastern coast of the U.S.

American casualties are up to 274,626 since D-Day. 59,043 of those have been killed. The fighting continues to be fierce as both the Japs and Germans offer stiff resistence. In the newspaper there was a story about evidence that the Nazis plan to destroy occupied cities before they retreat as a preparatory measure for another war. I guess Paris will be included despite its art treasures. Also, the Japs announced that all captured U.S. B-29 flyers will be executed. The same fate awaits all American airmen who bail out over Japan.

In terms of politics the big news was that F.D.R. will accept the nomination. He wrote a letter to National Democratic Party Chairman Robert E. Hannegan in which he elaborated on why he would accept another nomination for the presidency. The letter was published in full. In my opinion here are the significant paragraphs:

Dear Mr. Hannegan:

"If the convention should . . . nominate me for the Presidency, I shall accept. If the people elect me, I will serve.

"Every one of our sons serving in this war has officers from whom he takes orders. Such officers have superior officers. The President is the Commander in Chief and he, too, has his superior officer -- the people of the United States.

". . . if the people command me to continue in this office and in this war, I have as little right to withdraw as the soldier has his post in the line.

"For myself, I do not want to run . . . . All that is within me cries to go back to my home on the Hudson River, to avoid public responsibilities, and to avoid also the publicity which in our democracy follows every step of the Nation's Chief Executive.

"Such would be my choice. But we of this generation chance to live in a day and hour when our Nation has been attacked, and when its future existence and the future existence of our chosen method of government are at stake.

"To win this war wholeheartedly, unequivocally, and as quickly as we can is our task of the first importance. To win this war in such a way that there be no further world wars in the foreseeable future is our second objective. To provide occupations, and to provide a decent standard of living for our men in the armed forces after the war, and for all Americans, are the final objectives.

"Therefore, reluctantly, but as a good soldier, I repeat that I will accept and serve in the office, if I am so ordered by the Commander in Chief of us all -- the sovereign people of the United States."

Very sincerely yours,
Franklin D. Roosevelt

As Grandma Mendell and I road on the train to Chicago, I decided to ask her why I had not been told about our Jewish heritage earlier. She admitted that I should have been told earlier and that she knew my father hoped that the truth would finally come out and be shared with members of the family. She realized that he was waiting for Mother to tell us. However, Grandma reminded me that there was a reason for keeping it secret. She told me about the prejudice toward Jews. Over the years the Goldmans and the Mendells had tried to become part of America. They became Reform Jews in terms of customs and traditions. While the families attended synagogue, they did not send their children to Jewish schools. This often produced conflict within the family between the old and young generations. For example, when Grandma's Grandfather Jacob Goldman an Orthodox Jew lived with her family he strongly condemned those in the family who would not continue the orthodox traditions.

As time passed the families merged more and more into the "accepted" American community. She told me that the Mendells had altered their name in order to fit in -- to appear more part of the Anglo-Saxon culture. The Mendells changed their name from Mendelssohn to simply Mendell hoping that it would sound less Jewish. They often named their children with less Jewish sounding first names. As their children grew up, they married outside the Jewish faith and often changed to the faith of their gentile spouses. This is what happened to Mom. She met Dad, got married and then adopted his religion -- Presbyterianism.

Grandma admitted that she had experienced feelings of guilt and shame when she read about the death camps in Aaron's letters and from news stories. She said that she looked within herself and asked herself some painful questions. Hadn't she deserted the faith? Hadn't she turned her back on her heritage? Wasn't she a coward for not being willing to let people know about her heritage? What could she do to help the Goldmans who had fled to England? Aaron had asked himself similar questions and had experienced the same feelings. When he had married, he had married a gentile and had converted to the Episcopalian faith in order to fit in. Then, the request came from the Goldman refugees. Both Aaron and Grandma feel that they can not turn their backs on them and refuse to help. But, they realize that in helping them, they will have to reveal their Jewish heritage.

When we arrived at Union Station in downtown Chicago, Aaron was there to meet us. He looks a lot like grandma but just a bit younger by 4 years. He is short, with white hair, and wears very thick reading glasses. His smile is shy but engaging. He hugged Grandma, shook my hand and said that he was so happy to see both of us. Then, he drove us to his home in Oak Park. There we met his wife

Thelma who had prepared a late lunch for us. After we ate we sat in the living room while Grandma read the V-mail letters from Noah and the letters from the Goldmans who were now living in a refugee camp in England. Aaron and Grandma agreed that they had to welcome this as an opportunity to help. They never referred to the task as "a responsibility" or "duty" but always as "an opportunity" and "a privilege."

They also spoke about the reports of the death camps and speculated about what probably had happened to other relatives living in Paris and Brussels. Apparently the local populations in many areas under German control had been cooperating fully with the Nazis in handing over Jews. Of course, there were always exceptions. In Denmark the Christian population had been hiding and protecting Jews. But, most of our relatives did not live in Denmark but in France, Belgium, and the Netherlands. They had not been heard from for years, and they probably had been sent to the death camps.

Later in the afternoon my Aunt Ruth arrived with her two children -- Rachel and Ruben. Again the focus of the conversation was on helping the Goldman refugees now living in England. Grandma agreed with Aaron that he should contact them and indicate that he and others in the family are ready to help. He should go ahead and find out about the papers and requirements necessary to bring the family to the United States. He would also ask the Goldmans how we could help them now with clothes, money, and necessities.

The Passing Parade

News Story: "The Coming Battle for Germany"

Song: "La Vie En Rose" by Edith Piaf

Movie: "Double Indemnity" with Barbara Stanwyck

ACCEPTING OUR JEWISH HERITAGE, TWO DEATHS, F.D.R.'S NOMINATION

After Grandma and I got back home from Chicago, there was a big family discussion about what we had learned from Great Uncle Aaron. All agreed that we needed to help the Goldmans find a new home in the United States. Mom and Dad seemed happy that Grandma had told me more about her family. Mom told me later that she would have told me earlier but didn't know how to go about it. She felt that one of the good things that resulted from the Goldmans seeking help was that our Jewish heritage was finally being discussed within the immediate family. She told me and Dad that she shared her mother's guilt over hiding the past even though it was done for a very practical reason -- to escape being labeled "a Jew" and being discriminated against.

I must admit that I have had a hard time dealing with the situation and with the fact that the information was hidden from me for so long. Buddy and Carol seem to be able to take it in stride. Of course, I wonder if they really understand what being a Jew is and what the consequences of it may be. I doubt if they really understand how their lives may be affected when and if someone outside of the family gets wind of our Jewish heritage and acts in a hostile way about it How will Buddy and Carol deal with name calling or being ignored and left out? I guess the family will simply have to deal with these things if and when they develop. Personally, I feel very uneasy and a bit fearful that once my Jewish heritage is made public, that I will lose friends.

I have to admit that I had not realized what it was like to be considered different in a society. I remembered news stories about fights between white and Negro soliders at canteens. I recalled that the Japanese-Americans had been placed in relocation camps. Until now these situations did not mean much to me. But, now, they do. It is obvious that if you are too different, you are going to have some problems. I recalled Jim Banister telling Kelly about one of his pals in the service braging about shooting a Negro soldier who had gone into an outhouse on the camp to go to the bathroom -- about how he had imagined with glee how the "dumb S.O.B." had been surprised by the bullet coming through the side of the "john." Jim described it as something exciting -- like the killing of a wild dog. Suddenly, the idea that one could order the mass killing of Jews became a fact -- a reality in my mind. Now, I was one of the minorities too. It was hard to realize what had happened overnight to change my view of myself -- and how others would view me once "the news" about me got around. Even now it crosses my mind that I would prefer getting polio than being a Jew. In a way it would be more acceptable in some peoples' minds than being a "Jew boy." I had often heard that term but now it had a far more personal meaning. I now understood what Dave Patterson was going through

106

by being one of the few Negroes at McKinley High School. I was now able to feel what he must have always felt -- alone, different, and uneasy.

Two of our neighbors died this week. Miss Kline finally died in the hospital of cancer. She got thinner and weaker and finally died of malnutrition as the cancer spread throughout her entire body. She experienced a lot of intense pain too. Her funeral was held at the Riverside Presbyterian Church with burial at Riverside Cemetery. Miss Kline's estate went largely to her cousins. Nobody knows if Miss Whitman received anything in the will.

The other death was Irene's mother Connie Phillips. While she was still weak from giving birth, nobody expected her to die. Irene found her mother dead in her bedroom when she went up to check on her. She had brought Betty up the stairs with her to visit her mother. Irene told Mrs. McCoy that she knew something was wrong because her mother appeared blue in color. The doctor said that Mrs. Phillip's heart had been weakened by giving birth and it wasn't able to recover. The funeral was held at the First Methodist Church with burial at Riverside Cemetery next to her first husband.

Irene has been trying to deal not only with the death of her mother but what to do next. Her mother's sister Elizabeth and her husband Greg has offered to take her into their home. They live in Rockford, Ill. They told her that she could go to one of the nearby colleges in the fall and that they would help pay for her board and tuitioin. The big stumpling block is Betty. Mr. Phillips will not give her up. He has told Irene that Betty is his natural daughter and that he will arrange for a nanny to raise her if Irene leaves. Irene has grown to love Betty, and she feels that she can't leave her. She has also told people that her mother asked her to care for Betty if anything happened to her. After thinking it over, Irene has decided to stay with her step father and care for Betty. She was hoping to go to college but this will not be possible. She doesn't have any money of her own, and besides it is a full time job taking care of Betty. A lot of the neighbors -- especially Mrs. Moore and Mrs. Wells -- feel that Irene is making a mistake but hesitate to get involved. They admire her loyalty to her mother's memory, but wonder if there can't be a more sensible solution to the situation. If only Mr. Phillips was a different kind of man, things could be handled better. Dad feels that Mr. Phillips should cooperate with Mrs. Phillip's sister and work out a more equitable plan for all concerned.

Both Hitler and Roosevelt are making more news. Hitler appointed Himmler to stifle the revolt in Germany. He and his S.S. have conducted a Nazi blood purge; many high ranking military officials have been arrested and will stand trial. Hitler has tried to connect up the revolt with one supposedly similar to it in 1918 prior to the surrender of Germany. On July 22, Hitler claimed that the revolt had been crushed. While Hilter escaped a plot to assassinate him, he was seriously injured by the explosion that killed several members of his staff.

Meanwhile, on July 20, F.D.R. was nominated again for the Presidency at the Democratic Convention in Chicago. Dad is attending the convention and I'm looking forward to his account of the affair. Photos of F.D.R. are all over the newspapers and news magazines. While a few show a smiling F.D.R, most have shown a rather thin and sick looking picture of him. Of course, Dad reminded me that most of the news publications in the country are Republican so naturally they would want to present an unflatering image of F.D.R.

The Passing Parade

News Story: "Hitler Appeals for Army Loyality"

Song: "That Old Black Magic" by Glenn Miller

Movie: "Going My Way" with Bing Crosby

Report on the Convention, A High Society Wedding, and Some Heroic Vets

Dad returned from Chicago with Ben Gilbert after attending the Democratic Convention. They were both alternates to the convention. They stayed at the Drake Hotel in downtown Chicago along with other delegates and alternates. He told me that he really felt that he was helping to make history. However, he said he would never forget all the in-fighting over the vice presidential nomination. Of course, knowing that the "Boss" (F.D.R.) wanted Truman settled it. Dad had liked Henry Wallace's liberalism -- especially on farm issues -- but went along with what F.D.R. wanted. The tribute to F.D.R. was one of the events that he will always remember; the speeches were touching and the demonstrations enthusiastic. He admires F.D.R.'s willingness to forgo retirement to do his duty for the country and see the war through to the end. Dad feels that F.D.R. can and will win again because according to him "nobody wants to change horses in midstream."

Dad feels that Truman can help carry many farm states. Truman has a good record as a Senator from Missouri. He has a good reputation as a reformer and safeguarder of the public purse. Truman heads a committee that investigates possible wrong doings with regard to defense spending. This is giving him a lot of favorable press. However, Dad is concerned that Truman has little experience in foreign affairs and hopes that he will be able to learn a lot from F.D.R. Dad believes that F.D.R. is the only man who will be able to deal with the conflicting goals of the important nations united against the Fascists powers.

Dad said that he will always remember another emotional moment at the Convention -- the evening of July 20th when Roosevelt accepted the nomination. Since the President was on the West Coast -- I think at Camp Pendleton -- his acceptance speech was broadcasted through the loadspeakers while spotlights focused on a large photograph of him in the auditorium. F.D.R.'s voice was strong and confident as he declared, "Let us strive on to finish the work we are in; to bind up the Nation's wounds . . . . to do all which may achieve and cherish a just and lasting peace among ourselves, and with all Nations."

The Standstadt wedding took place this week too. I did not attend nor did any of our neighbors as guests. We only experienced it as sideliners to a luxurious and exclusive event of the high society of Milltown. Of course, we learned a lot about the details of the wedding from Arvid Gustafson and his wife Caroline. Arvid as head butler on the estate had the responsibility for making sure that everything went smoothly at the banquet and party that followed the wedding. He was told to plan to have the tables set up near the swimming pool and rose garden located west of the mansion. Caroline went over to help serve the guests. Since a lot of the Standstadt relatives stayed at the house, there was a lot to do. Caroline helped prepare and serve breakfast, dress some of the older ladies in the family, and later serve food at the banquet.

Arvid said that it was the most spectacular wedding he had ever seen. Elizabeth Standstadt had ten bridesmaids plus several flower girls and a ring bearer. Arvid said that a catering firm from Chicago handled the food. Believe it or not the food was transported in special containers by train from Chicago to Milltown. Cases of champagne were served at the party. The church and the setting for the party were decorated with flower baskets containing white, pink, and red carnations along with white baby's breath. The guest list included some of the most important business people in the country. There were some political leaders there too. All Republicans, of course. The Standstadts socialize with a lot of high society people when they winter in Florida. Also, they go to Chicago a lot -- to the so-called "gold coast" area -- where they stay with friends who own large estates along Lake Michigan.

The wedding was conducted at the St. John's Episcopal Church. We saw the wedding party pose in the front of the church for pictures. Later we saw the limousines go through the gates at the Standstadt estate. Still later one could hear the laughter of guests and the music from the dance band especially hired for the day. At times, I found myself tempted to dress up in a tuxedo (rented of course) and try to "crash" the party. My desire to do this increased as day wore on and the neighbors heard more laughter and splashing of water. It was obvious to me from the sounds that some of the guests had gone to the bath house to exchange their tuxedos and long formals for bathing suits and were now enjoying the pool. All these sounds echoed throughout the wooded ravines that surround the estate. They certainly made one feel very left out.

During the week Anna Swedson left for St. Louis. Glen has been transferred to a veteran's hospital there. He has to continue his physical therapy so that he can do a more for himself. Anna wants to find a job down there so she can rent a room to be close to Glen. She hopes to be hired as a waitress somewhere near the hospital. Everyone is impressed with Anna's determination. She has been a rather shy, clinging person most of her life. I guess it shows the strength of her love for Glen. Only that accounts for her sudden strength and willingness to take chances. As Mom said, "When you are truly in love, you will do everything -- risk all for that person. Anna knows that Glen needs her to get better -- and to adjust to his paralysis. She wants to meet that need -- and help him."

Buddy and Carol have been trying to help wounded veterans. They both made scrapbooks at Cub Scouts and Brownies for the veterans who are at local hospitals. The Scouts cut out all sorts of humorous cartoons and funny stories out of magazines and newspapers to put into their scrapbooks. During the week Buddy and Carol were part of several groups of Scouts that made visits to our local hospitals where many veterans are being treated. Carol told me that she felt strange around the patients but that she was glad she went. She hoped that the visit will help the men feel better. One veteran without arms smiled at her and asked all kinds of questions about her -- what she was interested in, and what she enjoyed most about being a Brownie. She was really impressed that he was interested in her. She wondered how he was able to think of her when he was in such bad shape. He told her that he has a little girl too who is also interested in horses. He gave her a lot of good advice about boarding a horse. Buddy admitted that he too felt self conscious as he visited the vets. And, like Carol, he felt better as he talked with them and saw how funny they found the jokes and cartoons that he had included in his scrapbook.

In **The Daily Herald** there was a story about a heroic vet by the name of Captain Ralph C. Fisher, who commanded a company of armored infrantry in Italy. He needed artillery in order to hold his position. When told that it would be too dangerous because some of our fire might hit American forces, he ordered the artillery to proceed because it was the only way to hold the enemy. He thought that it was worth the gamble. Well, he lost. Captain Fisher was killed by our own artillery. He received a D.S.C. for his bravery. The story brought home to me how much guts and courage it takes to be on the front lines -- and that this type of sacrifice is needed again and again to win the war.

The Passing Parade

News Story: "Paris Is Free Again"

Song: "It Had To Be You" by Helen Forrest and Dick Haymes

Movie: "Destination Tokyo" with Gary Grant

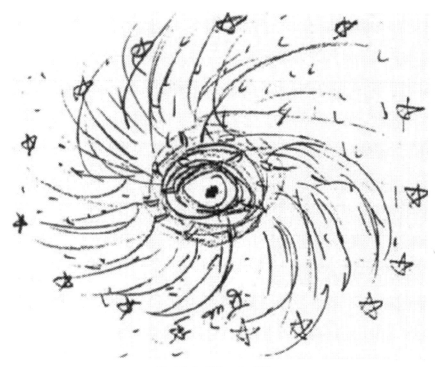

Buddy's Wheel of Fire

THE JOHNSON FAMILY REUNION AND AN END TO A WARTIME ROMANCE

I'm writing this on Monday because over the weekend we all went to Iowa City for the Johnson family reunion. Some of us stayed with Aunt Maude while others stayed with Uncle John or Dad's Aunt Sadie. I went out to Uncle John's farm to stay for one night, and had a swell time sharing a room with my cousin Phillip.

Aunt Maude had rented the pavilion at Lakeside Park for the event. Attendance was pretty good considering that many family members are in the service and others are not traveling because of gas rationing. A total of 73 people were counted at the business meeting. Before the war Dad told me that we often had 90 people or more at the reunion.

We saw a lot of people who we really like -- and a lot of others who we can take or leave. I guess that is rather typical with family relationships. Most of the relatives came from the Iowa City area or Des Moines. We saw a lot of our cousins -- first and second ones -- like Florence Hume, Velma Patchin, Rich Bolte, and Elizabeth Baker. Dad especially liked talking to his Aunt Sadie who is his father's sister. She would be my great aunt. Ever since Dad lost his mother back in 1938, he has been especially close to Sadie. She was there with her bachelor brother Ira. Both are in their 60s. Both are tall, big-boned people with naturally curly hair (now white) and blue eyes that are peering out of metal framed eyeglasses. Sadie had gone to live with Ira on the old Johnson family homestead after she lost her husband. Dad enjoyed talking with his Uncle Ira too -- especially about farming and the up-coming election. After Dad's father passed away in 1942, he has tried to find a replacement for his relationship with him. While Ira is interesting to talk to, Dad says that there isn't the same close emotional feeling that he had with his father. He said, "Once a relationship is ended by death, it can never truly be recreated again." The closest that he has come to doing it has been his relationship with his Aunt Sadie. She reminds him of his mother (Roberta Kelley) not so much in terms of her physical appearance but in terms of her caring attitude toward him and her dry sense of humor. Every time he visits with her he feels that he has as he puts it "revisited his mother in some way." Also, he has told me that he has experienced a feeling of revisiting a relationship that he had with a dead friend through a new friendship with another person.

Aunt Maude with the help of her husband Roy had organized the event very well. Aunt Sadie had posted the family trees on the side walls of the pavilian for all to see and to examine. There was also a table for family memorbilia. An old family Bible, letters written by Great Great Grandpa Edward C. Johnson, a pocket watch owned by him, and a lot of old faded photographs were on the table. As always the food was delicious. Every family had contributed something -- a casserole, a salad, a pie, a cake. Aunt Maude and Uncle Roy had purchased and prepared several stand- up roasts and hams. Also, Great Aunt Sadie with the help of her brother Ira had fried up some of their own chickens from the farm.

During the business meeting that followed lunch, relatives heard the minutes of last year's reunion read by the Uncle John, and then Aunt Maude invited anyone to share a a past rememberance or talk about an heirloom that they had brought. Cousin Florence had brought a log cabin quilt that had belonged to her grandmother, and cousin Rich had brought a tool box that had belonged to his great grandfather. Also, people were asked to tell everyone how many members of their family were in the armed services. The count came to a surprising 15. A prize was given to the family with the largest number of members present at the reunion. Also, a prize was given to the oldest family member in attendance. At the end of the meeting we all bowed our heads while the Rev. Theodore Johnson, who is a Methodist minister, led us in a prayer of thanksgiving for the family. Also, he called upon God to protect those family members who are serving our country overseas.

After the meeting, group pictures were taken of the various branches of the family. After that people either sat around talking or played soft ball or horse shoes. Some of the kids like Buddy and Carol went swimming in the park's public swimming pool. While some relatives started to leave about 4:00 to drive home, others stayed for a supper of warmed up left overs and some more conversation. By 7:30 everyone was either headed home or going to the place they had arranged to stay over night.

[Code: Phillip and I talked late into the night about our plans for the future. He liked the idea that I might attend the University of Iowa and stay with him and his folks. I told him about Dad's reservations about my doing this. Phillip told me not to give up the idea because we could help each other in basic courses like freshman Composition. He told me that "we can have a good time at college and still do well in terms of grades." He also brought me up-to-date on his girlfriends. He told me that he had been dating a girl named Peggy Thompson who lives on a farm nearby and that he had finally felt "her hole of creation." I asked him where it happened. He smiled and said that they had gone on a date and then parked on country lane that isn't used too much. They had started kissing and exploring and one thing led to another. Peggy had unzipped his fly and had reached in and started gently touching his "cob." Phillip had responded by reaching under her dress and into her panties. Peggy had opened her legs so that he could touch her "sacred temple of pleasure" as Phillip described it.

Well, things went from there to making love. Phillip said that he reached in the glove compartment to get a "rubber." He said Peggy was so wet that he found that it was easy to insert his "cob" into her. He told me that he had put some of his saliva on the top of his covered "cob" to start with. Anyway, he said that he was finding "husking his own cob" not as satisfying as being with Peggy and feeling "the hole of creation." Phillip said that if I would be able to stay up there with him and attend college, he could fix me up with a lot of girls who would love to go out with a college man -- and as he put it "give me some."]

[Code: On the way back home I came to the conclusion that living with Phillip and being tempted to spend time with a girl who would be willing "to give me some" did not go along with maintaining a good grade average. I thought to myself, "Dad is right -- I better go to St. Andrew and stay at home the first two years at least."]

On the war front, the big news was the invasion of Guam and the Mariana Islands. Again, the losses have been heavy as the Japs feel that it would be better to die -- or commit suicide -- than to surrender. It is part of the Samurai Code of conduct to preserve one's respect and dignity. To them suicide is better than surrender under any and all circumstances.

On the home front, one of the casualties has been a marriage. The divorce and what led up to it has been the talk of the neighborhood all week. It came as a complete surprise because nobody -- and I mean nobody -- knew what was going on in the McCoy household. It seems that Laura McCoy (George McCoy's wife and the mother of Patty) was having an affair with the doctor that she works for. As I understand it, she and a girl friend would go off for weekends to supposedly visit a mutual girl friend in Peoria, Illinois. Mr. McCoy became suspicious and so he followed them (I guess he used another car so that they would not recognize his coal truck.) Instead of driving to Peoria, the women drove to a hotel in Keyport where they met their respective employers (both doctors). When Laura was confronted with the evidence, she did not deny that she was having an affair. After George found out what had been going on, he told his parents to arrange for a divorce. While custody of Patty was given to Laura, the McCoys were given extensive visiting privileges.

Everyone in the neighborhood agrees that it was a very sad situation. Mrs. Moore and Mrs. Wells recalled when Laura and George had gotten married at the start of the war, and how they had been so much in love with one another. They feel, along with so many others, that if George had been home and not serving his country overseas that this divorce would never have taken place.

The Passing Parade

News Stories: "Yanks Cut Off All Of Brittany"
"The 1944 Campaign Begins"

Song: "Sleepy Lagoon" by Harry James

Movie: "And The Angels Sing" with Veronica Lake

Jewish Traditions, A Bloody Nose, and Skinny Dipping

War can bring out the best in people but also the worse. It was reported that President Roosevelt recently received a letter opener made from a bone from a dead Jap soldier. The President sent the thing back to the sender with the suggestion that it be given a proper burial.

Also, there were several stories coming out of France about how the local population is turning against anyone who helped the Germans or were simply too friendly with them. In one French town a seven man Committee of Liberation ordered 25 women to have their heads shaved for being too friendly with German soldiers. I've seen news reels about this too and the whole thing highlights how war brings out the worse in some people. Another story coming out of Rennes, France was about how one Frenchman offered to kill a pro-Nazi for a United Press cameraman.

After we got back from the reunion I had a long talk with Grandma. She told me that while she enjoyed the event, she was saddened by the fact that her own family didn't have such a spirit of unity. She said, "The Johnsons are lucky to be so proud of their past and who they are." Grandma wondered if the Mendells and Goldmans could ever be like the Johnsons some day. Could she plan some day to have a reunion for the Goldmans? for the Mendells? I told her that I thought it was possible. I voiced the opinion that perhaps after the Goldman family from England got to the States, she could plan a reunion. Such an event would give everyone in her family a reason to celebrate. Grandma thought the idea had real possibilities.

She also expressed her need to try to pass on aspects of the Jewish tradition. She said that she wanted to share with me memories of her family celebrating many of the Jewish holidays like Rosh HaShanah, Yom Kippur, and Chanukah. She said that she wanted to explain what being a Jew means. I told her that I would enjoy learning about Jewish customs, beliefs, and traditions. I stressed that I especially wanted to hear about her family and the traditions that they celebrated. Grandma was pleased to hear this. She said, "Mark, I'm happy you feel that way, and Mark, once you understand the traditions, I want you to explain them to Buddy and to Carol."

Grandma suggested that I go to the library and check out books on Judaism. She said it was a complicated faith and that there were Orthodox, Conservative, and Reform Jews. She reminded me that her family had practiced in the Reform tradition. She explained that a Reform Jew continues the traditions of the **Talmud** in everyday living. But, Reform Jews unlike Orthodox Jews accept changes that modern life has brought. She urged me to read about the various aspects of Judaism in order to get background for the discussions that she would have with me about the traditions practiced in her family. She also said that perhaps we could go to a local synagogue to talk to a rabbi. She knew about

115

one synagogue in Keyport we could visit. I told her that I was willing to start checking out books and thought the idea of going to a synagogue and meeting a rabbi sounded very interesting.

It is hard to believe but shy, mild-mannered Timmy gave Buddy a bloody nose. It started over a game of baseball. As I understand it, Timmy hit the ball and then failed to run fast enough to get to first base. Buddy blamed him for causing their team to get another out -- thereby losing the game. Timmy resented the criticism which he considered very unfair and out of frustration hit Buddy in the nose. Mom thought that she should do something to help the two boys mend fences. She called Dorothy Banister and asked her to send Timmy up to the house so she could sit down with the boys and help them restore their friendship. Dorothy thought it was a good idea and thanked Mom for taking on the job. After discussing the fight for about twenty minutes, both boys apologized -- Buddy for his unfair criticism and Timmy for hitting Buddy -- and then shook hands. When dad heard about the settlement of the dispute, he really was impressed with Mom's ability to restore peace and harmony. In fact, he said, "Let's write a letter to President Roosevelt suggesting that he appoint Mom to the World Court or perhaps to our delegation to this soon to be organized body called the United Nations." We all agreed that it sounded like a good idea.

During the week I managed to go out to the Boy Scout Camp for an outing. Camp Black Hawk is located 15 miles southeast of Milltown. It is on top of a steep hill which is surrounded by thick wooded ravins. Cole Steward substituted for me again at **The Daily Herald.** I rode out with several other guys -- Nick Temple, Fred Turner Mark Trotter, and Todd Keller -- who were interested in visiting their pals who are camp counselors. We spent part of the day walking along old Indian trails and doing some leather crafts. I got materials to make a billfold. We also helped the counselors teach first aid training to the younger Scouts. The training is part of the war effort. Just in case of an attack a good knowledge of splinting, bandaging, etc. by a lot of people will come in handy. Of course, the boys also earn a merit badge for achieving a high proficiency in first aid.

Later in the afternoon we went swimming in the outside pool. It was really swell because there weren't so many people in it. While some of the counselors taught a swimming class for younger boys, we swam in the deeper end and used the diving boards. We stayed in the pool after the swimming classes were dismissed. Todd brought us some food from the cafeteria so we could eat our supper along the side of the pool. [Code: When it started getting very dark, the guys decided to go skinny dipping. Although I felt uncomfortable about it, I went along with it. We dove off the diving boards and then played water polo in the pool that now was only lit by the light shinning from the moon and the few underwater lights. I have to admit that I felt a great sense of freedom -- and it seemed so natural in a way. As we played and horsed around, I began to feel that Nick and Todd were as interested in me as the ball. Several times I found that hands and arms were encompassing my body. When I stopped to see where the ball was or waited for the next round to begin, I often found Nick's or Todd's arms around my waist or chest. Instead of releasing me, they often stood there looking at me and then smiling or laughing. Once I felt Nick's stiff "cob" up against my buttocks. When we ended the polo game, we picked up our wet swimming suits and headed for the locker room. Nick and Todd and several others headed for the shower room. I was going to join them until I saw what they were doing in the dimly lighted room. They had formed a circle and were "husking" their peckers. When Nick saw my reaction, he yelled, "Come on Mark. We all do it. Why not join us? Or, are you saving it all for Maria?" I did not respond. I turned, got dressed and left. So ended my day at Camp Black Hawk.]

The Passing Parade

News Story: "U.S. Lost Battalion Is Rescued After 5-Day Fight Behind Nazi Line"

Song: "Serenade In Blue" by Glen Miller

Movie: "Dragon Seed" with Katherine Hepburn

Brave Soldiers, Polio, the Tunnel of Love, and the Rabbit Incident

Sunday, August 20, 1944

As the war heats up both in Europe and Asia, there are more news stories about the heroic actions of our fighting men and women. One story that I read to Buddy was about Second Lt. Norman Kimmel saving his flight engineer whose name is Don Carlisle. Their flying fortress was returning from Germany in bad shape. Two engines were gone; it was short of gas and riddled by flak. The bomb bay doors were still open. That's when Carlisle decided to drop down into the bay in an attempt to close the doors and relieve the drag on the plane. Well, when he did not reappear, Kimmel went down to see what was wrong. He found Carlisle unconscious -- his oxygen mask ripped off. Kimmel gave up his own mask in order to help Carlisle survive. They barely both made it back to base. Buddy cut out the article with Kimmel's photo and put it up in his room. Like I said before, war brings out the best as well as the worst in people.

The Standstadts decided to invite about 20 recuperating vets from local hospitals to spend the day at their estate. Arvid told us that the event was centered around the swimming pool. While not all the vets could enjoy swimming or wading in the pool because of their disabilities, they could enjoy playing cards, chess, and monopoly. And, of course, most could enjoy the buffet lunch that had been prepared. Caroline told us that the Standstadt had ordered a catering firm to supply a wide variety of dishes and deserts so that the men could find something that they would enjoy eating. Caroline was placed in charge of music and she got the latest hit records to play for the men. Anyway, the neighbors actually enjoyed hearing the sounds of laughter, music, and splashing water echoing through the wooded ravines surrounding the estate. At least this time, we did not feel left out but instead grateful that the Standstadts had taken the time to extend their hospitality to some vets who deserved the nation's thanks.

While we are all aware of the war going on in Europe and Asia, we are also aware of another war that is going on -- the war against polio. Toward the end of the week polio with lighting speed took one of our neighbors. Professor Olsen's wife Grace suddenly came down with the illness. She had been feeling tired and had a fever for a few days. Then came the paralysis. She was taken to the Milltown Public Hospital and placed in an iron lung. Professor Olsen phoned her parents to come as quickly as they could. They live on a farm outside of Newton, Iowa. Poor Grace did not last long enough to even say goodbye to her parents. She lingered only one day and then died. She wasn't even able to say goodbye to her little girls. The last they saw of her was when she had been placed in an ambulance. The doctors were fearful that they might be exposed to the disease if they visited their mother in the hospital. I was told by Dorothy Banister that Grace at the end seemed to be accepting of the fact that she wasn't going to make it. She looked upon it as God's will. She felt that if she did survived, she would be so handicapped that she would have a difficult time caring for her children.

Professor Olsen is beside himself with grief. It seems overwhelming. Grace's parents -- and also Professor Olsen's parents -- are taking care of the girls. They are trying to help the professor as best they can. They hope that for the the sake of the girls that he will be able to overcome his grief. Mrs. Moore told me that Professor Olsen and Grace had been sweethearts at St. Andrew College. They had married soon after graduation. To see the little girls playing on the walk in front of their home on 11ᵗʰ Avenue is really sad. According to Mrs. Moore, one of the girls -- I think it is Laura -- keeps asking, "Where is mommy?" It is really too much to bear for everyone in the neighborhood. Instead of an open casket funeral, there was a memorial service at the Firist Lutheran Church of Milltown with burial in Newton, Iowa.

I asked Maria to go on a date with me to Lake View Amusement Park which is about 25 miles west of Milltown. Dad let me use the car for the day. As we drove out to the park, we talked about our future plans. I told her that I was thinking of going to the University of Iowa or St. Andrew College. Maria said that she planned to work part time at the A&P Store and then take some courses at the Milltown School of Business.

We had a lot of fun on the rides. We rode the rollercoaster two times. As we decented the high peaks, Maria would grab hold of me for dear life. It was a nice feeling to be so close to her. We also went through the Haunted House which was filled with ghosts and wild animals that would jump out at us. At times we both found ourselves startled and wondering what was going to happen next. Finally, we went through the Tunnel of Love. We were in a small boat that seemed to be sailing on water. Actually, the boat was on a underwater rail. As we went through the tunnel we saw scenes of famous lovers such as Anthony and Cleopatra and Napoleon and Josephine. We also were taken through some areas where there were beautiful flowers and scenery. In the background we could hear the sounds of nature. Other parts of the tunnel were in total darkness except for a light that represented the moon. Romantic music was played in the background to help create the proper atmosphere. We made the most of the opportunity by embracing and kissing again and again.

[Code: At night we went swimming in the lake which was made romantic by the colored lights playing on the water. Instead of swimming out to the deep water we stayed near shore where the water was shallow so we could talk and explore. I playfully touched her breasts and then grasped her around the waist. She didn't protest but laughted and smiled. I felt my "cob" getting hard and extend itself. I think that Maria felt it because she suddenly began swimming to the shore. When we were both on the sandy shore again and lying on the beach towels that we had brought, we held each other and then kissed again and again. Finally, Maria pushed me away and whispered that she felt that things were going too far.]

Buddy got himself into hot water with Dad and Mom. It seems that Kelly Jackson was selling rabbits as pets to children in the neighborhood. Buddy really wanted to own at least two. Several of his pals were able to convince their parents to buy some for them. Dad refused to buy any for Buddy because he felt that we did not have a proper place to keep them. Besides, the price of 50 cents a rabbit seemed too high to Dad. After hearing dad's decision, Buddy stole the money from Mom's purse and purchased two rabbits. The funny thing was the way he tried to pretend that the rabbits had miraculously appeared at our house. He claimed that he did not know how they got there. Well,

Dad finally had Buddy confessing to his "wicked deed." He had a long talk with Buddy and told him that he could keep the rabbits as long as he agreed to the following:

1. make a cage for them,
2. pay for the materials for the cage.
3. do extra chores around the house to make up for the $1.00,
4. take care of them,
5. don't steal money again.

Buddy agreed to all of the above to show that he was willing to quote Dad "assume responsibility for his decision to buy the rabbits." Grandma got a kick out of how Dad settled the matter. She is referring to him as "our Solomon."

In order to raise money to pay for materials to build a cage, Buddy went into the jewelry business. Yes, he opened up a "store front stand" that sold jewelry. He convinced Carol that they could make some money by making and selling jewelry made out of buckeyes. They got the buskeyes free since they grow on several trees in the neighborhood. They made rings and necklaces out of them. Prices - 5 cents for a ring and 10 cents for a necklace. Carol and Buddy split the profits of $1.80. So, Buddy at least earned 90 cents to help him get out of debt.

The Passing Parade

News Story: "Reds Open Major Breach in East Prussia Line"

Song: "Mexicali Rose" by Bring Crosby

Movie: "The Seventh Cross" with Spencer Tracy

CANNING, A SECRET REVEALED, A WINTER PROJECT, AND OPEN HOUSE

A lot of women in the neighborhood are canning. Early in the week Mom and Grandma canned some of the tomatoes and green beans from the Victory garden. Also, they purchased grapes and peaches from a farm outside Andersonville for canning. It is hard work and hot too. They have been storing the jars down in the cellar. Some of the neighbors like the Jacksons have fruit cellars near their homes. While the work is hard, everyone feels that it will pay off in the winter. Mom always reminds herself and anyone who will listen that it will be great to have home made grape jelly and peach jam in the winter from our own cellar. Also, she reminds us that our own home grown green beans and tomatoes always taste so much better than the canned ones that you buy at the store.

Well, the secret is out. Buddy talked to Mr. McCoy and mentioned our Jewish relatives in England and how we were going to try to help them. Naturally, Mr. McCoy told his wife and now it is all over the neighborhood. Grandma wasn't too happy when she heard what had happened. But Dad told her that it was going to happen one way or the other. Besides, Buddy probably doesn't really understand how the information might be received by others. We sense that Kelly Jackson and Jim Banister have become stand-offish. They usually like to visit with Dad but they tend to run the other way now when Dad approaches them. Mrs. McCoy and several others have been less friendly. Of course, Grandma isn't surprised. She told me that she had experienced this sort of thing in Chicago as a child and later as an adult. Mom agreed with her. Grandma and Dad both agree that the only thing we can do is to be what we are and try to educate people about our family and the stereotypes that people have about Jews as well as we can over a long period of time. The main thing is to set a good example and show by our actions that we are good neighbors. "Some people," said Dad, "will never ask questions or bring up the matter in the open. That makes it difficult to educate them. That is why it is important that we continue to show them by our actions that we aren't a threat to them. Besides, actions are stronger and more clearly understood and believed than words."

Grandma and Dad both agree that we will find out who our real friends are in the next few months. "That word 'friend'," observed Grandma, "is too loosely used. A lot of so-called 'friends' are really job buddies or church buddies or lodge buddies or pals and chums. When the chips are down a lot of these so called 'friends' can't be found. A 'friend' is someone who you can call upon for help -- someone you can confide in -- someone who will give you honest advice -- someone who likes you for yourself no matter what -- someone who will stand by you in thick and thin." After hearing Grandma's dissertation on friendship, Dad looked at her and exclaimed, "Holy Cow Grandma! You really have your thoughts on friends down pat. You only forgot to say that a true friend will like you for yourself and not for what you can do for him." "Yes Fred," replied grandma, "I forgot to add that. You're right! A lot of people seem to be your friend until you can't do something for them. I have learned that from hard experience."

Grandma suggested to Mom that they think about a winter project to keep their hands busy and their minds off things that they can't change. Both like to quilt but they have done so much of it lately that they would like to try something else. Since they both can crochet, Grandma suggested that they make a table cloth. One advantage to the project is that the work can be done just about anywhere. Unlike quilting, there is no need for a frame to worry about. They can sit in the living room and listen to the radio or chat with a neighbor and continue to crochet. Grandma suggested that they make a table cloth for the dining room table. The table is quite long and square when it is fully extended with the extra leafs. Mom liked the idea. After a lot of thought they decided that the center of the tablecloth will be composed of white roses while the outer edges will be made up of rows of roses in various colors -- pink, purple, blue, and yellow. The flowers will be connected by crochet netting work. Both are very enthusiastic about the project and have already started working on the white roses.

I gave notice to **The Daily Herold** that I will be leaving after Labor Day. My boss tried to urge me to stay on for some night work and Saturdays but I told him that my family expected me to give my full attention to my studies. My boss said he will find a high school student to take my place as soon as possible. I told him that I would be willing to show him the ropes.

Before going to Open House at St. Andrew College I filled out the forms that were sent to me from the college and also called the high school to make sure that my transcript had been sent. On one of the forms from "St. Andy" -- that's the nickname for St. Andrew College -- it asked about my religious background and affiliation. I decided to be honest about my heritage and so I checked both "Protestant" and "Jewish" and then added a footnote about being brought up as a Presbyterian but having recently discovered that my mother's people were Jewish.

After church this Sunday, Dad, Mom, and I went over for the Open House between 2:00 P.M. to 5:00 P.M. The campus is very hilly and is divided into really two sections by Maple Avenue which runs through the middle of it. The part of Maple Avenue that runs through the campus has a tree-lined boulevard that adds a lot of character to the area. There are about nine buildings on campus: the book store and publishing building, the administration building called Old Main, the library, the science building, the music building, a gym, the Student Union, and two dorms -- one for men and the other for women.

We parked in front of the impressive looking Old Main which rests on a steep hill overlooking Maple Avenue. The building is a three story structure constructed of a cream colored limestone or granite (I'm not really sure which.) The most striking thing about the building is the dome which sits atop the building. It can be seen from miles around. After climbing up the stone staircase to the building, we entered and signed the guest book that was on a table in the main hall. The receptionist gave us all a copy of the college's handbook which related the history of St. Andrew College, explained the degrees offered, listed basic requirements, described all the courses, listed the names of the faculty with their degrees, and finally indicated what the school calendar was to be for the up-coming school year.

While we looked at the handbook, we were surprised to see Mr. amd Mrs. Patterson arrive with Dave. I was happy to see a familiar face. I knew that quite a few of my classmates from McKliney High School had decided to go to St. Andrew but I did not know that Dave was one of them. Mom and Dad greeted the Pattersons and learned that Dave was going to be a music major at St. Andrew. I smiled at Dave and told him that I was happy to see someone familiar. He replied, "I know what you mean. Starting college is quite a challenge and it's nice to know that someone from your old school will be on campus."

We were told that we could tour the buildings ourselves or be conducted around in a group by one of the professors who had volunteered to be a guide. We decided to take the group tour. A Professor Thomas Anderson of the Math Department greeted us and then conducted the tour. He is an outgoing, friendly person with a good sense of humor. At the start of the tour he told us a brief history of the St. Andrew and its liberal arts philosophy. He especially stressed the school's approach to education and its commitment to getting to know each student. Every once in a while he would stop to tell a funny story about a particular room or former president or professor of the college.

We were most impressed with Old Main which was built in 1870. While the outside is most imposing, the beauty of the inside of the building is something to behold. All the floors are made of fine walnut wood. The magnificant staircase rises three stories up the center of the structure. It is truly an experience just to climb the stairs and hear the echoing sound of one's footsteps on the wood. As we did this, we truly felt that we were in an institution of learning with a lot of history and character. We visited several lecture rooms which were quite large. Often there would be a portrait of one of the former professors on the wall. Usually Professor Anderson told us something about each one of them. Then, we came to the chapel on the east end of the building. It is truly magnificent and imposing. It is two stories high with entrances on both the second and third stories. There is a balcony that curves around where a second floor would normally be. Again, the use of wood makes the place unusual. The floor is of a fine walnut and the stairs to the balcony are too. The balcony has three tiers of seats and the stairs going to and from them are made of walnut. The chapel is dominated by a tall stained glass window that is rounded at the top. It is located at the front of the room directly above the stage. "The Risen Christ" is depicted in the stained glass window. Various shades of red, blue, and gold dominate the beautiful image of Christ. Above the window is written in large letters: "The Fear of the Lord is the Beginning of Wisdom." With the sunlight shinning through the pieces of stained glass, the chapel takes on an almost supernatural feeling. On the right of the stage is the console to a large pipe organ. Its pipes can be seen on either side of the stained glass window on what would be considered the upper level of the chapel. Because of the extensive use of wood, Professor Anderson's voice could be heard clearly throughout the chapel as he explained why students are required to attend services in the chapel two times a week.

The other building that is impressive was the Dickerson Library. It is made of gray granite with elaborate stone decorations around the entrances, windows, and corners of the roof. One especially notices the tall windows that are rounded at the top. Professor Anderson took us into the main reading room which is two stories high. Light comes in through the huge windows. Works of sculpture and painting add to its academic atmosphere. Again, there are portraits of former presidents of the college on the walls. The room is filled with long tables for students to study. Professor Anderson told us that the library contains about 250,000 volumes.

Before we left Dad asked Professor Anderson if I could make an appointment to see an academic adviser the following week. He felt that I needed to get some advice about the courses I should take. Professor Anderson directed us back to Old Main and to the counseling office. There, I was able to arrange to see a Professor Lillian Williams next week to discuss my academic program.

As we drove home, Dad said that he was impressed with the college -- and especially the friendly but serious tone that one senses there. He said, "One good thing about a small liberal arts college is that you will not get lost in the crowd. Classes should be reasonable in size and you should be able to get the attention that you need." He liked how Professor Anderson immediately responded to his request for some pre-enrollment counseling for me.

The Passing Parade

News Story: "Allies Drive for Reich on 200 Mile Front"

Song: "That Old Feeling" by Shep Fields

Movie: "Christmas Holiday" with Deanne Durbin and Gene Kelly

"St. Andy"

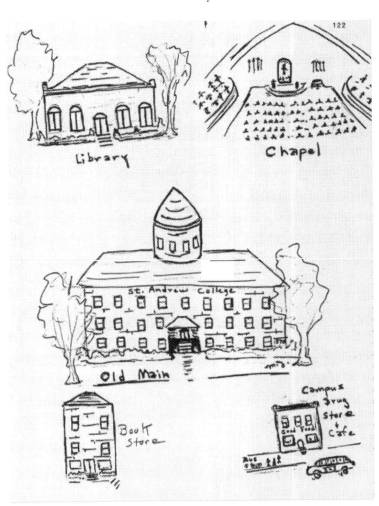

A Poison Pen Letter, "The Blue Danube", a Fire, and a Lesson on Judaism

The family received an anonymous letter this week. The address wasn't hand written or typed. Instead, someone had cut out letters and numbers from a magazine and then glued them to the envelope to spell out our name and address. Inside there was a short note composed of more cut out letters. It read: "Don't you think that you Jews should go back to Chicago and do the neighborhood a favor." Mom and Grandma were the first to read the note. They showed it to Dad and me when we got home. Mom wondered out loud to Dad if the note should be shown to Buddy and Carol. He said, "Yes, by all means, they are part of the family too." We spent some time speculating about who could have sent the letter but couldn't agree. Dad said, "The only thing we can do is to hold on to the letter until we have more evidence and meantime just go about our daily tasks as usual." He told us not to mention the letter to anyone. Then he reminded us again "to continue to reach out to others and be helpful to others." He believes that people in the neighborhood will judge us by our actions and not by what they may hear people say about Jews. I hope that he is right.

The big story about the war is that Paris is free. Today there was a large photograph of Allied troops on parade in the liberated French capitol. We all thought that it was going to happen last week. Even President Roosevelt had issued a victory speech about the taking of Paris. But then, everyone found out that it was premature. Thank God there was a city to liberate. Some thought that Hitler had ordered the destruction of the Paris. There was one report that said he had but then his generals had refused to carry it out.

Being a musician, Mom was interested in a news story that she heard over the radio. It involved Prt. Roger F. Fox who is with our forces in Resignavo, Italy. He had helped push the Germans back and in the process the American soldiers had taken a farm house. In the farm house Prt. Fox found a piano. He started playing it. Among the songs he played was "The Blue Danube." Meanwhile the Germans began shelling the house and advancing into the area. Two or three Germans who came near the farm house heard "The Blue Danube" being played and surrendered to the Americans. Why? Because they claimed the music made them feel homesick. Mom argued that this story, if true, proves the power of music to bring out the best in humans. Dad only laughed and said that he did not believe the story -- that some newsmen had made it up to provide a human interest story for the folks at home. I tend to agree with Dad -- but Carol and Buddy and yes even Grandma believe Mom and feel that Dad and I are just too pessimistic about human nature.

"Fire!" "Fire!" That was the yell that was heard throughout the neighborhood this past Tuesday. Mrs. Taylor who lives further up on 11ᵗʰ Avenue was out for a walk with her dog when she saw smoke coming from the wooded ravine that is part of the Standstadt estate. She ran up to our house and rang the door bell. When Mom and Grandma opened the door, they were met by a very frightened Mrs. Taylor. She told them to look at all the smoke coming from the ravine across the street. Well, they did and were horrified. Mom told Grandma to call the Milltown Fire Department while she went with Mrs. Taylor to investigate. According to what Mom told us all later, when she got to the top of the ravine she could see far below one of the Hansen boys -- Carl -- looking at the burning dry leaves and fallen dead braches. He held a box of kitchen matches in his left hand. Without a moment of hesitation Mom slowly started down the hill, reached Carl and took him by the hand and guided him up the steep incline. When she got to the top, she shook him by the shoulders and asked him why he had started the fire. He didn't say anything. By that time the fire truck had arrived to connect a hose to a nearby fire hydrant to put out the fire. Carl's mother arrived too and promised onlookers to take him home to discuss with his father what should be done to punish him. She thanked Mom for going down and getting him out of the ravine. We later learned that he had been assigned more jobs around the farm and restricted on his comings and goings for a month. When Mom heard about Carl's punishment, she wondered if that had been the right approach to what had happened. She said that she was really worried about Carl. Mom said, "Carl always seemed such a shy youngster. He often sucked his thumb and seemed to be by himself and afraid to play with other children. Could it be that setting the fire was a way to get attention? Or, could it be that he hoped that he would die in the fire that he had set himself?"

I received a letter from St. Andy telling about the events coming up for entering freshmen. On one day we will be given a battery of tests. The score in English will be used to place us. I hope that I don't have to take the so-called "dumb Composition I class." That is for those who score poorly on the English part of the tests.

On another day we will be given a physical exam in the science building. Finally, there will be a day of enrolling in courses after seeing an academic adviser. The enrollment will be in several large rooms in Old Main. We are supposed to get approval to take courses from the various department heads. Then, we will pay for the tuition at the Business Office and purchase books at the bookstore.

I told Dad about the details so that he could give me enough money to pay for the tuition and the books. I talked with Professor Williams and she told me to enroll in courses that fulfill basic requirements in science, foreign language, English and social studies. Her advice was to get as many requirements out of the way as soon as possible. That will help me graduate on time without having to go to school in the summer when I may need to work to make money for tuition and books.

Grandma and I started our own classes on Judaism. We talked about what makes a person a Jew. She said that a very simple definition of a Jew is "anyone born of a Jewish mother or anyone who converts to Judaism." She told me that the word "Judaism" is derived from the ancient Kingdom of Judah. We talked about circumcision as a ritual. Grandma explained that I and Buddy had been circumcized eight days after we had been born. She said that the Hebrew word for the ceremony of circumcision is B'rit which means covenant or agreement. This refers to the momentous covenant between God and Abraham. We also talked about the sacred books of Judaism -- the **Torah** and the **Talmud.** The **Torah** consists of the first five books of the **Bible.** The **Talmud** is actually many books written over a period of 300 hundred years, commenting on the **Torah.** Grandma told me that every synagogue has at least one **Torah** which is kept in an enclosure called The Holy Ark She told me that when we go Temple Israel in Keyport to visit the rabbi, we will see one. Grandma stressed at the end of our conversation that Reform Jews feel that by learning the traditions and relying on the individual conscience that they are fulfilling the commandments of "love thy God" and "love thy neighbor as thyself."

[Code: Later, I talked with Dad about circumcision. I asked him when he had been circumcised. He told me that he wasn't circumcised until he was about 20 years old and then it was for a very practical reason. He found that it was a lot easier keeping his penis clean and free of infection when it was circumcised. He had it done in Europe during World War I. In fact, he claimed that some of the army medical personel had recommended it to him and other service men. However, he did say that one drawback of having it done was the loss of sensation in his pecker. According to Dad in WW I the government didn't issue rubbers to the service men. Instead, they were told to abstain from having sex. Well, it did not work out and VD was a problem. Today, the men are issued rubbers along with their other rations.]

The Passing Parade

News Story: "War Casualties From Milltown"

Song: "By the Light of the Silvery Moon" by Ray Noble

Movie: "Andy Hardy's Blonde Trouble" with Mickey Rooney

"Christ Killers", Grandma's Birthday, Bar Mitzvah and Carol's New Horse

Another poison pen letter arrived. It read: "Christ Killers, do the neighborhood a favor and move back to the Jewish ghetto. If you don't, you will have to bear the consequences." As with the first note, we wondered who could be doing this. Mom remembered that Arvid and Caroline had received an anonymous letter about their nephew's entertaining women over night in their apartment while they were in Florida with the Standstadts. They had suspected Mrs. McCoy. Could she be the one sending these poison pen letters to us? Dad told us not to mention anything about this to others. He also warned us "not to jump to conclusions" or "accuse someone of doing this without proof." He voiced the need to continue to act normally and to continue to reach out to others in a helpful way.

During the week Grandma turned 75. Because of the arrival of the poison pen letter, we all had to make an effort to joyously celebrate Grandma's special day. Mom prepared her favorite dishes for supper. We had baked salmon along with a tossed salad, baked potatoes, creamed peas and carrots, and green beans from our own garden. For desert we had Grandma's favorite -- angel food cake. During the week she received a lot of cards -- some from her relatives in Chicago and others from Dad's relatives who have really gotten to know Grandma and hold her in high regard. Among her gifts were: bath oil, bedroom slippers (with fleece lining), a quilted blue bathrobe, and Betty Smith's book **A Tree Growes in Brooklyn.**

Throughout the week I have been trying to become a college student. Registration took a lot of time, and then came the first real week of college. It's going to take a lot of adjustment in meeting the demands of college courses. Like other freshmen I have suddenly come to the realization that it is going to be a lot tougher than high school. All the students in my classes seem to be intelligent and highly motivated. Competition will be keen. Also, the professors have high expectations and insist that students be prepared and meet their standards. Some of my professors are very old -- well into their 60s and in one case 70s. I was told by one of my new classmates that a lot of the younger professors were drafted and so a lot of retired professors were asked to come back to teach part time. Class size is low -- 18 to 25 -- again because of the war. A lot of young men volunteer for service before they are drafted. That way they can have some choice in terms of the branch of service in which they will serve. Of course, the number of females far exceed the number of males on campus. I have been told that the shortage of students has really been felt in the band, chorus, and orchestra.

Despite being busy I did have a chance to talk to Grandma about the importance of Bar Mitzvah. She said that my Great Uncle Aaron had gone through the ritual. She explained that to both Orthodox and Reform Jews it is a very important event. When a boy is 13 years old, he becomes a full member of the covenant and a son of the commandment at this ceremony. In order to participate in it Aaron, like all Jewish boys, had to study very hard to prepare himself for the ceremony which took place in the temple. Reading the Hebrew prayers to the congregation is one of the highlights of the service. Grandma said she knew for a fact that Aaron and his Hebrew teacher rehearsed many times to make sure he had it right. The ceremony takes place on a Saturday morning. The boy's father stands by along with the rabbi for the opening of the Ark. The handing of the **Torah** from father to son symbolizes the passing of knowledge from generation to generation. The boy says a brief prayer in English. Then, he reads from the **Torah** in Hebrew to the congregation. At the conclusion of the service, the boy receives the traditional kiss from his father.

Well, it finally happened. Yes, Carol has a horse and she is in "pig's heaven" as Great Aunt Sadie would say. Dad and Carol agreed on purchasing a pinto from a farmer who operates a stable north of Milltown. She cost $125.00. Since Carol's birthday is in about two weeks, the horse is her birthday present from the family. Also, Dad brought her a used saddle and bridle. The horse is only about two years old and is beautifully marked. She has brown, black and reddish calico spots on her sides. Carol has had a great time riding around the neighborhood and introducing "Cleo" -- that's what she has named her because she has the proud bearing of a queen like Queen Cleopatra. The horse seems to be good-natured and doesn't mind all the attention that she is getting. Everyone in the neighborhood --- including some who we suspect of writing the poison pen letter -- have taken an interest in Carol's new pet. I guess animals do help bring people together -- especially if they are beautiful like Cleo and seem to warm up to people. Carol rode the horse over to the Standstadt estate and introduced her to Mr. Standstadt who judged her to be "good horse flesh." He seemed to take a shine to the horse according to Carol. Let's hope so. We would like the boarding arrangement for the horse to work out.

The Passing Parade

News Story: "Roosevelt, Dewey 7ᵗʰ Cousins -- Election All in the Family"

Song: "Mairzy Doats" (Can't remember the group. I heard it on the juke box.)

Movie: "Marine Raiders" with Pat O'Brien and Ruth Hussey

A TYPICAL WEEK AT ST. ANDREW COLLEGE

After attending classes for two weeks I think that I can truthfully say that I will not have a lot of time for radio programs -- even the Tuesday night comedies -- or Hollywood films. There is a lot of home work for each course. I feel that I am expected to do twice as much work for each course as I did on the high school level. Also, as I mentioned before the professors expect you to have read the material. Tests also will be challenging. I have already been told by several professors that they do not use objective tests but essay exams. Another thing that I'm going to have to get used to is being called "Mr. Johnson" rather than by my first name. All the professors do this. I guess it is done to set a serious tone on campus. Well, it certainly does. Anyway, I believe that I did the right thing in not going to live with Phillip and his parents in Iowa City. I'm going to be lucky to do some dating and also keep up my grades here. [Code: I'm sure if Phillip came through with his promise of connecting me up with a girl who would be willing to service my "cob" that I would be thinking more of her and my "cob" than trying to study. Yes, I think that "Mr. Johnson" needs to try to meet the standards of St. Andrew College and not concentrate on getting some pussy.]

I did see Professor Olsen on campus and had a chance to talk with him. The students respect him as a person and for his teaching. He is demanding but humane. Despite the recent loss of his wife, he took the time to reassure me that once I got into the swing of things, I would adjust and do just fine. I hope that he is right.

Here is my typical week:

6:30 A.M.   I wake up, wash, dress and go down for breakfast.

7:15 A.M.   I get my books and notebooks and walk down 17th Street hill to catch a bus for Andersonville. I sometimes meet Dave Paterson and other students waiting in front of the Woolworths on 5th Avenue at the bus stop. I find myself doing school work on the bus. I'm either reviewing something or reading an assignment or rewriting a theme for Composition.

7:50 A.M.   I arrive at St. Andy and go to European History class on Monday, Wednesday, and Friday -- otherwise I go to the library to study. Dr. Donaldson is the teacher of the class. He is in his 50s, originally from Sweden, and looks very dignified in his dark suits with his watch chain displaying a Phi Betta Kappa key. His lectures are very well organized and given with a lot of enthusiasm. During the first week he has been trying to connect the present situation with the past. He gave a lecture about ideology and how it affects history. He drew a parallel between the stuggle of Fascism and Democracy with the

130

situation found in ancient Greece between Sparta and Athens. He also brought in the whole concept of the balance of power -- now and then. I found it all very easy to follow and interesting. He said that he wants us to write a research paper for the course. I think I will do it on the appeasement of Hitler during the 1930s. I'll try to determine why it was followed by Great Britain and France.

9:00A.M. At this time on Tuesdays and Thursdays I'm required to go to chapel. I say required because if you miss chapel you will be called in to discuss the matter by one of the deans. Chapel is a time for prayer, singing, and inspirational talks by the President of the college - Rev. Charles Bergman -- or professors on staff. The talks usually deal with making sure that what you do now and what you plan to do in the future will be of value. Of course, they stress the need to "uphold the simple religion of Christ and to further His gospel of peace on earth and good will to men." Sometimes we are treated to a musical presentation -- always classical -- by members of the Music Department. While some students resent going to chapel, I find it to be very rewarding. It certainly helps to built school spirit and understanding of the philosophy of the college. Besides, I find the talks very meaningful. The other day Dr. Bergman talked about "the need to look back and take stock of things" and "the need to search for the meaning behind events that you experience." When I heard his talk, I thought about this diary. That's what I have been trying to do in it.

On Mondays, Wednesdays, and Fridays I'm in Political Science. The teacher of the class is Dr. Frederick. He doesn't lecture but instead asks questions and encourages discussion. He is in his late 40s, bald, and wears thick glasses. He requires a great deal of reserved reading which I'm finding is very difficult to keep up with. He also expects us to remember what we have read so we can discuss it. He told us that he is going to give us a chance to work for political parties in the up-coming election. Anyway, I like his practical approach to the subject.

10:00 A.M. By this time I'm in Physical Geography. I have it five times a week; one day is set aside for lab work. A Dr. Hammond is the professor. He is about 35, tall (6'2"), intense, and very serious. He is originally from Belgium and talks with an accent. He also connects his subject with the war that is going on. He is an avid reader of **The New York Times** and likes to discuss the geography of the war. So, in addition to the regular course material we are also looking at maps where battles - on land and sea -- are going on in Europe, Asia, and any other place.

11:00A.M. I have Composition three days a week. A Miss Park teaches the class. She is about 29 and is working on her Ph.D. in English. She is quite intelligent, serious, and attractive with her warm smile and nun-like or madonna-like appearance. Those phrases are the best I can come up with to describe her. She always dresses in simple black dresses with high necklines, no jewelry or make up, and talks in a soft, earnest voice. She told us that she will expect a theme a week. She wants us to read stories in the newspaper and then use them as inspirations for themes in which we express our own feelings and our own creative thoughts. We may wish to write an essay about some moral question or perhaps finish the story that we have read using our own imagination. She also will assign two war novels to read and discuss during the first semester -- **Red Badge of Courage** by Stephen Crane and Farewell To Arms by Ernest Hemingway. So, she is using the war to teach Composition. I find myself admiring her creative techniques. I have never had an English teacher that used the newspaper to teach Composition.

When I'm not in Composition on Tuesdays and Thursdays I'm taking a religious class entitled The Old Testament taught by Dr. Parrington. He is well into his 60s, tall (6'1") with a full head of white hair, has glasses, and a very distinct manner of speaking. He always speaks in a slow manner so that his words are pronounced clearly and distinctly. He does this in almost a whisper. But, the the funny thing about it is that everyone hears what he has to say. I guess we are so entranced by his manner that we listen intensely to catch every syllable that he utters. I haven't found the class too difficult since I studied the **Bible** in Sunday school. He always brings in the war a lot. We always start and end the class with prayer -- always including a prayer for "the men and women in the military service." He also brings in the idea of God working through righteous men and women to defeat evil. He definitely feels Hitler is the Anti-Christ figure referred to in the **Bible.**

12:00 P.M.   I usually go to the nearby Campus Drug Store for lunch rather than the Student Union. It is closer and besides the food is better. A family by the name of Dayton owns it and they offer a lot of casserole dishes that have a real home-cooked taste to them. I usually sit at the counter. Their pies and cakes are good too. They are usually made from scatch by Mrs. Dayton. If I finish early I go back to the library to study. That's where I spend most of my extra time from classes. And, I need all the study time I can get because my heavy academic load includes a lot of reserved readings.

1:00 P.M.   By this time I am in U.S. History class. It is taught by Professor Olsen. While he lectures, he also requires extra readings that we discuss in class. His lectures are always well organized and filled with amusing anecdotes. He has told us that he likes to take a thematic approach to history which he defined as "tracing through the political, economic, social, and foreign policy trends." He also includes a lot of current events whenever he can and tries to draw parallels to past American history. When I don't have U.S. History on Tuesdays and Thursdays, I study in the library.

2:00 P.M.   I go to French at this time. It meets five times a week. It is taught by really delightful character by the name of Dr. Meyer. He is about 75 years old. He was asked to return to teaching after the young French professor was drafted last year. He has thining white hair, wears glasses, is rolly-polly, has a tongue in cheek type of humor, and a hearty laugh that is very catching. He lived in France for years and is full of stories about living there. Besides the grammar book, we have a reader that is filled with accounts pertaining to French culture. We translate these essays and discuss them. Also, he requires us to converse in French during lab. We are paired off for this. I'm happy that I took German because I find French easier in terms of word order. However, I am having some difficulty with speaking it properly. I had an easier time with German.

3:00 P.M.   I have P.E. on Mondays and Fridays. I decided to take Advanced Swimming since I like it so much. Again, a retired professor is my teacher. His name is Dr. Swan and is in his late 60s but is in great shape. He is 6'2" with a well built body. His white hair and blue eyes make him into a grandfather figure. I like him and the way he operates the class. There isn't any horsing around either like on the high school level. We are working on the basic swimming stokes plus water safety and games like water polo.

At this time on Tuesdays, Wednesdays, and Thursdays I have Introduction to Philosophy. I have a most unusual teacher for the class. He is Dr. Khrychev who is from Latvia. He is a short man -- 5'6" -- with a chunky figure and a mischievous smile. He is about 52 with grey thinning hair and glasses. He came to this country in 1938. He always says that he was one of the lucky ones; he was able to get out before the war. He is very well educated -- has taught at the University of Moscow and has three doctorates -- one in chemistry, another in math, and another in philosophy. He teaches philosophy in a most unusual way. He uses a lot of drawings on the blackboard to explain things like Plato's Concept of Ideas. He often gives us examples that one can visualize. I find that I am able to retain the material because I remember his illustrations and examples. He also uses the war to make his subject more meaningful. His introductory lecture was about how ideology has had such an impact on the world in the 20th Century. He pointed out that the philosophies of Fascism, Communism, and Democracy have been in conflict with one another and that these conflicts have shaped the events of this century. I feel lucky to have him as a teacher.

4:20P.M.   I catch a bus back to Milltown. I usually get off in front of the A& P Store on 6th Avenue. By the time I have walked up the hill to 11th Avenue it is 5:30 P.M.

5:45 P.M.   I turn on the radio to hear the news and at the same time plan my evening study time.

6:00P.M.   I eat with the rest of the family. Dad always asks, "What have you learned today Mark?" I usually have something to share with him and the rest of the family. Everyone seems to like hearing about my stories of college life. After that we all hear from Buddy and Carol. Then, of course, Dad, Mom, and Grandma have their turns if they want to.

7:00 - 11:00 P.M. Home work time. Once in a while I tune in a radio show but that isn't very often. Sometimes I use the car to go back to St. Andy to do some reserve reading at the library.

The Passing Parade

News Story: "Russians Heavily Shell Warsaw, Enter Sofia"

Song: "I Don't Want To Set The World On Fire" by the Ink Spots

Movie: "Since You Went Away" with Claudette Colbert

A Murder, Rules from the Torah, and the Election Heats Up

Sunday, Sept. 24, 1944

Like everyone else in the neighborhood I'm in a state of shock. Why? Because of a murder. In the early morning hours last Monday the milkman found a body lying on the sidewalk outside the Wellington estate. The dead man was lying on his back; his eyes were wide open staring up at the blue sky seeing, of course, nothing. The milkman said it was the scariest thing he had ever encountered. The police identified the man from papers in his wallet. It was Colonel Templeton. He had been severly beaten; his head was covered with blood. Later, it was determined by the coroner that he had died of massive brain damage. A bloody crowbar was found near the body.

Two days after the murder Mr. Berry was arrested for the murder. According to the newspaper story about the murder Mr. Berry claimed that his wife was running around with the Colonel and that he only wanted to scare him off when he confronted him with the crowbar. Mr. Berry said that angry words were exchanged and that Templeton had tried to seize the crowbar. In the fight that followed the Colonel was killed. Mr. Berry told the police and his lawyer that he was only trying to defend himself and keep his marriage together. The district attorney has decided to ask the grand jury to charge Mr. Berry with murder in the 2nd degree. Mr. Berry's own attorney feels that he should only be charged with involuntary manslaughter. A few feel that he is lucky to only be charged with the 2nd degree instead of the 1st degree because he had brought a crowbar with him and he had been following Colonel Templeton which shows planning and premediation. In fact, Mr. Berry had followed his wife and the Colonel that night and then had confronted him after he had seen them kiss before going their separate ways.

Of course, Dad was really surprised when he heard that it was his friend from the Arsenal who had been killed. He exclaimed, "Holy Cow! How in the world did he get involved with that woman? I thought he had more sense than that." By the way, nobody has seen "the purple lady." Mrs. McCoy claims that she left town to stay with her mother in Joliet until the trial.

Strangely, people seem to be more sympathetic with Mr. Berry than his wife. Most feel that Mrs. Berry was always tyring to show off and that her attraction to the Colonel was her undoing. They believe her husband's statement that he was only trying to keep his marriage together and that he did not mean to kill the Colonel. "The Bishop girls" again blame the war for this latest tragedy. They said, "Uniforms do strange things to some people. So many women seem to be attracted to any man in a uniform."

Grandma is happy that the first religious course at St. Andy is about the Old Testament. She feels that this will help both of us review basic ideas behind Judaism. She asked me to share any interpretation or insight that I either read in the textbook or hear from Dr. Parrington's lectures. We discussed some of the rules that orthodox Jews follow. She told me that Joseph Goldman her grandfather who lived with her family when she was a little girl followed these rules. The rules are all based on strict observance of the commandments of the **Torah** which was given to Moses on Mt. Sinai by God and which is intended to control every aspect of existence for the pious Jew, from the way he prays to the way he eats. Grandma told me that her grandfather as an Orthodox Jew always wore a hat called a yarmulke wherever he went. It was a sign of his respect and loyalty to God. The yarmulke is even worn indoors. According to Grandma when her grandfather woke up in the morning, he said a prayer to God praising the new day. Before eating any food, he would prepare himself for prayer. He began by putting on his blue and white tallith which is a scarf. Its fringes reminded him of the commandments of the **Torah.** Next he put on tefilins which are small leather boxes with passages from the **Torah** written on them. He placed one on his left arm near his heart. He tied leather straps to his hand so as to form the Hebrew letter "shin," which means "the Almight." A tefilin was also placed on his forehead symbolizing his total commitment of mind to one God. After the tallith and tefilin were on, Joseph Goldman prayed silently from his prayer book. He always stood while praying. After his prayer, he would eat breakfest.

Grandma told me that her grandfather only ate kosher food. Kosher means "proper" and can be applied to almost anything properly prepared and validated by a rabbi. Certain foods are prohibited at all times for Orthodox Jews, including meat that comes from the pig and all kinds of shell fish. Also, it isn't kosher to eat meat and dairy products at the same meal. If Joseph Goldman ate a steak at dinner, he had to wait several hours before he could drink a glass of milk.

I found all this very interesting. It explained why Mom and Grandma did not eat ham, hot dogs and anything with pork in it. Also, I found myself admiring the religious dedication of my Great Grandfather Goldman. Grandma told me that he disapproved of his own children and grandchildren as they drifted away from Orthodoxy and embraced Reform Judaism -- even more so if they converted to another faith. The latter he would never speak to; they were dead in his eyes according to Grandma.

The election is really heating up. F.D.R. has finally come out swinging. Dad felt that it was about time. Dad had feared that Dewey's charges that the New Dealers were too old and tired and that the President was in failing health were having their effect. Also, Dad and other Democrats were concerned that a lot of people who favored F.D.R. would not be able to vote because of the complexities and unfairness of the voting laws. Many of the soliders overseas and those who have recently moved to work in war plants in other states may not be able to vote.

The papers are filled with the accounts of the President's speech at a dinner for the Teamsters' Union and local politicians at the Statler Hotel in Washington, D.C. on the evening of Sept. 23. The talk was carried by radio and the entire family enjoyed hearing what he had to say. F.D.R. ridiculed those Republicans who attacked organized labor until an election was at hand when "they suddenly discover that they really love labor and that they are anxious to protect labor from its old friends . . . ." He asked, "Can the Old Guard pass itself as the New Deal?" Then, he answered, "I think not. We have seen many marvelous stunts in the circus but no performing elephant could turn a hand-spring without falling flat on its back."

Then the President enjoyed refuting several alleged misrepresentations by the Dewey Camp. Among them was the rumor that millions had been spent to rescue his dog Fala from the Aleutians. Supposedly Fala had been left there after a presidential trip to the area. Republicans charged that a special destroyer had been sent to get the dog. With tongue in cheek, F.D.R. stated, "These Republican leaders have not been content with attacks on me, my wife, or on my sons. No, not content with that, they now include my little dog, Fala. Well, of course, I don't resent attacks, and my family doesn't resent attacks, but Fala does resent them. You know, Fala is Scotch . . . his Scotch soul was furious. He has not been the same dog since."

At that, Grandma Mendell started laughing at this image of poor Fala trying to cope with his critics. Her laughter proved catching because we all joined in with a giggle or chuckle. Dad was really pleased with the President's tone; he felt that the old campaigner was back -- and in top form.

The Passing Parade

News Stories: "Families Speak for their War Dead"
"Roosevelt Calls G.O.P. Claims Common Fraud"

Song: "We'll Meet Again" by Guy Lombardo

Movie: "Mrs. Parkington" with Greer Carson and Walter Pidgeon

Carol's Cleo

STAR OF DAVID, VISITING A VET, LEARNING ABOUT JEWISH HOLIDAYS

Buddy told us about it first. He came into the house and first told Dad and then the rest of us that there was something painted on the garage door. He said that it looked like a star. We all -- including Peggy -- went to see for ourselves. As we all looked at the large Star of David painted in black along with the words "Fuck Jews" on the garage door, Mom said, "I can't believe that it would come to this!" We all agreed that whoever was behind trying to get us out of the neighborhood was becoming more bold and brazen. We went back into the house and discussed what we should do about it. Dad considered calling the police. Then, there was a knock on the door and when we opened it we found Arvid and Caroline. They told us that they had seen the garage door and came over to tell us how sorry they felt about it. They also told us that they saw Jim Banister and Kelly Jackson in the alley late last night. While they did not see them paint the star, they felt that we should know that they were in the area and could be responsible. Both Arvid and Caroline told us that most of the neighbors are still our friends and that we should not consider moving away. That made us feel better. There for a while we wondered if we had any real friends left in the neighborhood. Dad and Mom finally decided that the best policy would be to paint over the star, say nothing, and continue to be good neighbors. [Code: While Mom and Dad could explain the star to Buddy and Carol, they had a difficult time explaining what "fuck" meant.]

I saw Irene the other day pushing her sister's carriage around the block. She was happy to see me and to hear about my experiences at St. Andy. She wishes she were able to go to college. However, when I asked her about Betty, she smiled and talked about her in great detail -- from her attempt to say "daddy" to playing in her bath water. Irene really seems to enjoy taking care of her little sister; she has become like Irene's own daughter. Irene told me that Ed Harrington was discharged from the mental hospital and is now at home. Nobody has seen him. He keeps to himself. Sometimes he goes out for walks late at night. That's what Mr. Jackson reported. He thought that it was Ed that he practically ran into as he took an evening walk with his dog Pal. We also talked about the Berry case. I told Irene that Mr. Berry's case will come up in about two weeks or so. The grand jury did indict him on the charge of murder in the second degree.

I am having problems with Composition. Professor Park often reads good themes and bad ones to the class. The other day she started reading a theme -- and it was mine. It was about attending a funeral for a soldier killed in action and how I felt about it. I based it loosely on my feelings about Doug's funeral. Well, she read it as an example of how not to write. She never mentions the name of the author. Thank God! Anyway I'm going to have to do better. I'm determined to write an outstanding theme next time. We are supposed to write about different types of a topic. I'm going to write about different types of war propaganda. Hopefully, I'll make at least a B on it. I only received a D on the theme read to the class.

Dr. Frederick has arranged for us to either work for the Republican Party or the Democratic Party during the election. Naturally, I told him I would like to work for the Democrats. I went to a caucus meeting and later helped with a rally over the weekend. I basically hand out literature and pins, answer phone calls, and do whatever is needed. I really like this approach to the study of political science. Of course, Dad thinks that getting out in the real world of politics is a fine introduction to what he calls "that noble art in understanding human motivation and behavior."

Mom received a telephone call from Anna. She told Mom that she and Glen were back in town. He was discharged from the Veteran's hospital; he will go back on an outpatient basis. He and Anna are staying at his mother's home until they can get a place of their own. We all went over to see him. At first, I found it difficult to look straight into his eyes and talk to him. I remembered him as a tall (6'2"), handsome man who was very out-going and physically active. While his smile was the same and his manner friendly, it was hard to see him confined to a bed. When we arrived he was using some weights to strengthen his arm muscles. There was a wooden pole in a frame over his head. In order to sit upright he would grap the pole and use his arm muscles to pull himself up. We were all a bit ill at ease as we started talking to him. But, thanks to Glen's calm and friendly manner, we began to relax and feel that we were with the friend that we had known so long. The fact that he seemed to be accepting his disability and handling it helped us accept and deal with it too. He told us that the government was going to help him buy a home and also a car that would be equipped with special levers so that he could drive it by using only his hands. He observed, "If President Roosevelt can drive a car, I should be able to learn to do the same." Later, he showed us the Purple Heart that he had been given by General Eisenhower himself. It was quite a visit -- one that touched all of us.

Grandma and I spent an hour talking about some of the Jewish holidays. She described Pesach or Passover as a festival of Jewish freedom based on the exodus of the Jews from Egypt. She said that unleavened bread called Matzot is served at a special dinner. She told me that Passover usually talkes place in April. We talked about Rosh HaShanah that usually occurs in Sept. It is a holiday set aside for introspection and self-inspection. It is a day of rememberance during which the past year is analyzed. Grandma said that during Rosh HaShanah white robes are worn and a ram's horn is blowen. Yom Kippur takes place ten days after Rosh HaShanah. Grandma stressed that it is considered a day of judgment and atonement for sins against God committed during the year. According to Grandma, my Great Grandfather Goldman aways celebrated this day. He recited the Kol Nidre prayer and put on a white robe. In Oct. Sukkoth is celebrated. It is a harvest festival during which Orthodox Jews take meals and sometimes sleep in lean-to-like structures with thatched roofing to remember their ancesters. On this occasion various types of foods from the fall harvest are served at a special meal.

In December grandma's family always celebrated Chanukah. She told me that "it is a festival of eight days celebrating the restoration of the Temple to the Jews in 165B.C." Specifically, from one of the books that I read, I learned that "it commemorates the great victory of the Maccobees over the forces of Antiochus Epiphanes who in 168B.C. strove to destroy the Jewish faith." The observance of the festival, however, is built not upon the military victory as such, but upon a legend which tells of how a one-day supply of consecrated oil which the Maccabees used for the re-dedication of the desecrated temple lasted for eight days until more could be obtained. An eight-branched candle-stick called a menorah is lighted as part of the celebration. Sometimes gifts are exchanged. Grandma said that in her family Chanukah was always the favorite holiday -- especially among the children -- and was celebrated with a lot of enthusiasm. I suggested that we plan to celebrate it along with Christmas this coming December. She liked the idea. When we told Mom and Dad, they agreed that it would be a good way to rekindle our Jewish heritage.

The Passing Parade

News Stories: "Reds Push 6 Miles Into Yugoslavia"

"Our Next War President -- Roosevelt's Record, Dewey's Qualifications"

Song: "Mam'selle" by Art Lund

Movie: "And The Angels Sing" with Veronica Lake

A Suicide, New Friends, A Reassurance

Sunday, Oct. 8, 1944

They say that things come in twos. I'm beginning to believe it because we had two deaths again at Hilltop. The first wasn't totally unexpected. Mrs. Walters died peacefully in her sleep of an apparent heart attack. Her husband Josh said that he awoke about 2:45 A.M to hear a loud series of gasps for air and then a sound like a long sigh. According to her obituary Mrs. Walters was 78. The funeral was held at the Kaiser Funeral Home with burial at Green Lawn Cemetery. Ethel who rents the upstairs apartment from Mr. Walters has been a great comfort to him. His daughter's family drove up from Florida to attend the funeral. She would like her father to sell his home and move in with them but he is resisting the idea. He is an independent sort and would like to do for himself as long as possible. Besides, he is an out-going, friendly man who has a lot of friends through his church and Masonic Lodge here in Milltown. As it stands now, he has promised his daughter that he would visit her more often, especially on holidays.

The other death was unexpected. Mrs. Taylor was found hanging from a rope in the attic. Her children found the body after they got home from school. When they got home, they couldn't find their mother anywhere. They searched everywhere -- the laundry room in the basement, all the bedrooms, and the garage. Then, June went up to the attic and discovered the body. The police were called to investigate the matter. It looks like a suicide. It is difficult for people to accept it because Mrs. Taylor was a good Catholic -- and Catholics consider suicide a sin.

Some of the neighbors are now reporting that she had been acting strangely. Mrs. Moore said that she had seen Mrs. Taylor outside of her home dressed only in a slip. Others remembered seeing her crying on various occasions. Mrs. McCoy claims that she heard that Mr. Taylor was having an affair with another woman. Nobody knows for certain what had gone wrong. Mrs. Mario, Mrs. Hansen and others have gone over to the Taylor household to help out during this difficult time. The children are having the most trouble accepting the situation. To add to their pain the Catholic Church has refused to allow Mrs. Taylor to be buried in St. Mary's Cemetery since she committed suicide. She will be buried at Riverside Cemetery instead. Most of the neighbors feel that the Catholic Church is wrong for not accepting the body for burial.

The big news at St. Andy concerns the debate team. It won the West Point Debate Turnament. It is the first time that it has won this important national debate contest. It was up against some of the top ivy league colleges and universities in the country. The debate topic was: "Fascists Leaders Should Be Tried By An International Court For War Crimes." The St. Andy debaters defended the proposition. When the debaters returned from New York, they were honored. President Bergman asked all the students on campus to come to the bell tower at 10:15 A.M. to congratulate the debaters. They started ringing the bell at 10:00 as the students and faculty began to assemble to hear a short address by President Bergman and to applaud the debaters and their coach. The debaters -- Jim Anderson and Martha Hultgren -- showed us the trophy that they had brought back. It was 20" bronze Statue of Liberty mounted on a wooden base. We all hoped that President Bergman would dismiss the school for the rest of the day but he did not. Instead, he urged us to continue developing into "disciplined and dedicated students in the St. Andrew tradition." It was somewhat of a let down but not totally unexpected. I have learned that this is pretty typical behavior at St. Andrew College.

I'm doing better in Composition. While my latest theme about different types of war propaganda wasn't selected to be read to the class by Miss Park at least she wrote the following favorable comment at the top of the theme: "This shows a lot of good thinking about the topic of propaganda. I especially liked your good examples." While I received a B for content, I only received a C on mechanics. Boy, is Miss Park a tough task master. Perhaps one of my future themes will merit an A.

"Up In Arms" with Danny Kay is playing at the Paradise theatre and I called Maria to see if she would like to go with me to see it. Much to my surprise she turned me down. She has a date with a guy that she met at the Milltown Business School. The way she talked about Patrick (that's the guy's name) she has been seeing a lot of him. I mentioned being turned down to Dad and he said that he wasn't too surprised. He told me that "people form close relationships because they share something in common -- like going to the same school or working in the same place -- and then when that changes, they go their separate ways." What he told me makes sense. I have been making a lot of new friends at St. Andrew College too. Anyway, I took a break from my studies and went to see the movie myself and had a lot of laughs. Just what I needed. Danny Kay as always was very funny in a crazy way. Also, I enjoyed Dinah Shore's singing in the movie. She really has a warm personality that you remember long after seeing the film.

At St. Andrew College I have gotten to know a student by the name of Eric Fitzgerald from Wisconsin. He is very short (5'2"), lean, with glasses, and an intense look on his face as if he is concentrating on something very complicated. He is in my Introduction to Philosophy class. He wants to be a writer too --- but a writer of fiction. Of course, I have told him about my desire to be a journalist. He is working on some short stories that he hopes to sell to magazines. He even let me read one to get my reaction. I was impressed with his effort. The story was about a G.I. who falls in love with a Japanese-American girl who is placed in a relocation camp. I plan to show him parts of this diary to get his reaction. We sometimes eat together at the drug store or at the Student Union. He loves to smoke cigarettes, drink coffee, and talk about his ideas for stories.

Another person that I have gotten to know is Kara Larson from Minnesota. She told me that she grew up on a farm outside the small town of Hutchinson. I met her in my French class when our professor paired us off to practice speaking French. She enjoyed hearing about my family and especially about Carol and her love of horses. Of course, Kara has her own horse too; she started riding horses when she was 5 years old. Kara, with her long blond hair, large expressive blue eyes, and radiant smile draws people to her. I think part of her popularity is the fact that she listens and reacts to what you have to say. She makes you feel important. I finally got up the nerve to ask her to have coffee with me at the Student Union. There, we met Eric and the three of us have been palling around campus quite a lot. Perhaps sometimes in the future I'll ask her out for a date to see a movie or go to a dance. If it is to a dance it will have to be off campus because the Lutheran leaders discourage dancing; they feel that too much closeness can lead to improper behavior.

The Passing Parade

News Story: "6000 Planes Blast Reich in Record Blow"

Song: "Maria Elena" by Jimmy Dorsey and Bob Eberly

Movie: "Wing And A Prayer" with Dana Andrews

A Fire Side Chat, Indian Summer, Helping the Goldmans, A Pervert?

On Oct. 10, we listened to the President's fire side chat. He opened by urging all Americans regardless of party to register and vote. Again, he claimed that the Republicans were making it difficult for servicemen to vote. He said, "There are politicians and others who quite openly worked to restrict the use of the ballot in this election, hoping selfishly for a small vote." Then, he addressed Dewey's charge that the Roosevelt Administration desired to keep "the boys in uniform" because "the New Deal is afraid of the peace." F.D.R. stated, "It seems a pity that reckless words, based on unauthoritative sources, should be used to mislead and weaken morale." Finally, he turned down the support of the U.S. Communists headed by Earl Browder. Roosevelt declared, "I have never sought and I do not welcome the support of any person or group committed to communism or fascism, or any other foreign ideology which would undermine the American system of government." After the talk, Dad told me that he was happy that President Roosevelt had disconnected himself from the Communist Party because the Republicans would love to use any Communist Party support for F.D.R. as another reason why people should not to vote for him.

We are enjoying a beautiful Indian Summer. The temperatures are cool in the morning (about 35 degrees) and then heat up into the 70s during the afternoons. It is hard to know what to wear. In the morning you need a sweater but by 2:00 P.**M.** you find yourself wanting to take it off.

Milltown is famous for its trees -- especially elm, red oak and maple. There has been enough cold air to turn the leaves from green to brilliant shades of yellow, red, and orange. There are a lot of red oak trees in the woods that border the neighborhood to the north and east and they are really putting on a show of radiant color. The Bishop, Wellington, and Harrington Estates have plenty of maple trees and they are turning out in vivid shades of yellow and orange.

Some of the leaves have already started to fall and Carol and her girl friends are using them to play house. In our front yard the girls rake the leaves into rows to use as walls. The finished floor plan usually includes a living room, dinning room, kitchen, and three bedrooms. Then, the girls use old blankets to create make-believe beds, tables and davenports. The girls along with Buddy and other boys interested in playing house assume roles (moms, dads, grandmas, children, etc.) and act out situations (cleaning the house, taking care of a sick child, giving birth to a baby, putting out a fire, being attacked by the Japs) imagined by the girls. Some props like toy dishes and dolls help them to act out their roles. When they are finished playing, they often rake the leaves to the curb and burn them with Dad or Mom supervising.

Arvid and Caroline are helping the Standstadts to move to their Florida estate. That is a sure sign that the seasons are changing. They have already left for Florida with each driving one of the "master's" cars. The Standstadts themselves will be traveling by train to Palm Beach.

Grandma received a letter from her brother telling her more about the Goldman family living in England. He wrote that they are living in a refugee or displaced persons camp in the northern part of the country. There are about a thousand people living in the refugee camp. He said that the family had to leave most of their belongings in Denmark. He told Grandma that they need winter clothing, shoes, soap, wash coths, towels, underwear, and blankets. Great Uncle Aaron included their sizes. Mom and Grandma are going to mail several boxes to the Goldmans with the things they need. Some of the items like towels and blankets they have around the house. Other items like soap, winter coats, underwear and shoes they will have to buy. Aaron said that they could use some money too. $75.00 was collected by pooling the resources of several families. Our family and Grandma contributed $40.00. Aaron is going to send it in the form of a money order which they can convert into British pounds.

I received another good mark on a theme for Composition. Miss Park had assigned us to write a theme using the topic of conflict. I wrote about the conflict between Judaism and Christianity. I addressed it on two levels -- the international level as seen in the war and on a personal level as seen in my own life. She liked the theme so much that she read it to the class. Usually, she doesn't give the writer's name but when students pressed her for a name, she nodded in my direction. So, my secret is out and I already feel that my classmates are viewing me differently. Whether this will be good or bad I do not know. I am only sure of one thing and that is that I wish Miss Park hadn't identified me as the writer of the theme. I did earn an A for the development of the topic and believe it or not a B on mechanics.

On Friday, Irene came over with Betty to see Mom and Grandma. She was very upset and started crying as she spoke. She told them that her step father had tried to get into her bed with her. Irene said that even before this he had often started undressing in front of her. On one occasion he had hugged her and then felt her breasts. Both Mom and Grandma were shocked to hear this and said the they were going to talk to Dad about what should be done. Mom told Irene that she could come over to our house at any time if she ever felt afraid of her step father. She suggested to Irene that she phone her Aunt Elizabeth and Uncle Greg about what was going on as soon as possible. Meanwhile Mom said that she would get back to her as soon as she talked to Dad about it.

Our neighbors are talking about the results of Mr. Berry's recent trial. The jury found him guilty of murder in the second degree and he was sentenced to 25 years in prison. The Purple Lady (Mrs. Berry) took the stand in her husband's defense and told the jury that she was a witness to the crime and claimed that her husband only acted in self-defense. The jury did not buy her story. They felt that the physical evidence suggested that Mr. Berry had attacked the Colonel from behind and had hit him again and again until he was dead. Mr. Berry did not have any injuries. Also, he had brought a crowbar with him which showed intent to harm the Colonel. That is what really hurt him. When he was sentenced, he broke down and started yelling that it was all his wife's fault "because she started fucking the Colonel" and that "she is the one who should go to jail because she is a fucking bitch." All this from mild mannered Mr. Berry. It was too much for most of his neighbors. They couldn't believe that he was saying such things. I guess it only proves that anyone can break under pressure due to a situation that is beyond one's control.

We heard that Mr. Taylor's parents have moved into his home to help care for the children. We still do not know the entire story behind Mrs. Taylor's suicide. Some in the neighborhood claim that Mr. Taylor wanted to marry his secretary. Others claim that Mrs. Taylor found out that she had a fatal illness. I guess we will never really know what happened. Some of the kids in Hilltop Place feel that the house is now haunted by Mrs. Taylor's ghost. Buddy claims that he and Timmy saw her ghost appear at one of the dormer windows in the attic. It has even been reported by the Taylor's clearning girl that she heard the sounds of a crying woman coming from the attic. When Dad heard about these reports, he speculated that some people -- and kids in particular -- are getting into the spirit of Holloween early. He observed, "People are just jumpy because the neighborhood has had both a suicide and a murder. It is understandable if some people start thinking that they are hearing and seeing things that aren't real. At a certain point the imagination takes over."

The Passing Parade

News Story: "Allies Occupy Athens; Russians in Begrade"

Song: "Dancing In The Dark" by Artie Shaw

Movie: "Rainbow Island" with Dorothy Lamour

F.D.R.'s Campaign, Helping Irene, Mom's Birthday, the Jewish Sabbath

The newspapers have been filled with stories about General Mac Arthur's landing in the Philippines and the President's campaign swing through New York City. The landing on Leyte was a surprise to the Japs and the invasion is going well for us. Roosevelt had helped plan the move with MacArthur when the two met at Pearl Harbor. Also, F.D.R.,'s 51 mile motor trip through Brooklyn, Queens, the Bronx, and finally Manhattan was a big success despite the hard rain and gale. Between 2 to 3 million people saw him pass in his open car. The President only had his cape and hat to protect him. But, he seemed to really enjoy the ride and smiled and waved at the tremendous crowds. Mrs. Roosevelt and Fala were with him for part of the trip and seemed to enjoy themselves too. Dad hopes that this will end the health issue for good.

Dad and several members of the local Democratic Party plan to drive to Chicago to hear the President speak at Soldier Field on Oct. 28. Dad asked me if I wanted to go and I jumped at the chance. I would like to see a President of the United States in person and of course I really admire Roosevelt. I told Professor Frederick about the trip and he told me that he wanted me to report to the class about it when I get back.

My parents are trying to help Irene deal with her step father. They took it upon themselves to call Irene's Aunt Elizabeth in Rockford to tell her about the situation. She told them that she had already talked to Irene and was shocked when she heard about what was going on. She also told them that she and her husband Greg had phoned Mr. Phillips and had told him that they wanted to talk to him again about a different arrangement for Irene and Betty. His response was a very hostile one but he agreed to see them next week.

After Mom and Dad talked to Irene's aunt, Dad went over to talk to Mr. Phillips about the situation. He later told us that it was the most difficult thing that he had done in quite a while. He told us that he talked with him about other things before he discussed Irene's charges. Dad asked how Mr. Phillips was doing and whether or not he was dating again and trying to get on with his life. Dad told him that he knew a lot of suitable ladies that would be happy to go out with him and that he would be happy to make the introductions. Then, Dad got to the subject of Irene and Betty and the way that Irene had interpreted Mr. Phillip's actions. Bill (Mr. Phillips) denied any improper feelings and actions toward Irene and told Dad that he resented "a Jew lover" coming over to talk to him about such private matters. "At that point," Dad said, "I had a very difficult time holding my temper." He said that he told Mr. Phillips that "his love for Jews had nothing to do with the matter at hand." Dad told Bill that while he might believe his statement of innocence, others may have a difficult time with

146

it. Dad pointed out that the situation that now exists in Bill's household as a result of his wife's death may lead people to form wrong impressions. Dad suggested that Mr. Phillips work out a different arrangement that would remove any suspicion of impropriety. He told Mr. Phillips that some neighbor may turn him into the police if Irene claims that he is continuing to make improper sexual advances toward her. Dad feels that Mr. Phillips got the message. Let's hope so. We will have to wait and see what will happens when Irene's aunt and uncle visit Mr. Phillips next week.

Temperatures are falling. Most of the neighbors are taking down their screens and putting up storm windows and doors. Also, trucks with coal are making their deliveries. McCoy's coal truck usually backs into our yard from the alley and gets as close to the coal bin as possible. Then, he takes a metal coal shoot and runs it from the truck down into the coal bin through a basement window. Usually, he has to take a shovel and guide the coal down the shoot. It usually takes about 35 minutes to fill up the bin. Some of us also stock up on kindling to use to help start fires in the furnace.

The Bishops, Wellingtons, Harringtons and Standstadts have oil heat. The oil trucks have been seen in the neighborhood refilling the storage tanks. Another thing that is being done by everyone is changing the oil and putting new anti-freeze in their cars. Most are checking to see where they put their chains for their tires too. Of course, heating oil is rationed and you're supposed to keep your thermostat set at no more than 65 degrees. Whether the people on the big estates abide by this nobody knows for sure. We have more confidence in the Bishops than anyone else. Naturally, the Standstadts don't have to worry about it most of the winter because they are in Florida.

Anyway, everyone is preparing for a cold winter which is typical for this area. Milltown has a lot of snow plows to clear the snow so that people can get to work and school. Most of us are used to the low temperatures that will come and the challenges of driving -- and especially getting up and down the steep hills of our river town.

Well, Mom turned 42. Dad decided to take the entire family out for dinner to celebrate the occasion. We ate at the Walnut Groves Restaurant so that each of us could order what we wanted. For desert a special birthday cake was served to our party. It was a yellow cake with white frosting and lots of pink roses on it and of course "Happy Birthday Mom." Dad ordered a red wine to go with the meal. Everyone including Carol and Buddy got a glass of it. Dad's toast was: "To the most loving woman in the world." After we sang "Happy Birthday" to her, Mom opened her gifts.-- a handbag from Buddy and Carol, a set of long white gloves from me, a quilted lap blanket made with various shades and patterns of pink blocks from Grandma, and a gold bracelet with pearl settings from Dad. She enjoyed opening all her gifts and then gave her own toast to us: "To the best family a woman could ever have."

During the weekend St. Andy had its Homecoming. I did not take an active part in it. Perhaps next year I will become more involved as I feel more comfortable with college life. Right now I feel that I am trying to just survive in the classroom. I expect my mid-term grades to be mainly Bs and As but I am really having to work. Of course, finals may change everything. They count the finals for about 50% of the grade so a person could really do himself harm at the end. I did go over to campus to see the parade and the football game between St. Andy and St. Olaf. I have to admit that I was surprised that the Lutherans could really kick up their heels and have some fun. After experiencing the daily serious atmosphere on campus -- in chapel and in the classroom -- I was taken aback by all the laughter and down right silliness that was evident in many of the festivities. The Viking Royalty lead the parade which consisted of a lot of floats entered by various fraternities and sororities on campus. The college band played a lot of Broadway tunes as well as the traditional Sousa marches as it lead everyone to the football field. I was very impressed by the fact that so many Alumni had travelled quite a distance to see the Homecoming game. The ladies were given mum corsages by the welcoming student representatives. Anyway, it was an exciting event and I hope to participate more next year.

Grandma and I had a little time to talk about what her family did on the Sabbath. She told me that every Friday at sundown her mother lit two candles and said the prayer that marks the beginning of the Sabbeth. Then, her father recited the Kiddush which is a prayer recited over a cup of wine which sets aside the Sabbath as a holy day for joy, peace, meditation, and study. Then, he broke off pieces of the special Sabbath bread called Challah and distributed them to his family. During the meal the family relaxed together. This sharing and closeness is part of what Judaism meant to the Goldman family. Often Grandma said stories, lessons, riddles related to the lessons of Judaism would be discussed during the meal. After dinner Grandma said that the family would remain together, talking, reading aloud or playing games. To Grandma, the Sabbath was a time to draw closer together and to reflect on what it meant to be a Jew.

Well, the leaves are really falling now as the temperatures drop and the winds become stronger. I always feel that the sounds of the trains, factory whistles, and even people talking to each other outside in the neighborhood sound different to me at this time of year. I guess I feel that the sounds are more penetrating and in the case of the trains more sad as they sound their whistles as their steel wheels make their way down the tracks and through the town. One becomes more aware of the passing of time, of one season dying and giving way to another. In some way it is sad but at the same time reassuring that the cycle of life is continuing and is a constant in this world where man has caused so many things to be unpredictable.

Most of the neighbors rake the leaves to the curbs and then burn them there. The smell is really aromic -- nothing like it except the smell of wood burning in the fire place. Of course, every once in a while someone gets carried away and tries to burn too many leaves at once which results in a lot of heavy smoke. This also happens when someone tries to burn leaves that are too wet. But, even then, the smoke and the penetrating sounds make for a very different kind of atmosphere -- especially when they all come together at dusk.

The Passing Parade

News Story: "Roosevelt Text: Leadership in World Community Our Duty"

Song: "White Cliffs of Dover" by Kay Kyser

Movie: "Step Lively" with George Murphy and Frank Sinatra

Fuck Jews!

Seeing F.D.R., A Problem Solved, and Halloween Parties

I was too tired from the trip to Chicago to write anything on Sunday so I decided to wait a few days before I made any more entries. Instead of taking our Chevy to Chicago we decided to take the train up and back.

As we rode the train to Chicago, we talked about the war and politics. The big news on the war front was the smashing defeat of the Japanese navy in the Battle of Leyte Gulf. This has really given a lift to morale on the home front. It has caused people to say to themselves, "Perhaps there is an end to the war after all." Dad felt that this news would really help F.D.R. and the Democratic Party in the election. It would be obvious to everyone now that the Democratic leadership had put together a mighty war machine that was winning the war.

The President's train was late getting into Chicago. According to the newspaper that I read later he was supposed to have been in a parade organized by Mayor Kelly. Nobody seemed to mind when F.D.R.'s train finally arrived. According to the news article, the large crowd that had gathered at the station was still there, and it gave out a thunderous cheer as the train pulled in and an even louder one when the President was seen leaving it. He was immediately taken to the stadium for his speech.

I felt that I was participating in history by seeing the President. He was in a fighting spirit as he addressed the huge crowd. Every seat was filled. Dad told me that he heard that the stadium had about 110,000 seats. Another 150,000 must have been jammed outside the stadium to see the President enter and leave. Dad made sure that we got there early so that we could get seats. It helped being a party member too -- and being an elected official like Dad.

F.D.R. spoke from his automobile that appeared to be on a special ramp. A spot light lit up where the President was sitting in the car. I could see in front of where he was sitting a board holding several microphones. He had to wait to speak, The huge crowd stood up (including me and Dad) and cheered him for at least 10 minutes. I noticed that some people had tears in their eyes as they applauded. I too felt a surge of emotion when I saw him. He looked thinner and much older from the photograph of F.D.R. that Dad keeps on his desk at home. I felt like others in the crowd that the war had taken its toll on him too. I think much of the applause was a way for us all to say, "Thank you, Mr. President for all your hard work."

When F.D.R. spoke his voice was strong and clear as he denounced the Republican campaigners for calling Democratic leaders "incompetent blunderers and bunglers." The crowd applauded again and again as he defended his administration's record -- both on domestic issues like farm relief and

150

Social Security and on foreign issues like the effort to mobilize the nation to win the war. He ended his speech by saying, "We

At Soldiers' Field

are not going to turn the clock back. We are going forward, my friends, forward with the fighting millions of our fellow countrymen. We are going forward. And that tonight is my message to you -- let us go forward together." At that the crowd roared its enthusiastic endorsement of his words -- and his bid for a 4th term.

We had to take a late train back after Roosevelt's speech. We were lucky to get seats because thousands of people had gone to Chicago to see the President too, and they were trying to get back home after his address. Before the train left Union Station we had a sandwich at one of the small eating places near the station. It was a good thing too because the dining car was too crowded and then later it was closed.

My report about the President's speech was not met with a lot of enthusiasm by my classmates. There are a lot of conservative Republicans at St. Andy and they tend to really hate the Roosevelts -- especially F.D.R. and the First Lady. They feel that he is really a socialist who has become a dictator.

In the case of Eleanor Roosevelt, they label her a "Communist." But, Professor Frederick liked my account and encouraged others in the class to report on politicans that they go to see. He hoped that one of the Republicans in class will make an effort to go to a Dewey rally.

In most elections there are many rumors and accusations floating around, and the current election is no exception. In fact, it has been marked by an especially large number of false and in some cases silly rumors. The one about the President sending a ship to get Fala is a good example of the latter. We heard about another rumor or election gossip by way of Buddy. He came home from school and informed us that one of his pals -- a Republican -- had told him with a great deal of pleasure that President Roosevelt had a girl friend and was not being faithful to Mrs. Roosevelt. The boy told him that the girlfriend was a WAC who had been seen leaving a military plane with F.D.R. and getting into his private limousine. Mom and I both laughed at this story and told Buddy that it just showed that the Republicans were getting desperate and that they have been telling such hate Roosevelt jokes and stories for years.

During our absence Mom had a chance to visit with Irene's Aunt Elizabeth. She told Mom that she and her husband had confronted Bill Phillips about becoming too familiar with Irene. While he did not admit anything, he agreed that the living situation might cause some people to draw the wrong conclusions. Elizabeth said that he agreed to allow Irene and Betty to live with them until he remarried. Naturally, he would visit often and take Betty for long periods of time and would provide for her financial support. Elizabeth said that she intended to see that Irene got to attend a college in or near Rockford, Illinois. Also, she voiced her hope that down the road Mr. Phillips would give full custody of Betty to them. While we will all miss Irene, the neighbors agree that this new arrangement would be best for all concerned.

The kids in the neighborhood really enjoyed Halloween. The mothers from the local scout troops got permission to use one of the barns on the Standstadt estate as a haunted house, or in this a "haunted barn." They worked very hard making up scary experiences for the kids. Buddy and Carol really got a laugh out of seeing the ladies dressed up as witches and gobblins. Buddy claimed that he recognized Mom right away despite her attempt to look and sound like a mean and vicious demon from hell.

Mrs. McCoy had a Holloween party for her two granddaughters -- Joyce and Patty. All the kids in the neighborhood were invited to attend. The McCoys had decorated their basement with corn stalks and jack-o-laterns for the party. The kids bobbed for apples and won prizes for answering questions about Halloween or having something spooky (like a spider) on their costumes. Buddy went dressed as a clown thanks to Grandma who spent at least four days making his outfit. Carol was dressed up like a gypsy fortune teller. Mom and Grandma gave her a lot of their old clothes, a turban and lots of jewelry for her outfit. She used a round glass hurricane lamp shade for a crystal ball. The final touch was make-up to complete the transformation into a darker and older looking woman.

Mom had purchased a jack-o-latern and a cat-o-latern from Woolworths for them to use on the scary night. She reminded Buddy and Carol to be careful with them because they were made of cardboard and paper and that they could easily catch on fire. Dad also brought home some real pumpkins and helped them to make some friendly and not so friendly looking laterns to put out on our front porch The hard part was getting candles in the laterns and then using kitchen matches to light them.

Mrs. McCoy had made a lot of good things for the children to eat. Buddy reported that they had popcorn balls, gingerbread men, and pumpkin cake. Naturally, cider was the drink of the evening.

After the party the kids went trick or treating around the neighborhood. They even went to the Wellington estate. According to Carol, they were met by a butler at the front door. He threw 3 dollars worth of 50 cent pieces at the "gobblins." Carol said that the kids immediately began to argue over who would get what. The issue was never settled; Eldon, a neighborhood bully, got most of the money.

The Bishops had their annual Halloween party in one of their rental garages. Mrs. Moore and Mrs. Wells were dressed as witches as they served cookies and apple cider. Mr. Bishop had a great time demanding that the kids do tricks before he would give them a treat. Fred played his fiddle so that some of the adults could dance. The garage was decorated with straw, real pumpkins, corn stalks, and a scare crow.

On the morning following Halloween we found a large Star of David painted on the side of our house. Underneath it was printed: "Death to Jews." Thus, Halloween ended on a sour note for us. This time Dad called the police and reported the vandalism.

The Passing Parade

News Stories: "B-29 Raid on Tokyo Reported by Jap Radio"
"Casualties From This Area"

Song: "Dear Hearts and Gentle People" by Dinah Shore

Movie: "Summer Storm" with Linda Darnell

"The Bishop Girls"
as Witches

153

F.D.R. Wins!, An 18th Birthday, Causes of Discrimination

Boy, were we all surprised this morning. We woke up to a cold -- very cold house. Overnight the temperature had dropped and we got a two inch snow fall along with it. Frost had formed on some of the storm windows. Nobody had built a fire in the furance because we weren't expecting the sudden change in the weather. I got up and put my pants over my pajamas and went down to start a fire. I grabbed some of last night's newspaper and some kindling and got busy. I also turned on the oven in the gas stove. By breakfast time the house felt a lot warmer -- at least in the down stairs.

There's good news to record. The Democrats are back in power again. After going to Chicago Dad felt that the Democrats had the edge and he was right. F.D.R. received 432 electoral votes to 99 for Dewey. The popular vote was closer -- 25,600,000 to a little over 22,000,000 for Dewey. The Democrats also retained control of congress; in fact, they picked up 20 more seats in the House. Only about 56% of the people voted; that is down from 58% that voted in 1940. Dad said it was due to the number of people who had moved during the war to find work in war plants. They had lost their right to vote until they had lived long enough in their new states. Of course, I mentioned the fact that in 1940 the controversy over breaking the two term tradition probably generated more interest in that election. Dad agreed with me on that.

We analyzed the results of the election in Political Science class. We concluded that Roosevelt was helped by the success of D-Day and also the defeat of the Japanese navy at Leyte Gulf. This showed everyone that Roosevelt's direction of the war effort had been successful. Also, by Roosevelt getting out and making public appearances he had been able to reassure people about his health. The so-called "Fala speech" while dealing with a silly topic had been well received by the people at large. It showed that Roosevelt was still a fighter and could really turn the knife of humor against his opponents. To a lot of people F.D.R.'s comments about the Republicans wanting to undo the New Deal hit home. Most agree with the reforms -- like Social Security -- and fear that the Republicans would endeavor to undermine them if given power. Professor Frederick pointed out to the class that the coalition created by F.D.R. had held together. By the coalition he meant the big city vote, the Solid South, labor organizations, and minorities (Negroes, Jews). Finally, some of us felt that Roosevelt's comments about Dewey's dog (a grey hound) and Fala (a Scottish terrier) summed up the election to a lot of average people. F.D.R. said, "The big man has the little dog and the little man has the big dog." While it was in a way a ridiculous statement, it had its effect. People began looking at Dewey and F.D.R. and evaluating them in terms of the types of dogs they owned. Dr. Frederick felt that if Dewey had only taken the high road and offered the nation new ideas rather than making personal attacks, he would have won more votes and who knows even the election. Of course, he admitted that people tend not to want to change horses in mid-stream -- and this is all the more true during a crisis like a war -- and especially if the person in charge seems to be doing the job.

I did two important things on the 10th. I turned 18 and also registered for the draft. I didn't expect much for my birthday because Mom and Dad are helping me a lot by paying for part of the tuition and textbooks to go to college. So, I was surprised by what was done for me. Mom and Dad gave me a new blue tweed sports jacket. Buddy gave me a tie clip, and Carol a bow tie that she had made herself with Mom's help. It was dark blue with white polka dots in it. F.D.R. has one like it. Then,. when I thought that I had received everything, Grandma presented me with something that I had really wanted --a red vest. She had made it herself using fine red silk and gold metal buttons. It was patterned from a red vest that I had seen in the window of Carlson's Clothing Store on 5th Avenue from the bus as I was going to St. Andy. Grandma told me that she had gone to the store and had asked to see that vest to help her with her own effort. Anyway, I had a great birthday. I guess it pays to get good mid-term grades. I received 3 As and 5 Bs.

I had a chance to talk to Grandma about some of my reading dealing with Judaism. In one book I found an entire chapter about discrimination toward Jews; it dealt with the causes of it. I told Grandma that the author feels that the discrimination occurs because Jews appear to be different in terms of customs and traditions and hence a threat to the dominant and accepted culture. He claims that the majority in any community usually turns on any minority that is perceived as being very different. That plus the fact that the Catholic Church had taken a strong stand against Jews for killing Christ and rejecting Him as the Son of God accounted for the extreme persecution of Jews over the years. Also, the author pointed out that economics played a role too. For centuries Europeans did not want to share any of the economic pie with people who they considered outsiders and a threat to the accepted beliefs. Hence, Jews were forbidden to own land. They were forced to turn to business and banking to make a living. Jews were also forced in many countries by the king or nobles to pay protection money for the safety of the Jewish community. This took place especially during the Crusades.

Finally, the author pointed out that many individuals need scapegoats to vent their anger or to explain problems in the community. Jews over the years became good targets for many individuals. This information did not come as anything new to Grandma. She had heard about a lot of these things from her father and grandfather as a child. However, she said that the thing that still amazes her is the role of the Catholic Church in the persecution of Jews. She finds it very difficult to forget or forgive its role in labeling Jews as "Christ Killers." Also she felt that the Church had not done much of anything recently to stop the persecution of Jews under fascist regimes. By not speaking out against the persecution of Jews, the Catholic Church and other Christian churches had aided and indirectly supported an official policy of discrimination and murdering Jews.

Grandma and I both agreed that it took a lot of courage for Jews -- especially Orthodox ones -- to live in a world with this type of persecution. We both could understand why some Jews tried to blend themselves into the dominant culture and to do everything to achieve it -- such as changing their names, marrying gentiles, becoming Christians. It was a very natural reaction to the obvious evidence of widespread discrimination. We could also understand why some would commit suicide or become depressed or suffer from mental illness as a result of the anxiety of living in an atmosphere of persecution. Many Jews felt caught between being loyal to their heritage and at the same time wanting to be accepted by the dominant group.

The Passing Parade

News Story: "Roosevelt Wins; Leads in 35 States"

Song: "Love Letters" by Dick Haymes

Movie: "Carolina Blues" with Kay Kytser and Ann Miller

The Disappearance and the Letter from Joseph Goldman

Josh Walters has disappeared! As Mrs. Wells said, "Poor Josh has vanished into thin air." He was on his way by bus to visit his daughter's family in Miami. He had taken the Greyhound Bus to Chicago where he was supposed to transfer to a bus headed for Washington D.C. From there he was to transfer to a bus headed south to Florida. We know that he checked in his luggage at the bus station in Milltown. It was to be transferred to different buses and reach Miami the same time he did. He only carried a small bag with some personal items on to the bus. We have been told that Mr. Walters had about $200.00 in his wallet for the trip. His daughter knew something was wrong when his luggage arrived in Miami without him. Naturally, she was frantic with worry and asked the police to trace his steps if they could.

After a lot of looking and checking the police concluded that he disappeared while waiting in the Chicago bus station. One witness -- the woman who sells bus tickets -- claimed that she remembers him waiting in the station and that he did strike up conversations with some of the service men waiting there. She did not remember when he left or if he left with someone.

His daughter ran an ad in all the major Chicago newspapers with his picture hoping that someone would come forward. She even offered a $500 reward. Nobody ever came forward. The neighbors feel that his daughter was wrong in allowing him to make the trip by himself. "Afterall," Mrs. Moore pointed out, "Josh is in late 70s and is simply too trusting." The neighbors theorize that Mr. Walters was lured outside the station and probably murdered for the $200.00. Someone who appeared to be helpful and friendly may have asked him to join them for lunch -- or they may have invited him to their home with the promise of getting him back to the bus station on time. Who knows? One thing that is certain is that life is very unpredictable. You don't have to be in the war zone to get killed. Sometimes it happens near a bus station -- and the killer doesn't have to be in uniform either; he might be a very ordinary and charming person.

Ethel who rents the upstairs apartment over Mr. Walters has taken his disappearance very hard. She knows that he would not have deliberately disappeared. He often talked about his late wife and his love for his daughter and his grandchildren. He was looking forward to visiting them for Thanksgiving and Christmas. Ethel certainly did not need to think of him coming to a violent end. It reminded her that life can be so unfair. In fact, the incident has increased her worry about her husband who is fighting somewhere in France. Bob escaped death during the D-Day invasion and she hopes that he will be able to come home in one piece to her. It has been over a week since she has received a V-mail letter from him.

Irene and Betty left to live with their Aunt Elizabeth and Uncle Greg in Rockford. Mom had all four over for supper before their departure. Irene is really looking forward to the change. She told us that she found it hard living in the house where her mother died. She will be happy to have some new memories -- hopefully happy ones. She is looking forward to going to college next semester. Later, I got to say my goodbye to her. I told her that I'll always cherish the memory of taking her to the prom, and I promised that I would try to visit Rockford some weekend after she starts college. She smiled and said that she "would be looking forward to it and comparing notes about college life."

Grandma received a letter from Mr. Goldman. He wrote the letter in English. That didn't surprise her because Uncle Aaron had told her that Joseph Goldman had a good command of several languages. In Denmark he had received an excellent education and when the Nazi invasion occurred, he was an executive with a bank in Copenhagen. In the letter he said that his family had been overwhelmed by all the items that they had found in the care packages. He thanked us all and hoped that he and his family could come to America in the near future to meet us and thank us personally.

Each member of his family wrote a short note thanking us for a particular item that they really found helpful. They included a black and white photograph of themselves too. It had been taken in 1942 before they were forced to leave their home and go into hiding and eventually flee to England. The photo showed a nicely dressed family. Joseph Goldman appeared to be about 5'8" and was dressed in a pin-stripped suit. He wore glasses and had a beard. Next to him was his wife Sarah. She had on a long dark dress with a lace collar. She wore her hair in an upsweep. Unlike her husband she seemed more relaxed and smiled out at us from the photo in a very engaging way. The lean girl next to her was Greta their daughter. She wore a white blouse and a straight skirt with a belt. She had long hair and looked as if she was a bit shy of the camera. In front of Mr. Goldman was their young son whose name is Benjamin. He seemed to have a school uniform on and looked very outgoing and mischievous. He had a very relaxed stance and a friendly grin on his face. Mom said that she thought that he looked like a young version of his father -- minus the beard and, of course, the addition of the smile. We were happy that they had sent us the photograph. It made them a reality, and we talked about possibly seeing them during the coming year if things work out.

Here is some war news that a lot of people may not know about. The Japs are sending across the Pacific thousands of paper balloons with bombs timed to explode when they reach the United States. Some have reached the U.S. and have caused some damage. Dad got this information from one of his Masonic pals who works at the Arsenal. The government hasn't allowed publicity about it because it doesn't wish to cause a panic, and it doesn't want to tip off the Japs that their balloons are arriving and are somewhat effective.

The Passing Parade

News Story: "British Join Yanks in Thrusts Toward the Ruhr"

Song: "Ding Dong - The Street Car Song" by Judy Garland

Movie: "Something for the Boys" with Carmon Miranda and Vivian Blaine

THANKSGIVING AT THE OLD JOHNSON HOMESTEAD

Sunday, Nov. 26, 1944

As usual we celebrated Thanksgiving with Uncle Ira and Aunt Sadie at the old Johnson Homestead outside Iowa City. Dad especially likes to return to the homestead because he often visited his grandparents there. And, besides, as I wrote earlier, Aunt Sadie has become like a second mother to him.

It had snowed earlier in the week but we didn't let that stop us. We had only gotten about 3 inches and Dad consideres that "a light dusting." We all piled in our Chevy and took off after packing 4 overnight suitcases. Dad put the tire chains in the trunk too just in case we needed them. As we approached the outstirts of Iowa City, we took a slide road that runs to several small towns like Kickapoo and Miller's Creek. About ten miles down this road is the Johnson farm. It took us over an hour to drive there because the Victory speed is only 35 on many of the roads.

The old Johnson farm house sits in a wooded valley about a half mile from the road. The house is a two story Victorian structure with a gabled roof and plenty of so-called gingerbread trim on the hugh porch that runs across the front and around the right side of the house. As we approached the house we could see the outbuildings, the barn, and silo. Ira keeps 4 cows and 2 bulls, about 12 pigs, and about 30 chickens on the place. Of course, there are the usual large numbers of cats and dogs that one finds on most farms.

Despite its charm and elegance the farm house lacks indoor plumbing, electricity, and central heat. But, Ira and Sadie prefer it this way. Water comes from a pump in the kitchen. Kerosene lamps with chimmeys of several sizes, shapes, and colors dot the rooms. Pot bellied stoves in the main rooms provide heat as well as the cook stove in the kitchen. A telephone is one of the few concessions to the modern world; it hangs on the wall in the kitchen. On the main floor there are two parlors, one for everyday use, the other for special days. Sliding wooden doors can be pulled out of the walls to separate the parlors and conserve heat. There is also a large dining room and kitchen. The open staircase in the front hall leads to the four bedrooms on the second floor.

As we got out of the car, Uncle Ira and Aunt Sadie came out to greet us and gave us all big hugs. As usual they were in their "farm chores duds" as Sadie calls them -- he with his blue overalls and plaid wool shirt and she with her printed house dress with a long apron. We were also welcomed by several dogs -- General Sherman and Robert E. Lee. Uncle Ira likes to name his animals after famous people. Also, there were about 5 cats who came up to rub their bodies against our legs. I only recognized one -- a tabby named Eleanor Roosevelt. When we got into the house, we took off our heavy coats and boots and headed either for one of the potbellied stoves or the cook stove to warm ourselves. We could smell the turkey and oyster dressing cooking in the kitchen. Sadie told us that she had been baking the last 2 days in order to serve her orange nut bread and pumpkin and mince-meat pies for Thanksgiving.

As always the dinner was really "a spread" as Uncle Ira refers to it. He ordered, "Put on your feed bags and come to the table." Grandma, Mom and Carol helped Sadie set the table and serve the food. Dinner consisted of turkey, oyster dressing, sweet potatoes, cranberry sauce and several vegetables. This was accompanied by huge slabs of Sadie's home-baked bread, covered with freshly churned butter.

After dinner, we were so stuffed that some of us (me, Buddy, Carol, Dad and Ira) took a walk around outside while the women cleared the table and washed dishes. Halfway up the hill from the house is an old cemetery where Saide and Ira's parents and grandparents are buried. There is also a stranger known only as "Fred" buried there. He showed up at the farm one day years ago. He was sick and didn't last the night. Dad's great-grandfather conducted a simple funeral service and laid Fred to rest in the family cemetery. His sons had built the casket of walnut; great grandmother had carefully sewed in a lining for the casket of left over printed cotten material.

We also headed for the barn to see Uncle Ira's new arrivals. We found 2 new calfs nestled next to their mothers. Ira names the cows after famous women. Since the start of the war, he has been keeping up with the names of the the famous pinup girls that the G.I.s like. So, he has named his most recent cows: Betty Grable, Lana Turner, Rita Hayworth and Veronica Lake. The bulls are named: Clark Gable and George Patton.

Back in the house we entertained ourselves with Monopoly, charades and card games. This time we got to use the special parlor. The empire sofas, floral patterned wallpaper, lace curtains and tie back drapes, along with the intricately carved fireplace, always make us feel as if we are back living during the turn of the century. There is even an old pump organ in the room. Toward the end of the evening Aunt Sadie went over to it and played what she calls "the oldies but goodies" for us.

Before we headed for bed, Uncle Ira and Dad went out to bring in more firewood for the stoves. We carried kerosene lamps as we climbed the stairs. In the bedrooms are heavy fruitwood armoires, dressers, bedsteads, and headboards. Wash basins and pitchers are available in each room. Also, chamber pots can be found tucked under the beds. Quilts and comforters were brought out of the armoires to make sure that we would be warm enough during the night. Buddy and Carol started laughing and giggling as if they were preparing to camp out in the woods. Soon everyone stopped chatting and fell into a deep sleep.

The next morning we were awakened early by crowing roosters. After one of Aunt Sadie's country breakfasts, we collected walnuts and pinecones. Aunt Sadie whipped up some of her famous fudge for us to eat in the car. Uncle Ira showed us how to make wreaths out of pinecones.

After a lunch made up of left overs from yesterday's fest, we said our goodbyes all around and piled into our car. Then, we slowly drove up the hill and on to the country road, waving for as long as we could see Aunt Sadie and Uncle Ira.

The Passing Parade

News Story: "U.S. Smashes 4th Leyte-Bound Jap Convoy"

Song: "My Heart Cries for You" by Dinah Shore

Movie: "Heavenly Days" with Fibber McGee & Molly

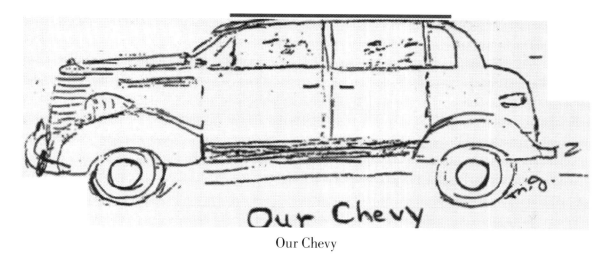

Our Chevy

The Johnson Homestead

VISITING RABBI SOLOMAN

The entire family heard over the radio that the 4 chaplains who went down with the U.S. Army transport **Dorchester** were awarded Distinguished Service Crosses by the U.S. War Department. Clark V. Poling and George L. Fox were Protestants while John P. Washington was Catholic and Alexander D. Goode was Jewish. The 4 had calmed the fears of many on board the sinking ship, convinced many to go into the water to await rescue, and finally gave up their own life jackets to others. Survivors reported that as the ship sank the chaplains were seen linking arms and raising their voices in prayer. They were still on deck together, praying, when the stricken ship made its final plunge.

Grandma received another letter from Uncle Aaron telling her that the Goldmans were scheduled to arrive in the United States in January. Aaron said that all the paper work had been filed with the government. Aaron indicated on the forms that the Goldmans would live with his family until they were able to get their own home. He admitted that it would be crowded in his three bedroom house, but that he and his wife were looking forward to the company. They felt that they could set up a daybed in the living room and make a bedroom in the basement. Aaron had also arranged for a job interview for Joseph Goldman at a bank in Chicago. The job called for someone familiar with foreign currencies. With Joseph's background working at the bank in Copenhagen, he should not have too much trouble convincing the manager that he can handle the position with great expertise. So, if all goes well and the Allied Forces remain in control of the North Atlantic, the ship carrying the Goldmans and other refugees should be able to sail on schedule. Aaron wrote Grandma Mendell that he would keep her informed about any change in plans. We were all excited about this news and look forward to meeting the Goldman family that we have gotten to know through their letters and the black and white photograph that they sent us.

Grandma, Mom and I finally got around to visiting Temple Israel synagogue in nearby Keyport: It took us 45 minutes to get to the temple which is located on Main Street. The building is very simple but impressive. It is a three story, red brick building with no windows in the front and topped by a dome. It has several decorative features -- balastrades, pilasters, railings -- made of limestone and granite. A Star of David is in the upper center of the front of the building. It appears to be made of limestone.

Rabbi Soloman was waiting for us as we walked into the lobby. He is a small man (about 5'3"), with a heavy figure, a white beard, and glasses. He is very impressive in his flowing robes and prayer shaw. He was very attentive as we introduced ourselves and told him how grateful we were that he had agreed to meet us and give us a tour of the temple. He indicated that he wanted to give us the tour before we sat down and talked.

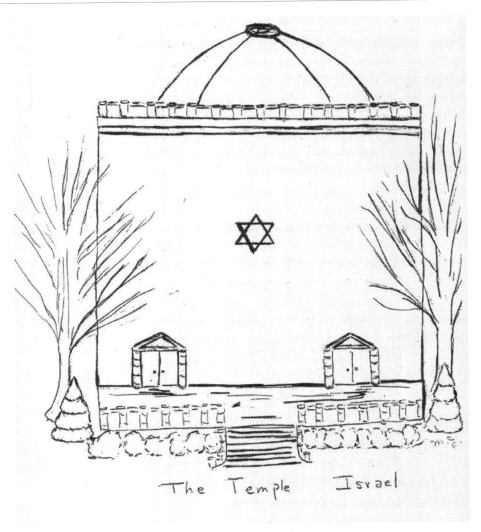

The Temple Israel

He gave me a yarmulka to wear before we entered the sanctuary. It is a very large square room with a balcony running around three sides of the room. We were told that the men sit on the main floor while the women and children are seated in the balcony. The room is decorated with paster work in the form of laurals. They are drapped around the upper walls. The laurals are composed of plaster grapes, apples, and other types of fruit. Several elaborate chandeliers hang from the ceiling. They are composed of small electric candles and plenty of crystal. In front of the large room is a podium and behind that the elaborate hiding place for the **Torah.** Rabbi Soloman identified it as the Ark. The Ark is really an opening in the wall which is surrounded by elaborate stone work and enclosed or covered by wooden doors that have been decorated with floral carvings. There are two marble pillasters which support a pediment which frame the doors. Rabbi Soloman then opened the doors of the Ark and showed us the **Torah.** It is actually a scroll made of parchment sheets rolled around two wooden poles. Then, he pointed out where various ceremonies like Barmitzvah are performed in the sanctuary.

After we had seen the sanctuary we went to the rabbi's office to talk about ourselves and our concerns. Grandma told him about her family and how it had gradually deserted Jewish traditions. She talked about her brother Aaron and the Goldman refugees in England. She talked about her feelings of guilt about the past. Mom joined in at that point and indicated that she had experienced similar feelings. Rabbi Soloman listened quietly. Then, he told us that he was not surprised by the story. He reassured Mom and Grandma that their experiences were very typical of many Jews in America. While he regretted the desertion of so many Jews from the faith, he said that he could understand it because of the prejudice and discrimination against Jews. He told Mom and Grandma that he was happy that they wanted to rekindle their Jewish faith and to pass Jewish traditions on to the next generation. He told them that they were welcome in his congregation. He also applauded their efforts to befriend the Goldman family. He told us that the Nazis had been killing Jews for years -- that Jewish leaders throughout the world had tried to tell leaders in the West what was going on but they had not been believed. Then, he predicted, "Once the Allies liberate the prison camps behind German lines, they will find only death and brutality." He urged us to stand up and be counted for the Jewish faith. Both Mom and Grandma were overcome with emotion at this point and tearfully asked the Rabbi Soloman to pray for them as they make their way back to the faith. He nodded, and then said quietly, "I will say a daily prayer for you because we, your Jewish brothers and sisters need you -- and you need us -- and God needs us all."

The Passing Parade

News Story: "Patton's Men Capture Most of Sarrlautern"

Song: "Baby, It's Cold Outside" by Dinah Shore

Movie: "Thirty Seconds Over Tokyo" with Spencer Tracy

GETTING READY FOR CHRISTMAS

Since Thanksgiving people are slowly getting into the spirit of Christmas. It is difficult because of the war. The newspaper and our local radio stations continue to tell us about Milltown citizens who have been either killed or wounded or missing in action. However, there is a feeling that we should make an effort to be happy for the children. Even those wives whose husbands are fighting overseas want their children to receive gifts and have a tree as usual. They talk about how the happy reactions of their children to the trappings of Christmas make them feel better. Besides, as many point out, the Christmas story is a story of hope for mankind and hence deserves to be celebrated. Everyone hopes that this time next year their loved ones will be back home with them and gathered around the tree.

Despite the war the mayor of Milltown ordered the Street Department to put up some festive Christmas decorations while omitting the usual colorful lights in order to save on electric power. Each lamp post has two real trees attached to it. The trees are decorated with red garlands. Across the intersections real evergreen laurels with red garlands have been strung. While we miss the bright Christmas lights, we understand this small sacrifice may help end the war sooner. Some of the department stores like Penney and Sears have outside decorations. The New York Store on 5th Avenue is especially festive with evergreen laurels strung with blue lights cascading down the front of the six story building. There must be at least 6 laurels of lights with evergreens that have been hung from the top of the building down to the street where they are attached to lamp posts. The Salvation Army has stationed several of its workers dressed as Santas on at least 5 of the busiest downtown intersections. The Santa next to the New York Store is accompanied by several musicians from the Salvation Army. The small band plays everything from "Silent Night" to "Little Town of Bethlehem." Of course, as you approach it, you can hear the ringing of the small Salvation Army bell that is being held by one of the S.A. "soldiers" standing by the red metal collection pot.

Christmas trees are being sold on lots throughout the city. Even some of the mom and pop stores are selling a few trees. Some organizations like the Boy Scouts have their own tree lots to raise money. Also, lighted trees are appearing in the schools. Carol told us that the one at Willard this year is really tall -- about 10 feet and covered with lights and ornaments. Also, Christmas programs are being planned at the schools. The high school chorus will present a medley of Christmas songs soon. As usual the members of the chorus will hold evergreen branches and lights so that it will appear that they are part of a living Christmas tree. At the grade schools skits and musical programs are being practiced. Naturally, every church -- including our own Riverside Presbyterian Church -- is planning the traditional nativity play accompanied by appropriate music. Of course, this year I'm looking at all this preparation for Christmas in a very different way. Now being a Jew I can understand how those of other faiths feel left out of the Christmas season -- and experience a feeling of isolation from the rest of the community.

Mom spent a lot of time addressing Christmas cards; she asked Carol to help her check names and addresses. She usually sends out about 100 cards each year to friends and relatives. She has also done some shopping for presents for the family and for the Goldmans too. Uncle Aaron plans to send some more packages to them in the near future and promised to include anything that Mom and Grandma would like to mail. Buddy and Carol are busy making some gifts at school during art class. Buddy told me that he is making a clay ash tray for Dad -- one that can accommodate a pipe -- and a small jewelry box for Mom. Meantime, Carol is making a spoon rest for Mom and a small needlepoint box that is lined with felt for Dad's tie clips, cuff-links, and Masonic jewelry. They won't tell me what they are making for me and Grandma. Several things have already been wrapped and set aside in a box in one of the bedroom closets until we get a tree. Most of our packages will be wrapped in white, red, or green issue paper. In the past few years we have been using old Christmas cards to help us decorate the packages. We have salvaged all the gold and silver tin-like sheets from the old cards (not used in the new cards because of the war) to make stars and other ornamements that we paste on the packages. Also, we cut out some of the more beautiful illustrations from the old cards and make seals out of them. We all agree that they really give each package a unique touch. For the past few years we have been using the old stand-by-- paste made from flour, water, and a little salt. It works very well. We recycle our ribbons too from year to year. Anyway, each package is an example of what you can do when you have to improvise. We all agree when we see what each one of us has come up with in terms of creative wrapping ideas that we all deserve top designer awards. Of course, Mom and Dad point out that we should be good at it because during the Depression we got plenty of practice improvising.

Since the family has decided to celebrate Chanukah as well as Christmas, Grandma Mendell went to Larson's Religious Store to buy a menorah. She told me that she was able to buy one that she liked for $7.50. It is a simple silver candelabrum consisting of eight candle holders. She also purchased eight white candles and another (she calls it a servant candle) to light the others. Now, where will we display it? Perhaps we will place it on the mantel or on the dinning room table. Grandma will decide.

We had another 5" of snow which the kids in the neighborhood really welcomed. Some of them decided to use the hill in front of the rental houses on 18th Street for sleding. It isn't as steep as a lot of hills in the area and it is long enough -- and yet not too long -- for a good run with a sled. It doesn't take too long for the little kids to climb it again for another run. Another hill in the area -- the one on 11th Avenue that runs down in front of where Arvid and Caroline live -- is reserved for "skiing only." The older kids chase off any of the younger kids who want to use it for sleding. They claim that the sleds will ruin the snow for skiing. Meanwhile, Buddy and Carol have made a large snowman and snowwoman in our back yard. Mom gave them some old clothes to put on them so that they really look like a couple. They used pieces of coal for eyes and mouths. Timmy and Joyce joined in and they made several snow children to go with Mr. and Mrs. Snow. So, now we have a complete snow family in the back yard. All they need now is a snow dog or cat.

The Cub Scouts have also made use of the snow for a project of their own. Mr. Hanson taught his troop how to make igloos. They rolled up gigantic snowballs and then carved out the insides to make what they affectionately nicknamed their "Eskimo huts." After that Mr. Hanson suggested that they spend the night out in them to get a good idea of Polar living conditions. Well, despite the fact that most of the boys had sleeping pags and oil lamps, they all deserted the Eskimo huts by 11:00 P.M. It was just too cold.

Even Cleo has been introduced to the snow. Carol hitched her up to an old sled that she found in one of Mr. Standstadt's barns and took her girl friends for a ride around the neighborhood. They loved the experience of gliding along the snow covered streets and waving at the startled Hilltop neighbors who peered out from doorways and windows.

Some of the kids in the area have gone down to Riverside Park to ice skate on the city pond. The city maintains a shelter near it. That plus a bon-fire and several street lamps make for an ideal skating area. Others have taken up their mock war again. They have sought out the military camps that they made during the summer and have reactivated them -- but now as "winter military headquarters." They have divided into Allied and Fascists forces again and continue their version of the war with their toy rifles and hand guns. Oh, yes, once in a while you hear an explosion. Some of the kids saved their fireworks from the 4th of July to use as handgrenades and rockets to use against the "enemy."

During chapel Professor Hugo Vetter, Director of the St. Andrew College Choir, talked to us about the annual performance of Handel's **Messiah.** He has been presenting it for almost twenty years and is well known for his excellent interpretation of the work. Of course, it has been difficult to put on the work because of the war. The number of men in the chorus and in the orchestra has been reduced significantly. In desperation, Dr. Vetter has relied upon more musicians and singers from Andersonville, Milltown and Keyport. Like a lot of students I knew very little about the composer or the work before coming to St. Andrew College. Of course, earlier in the year I had heard some parts of it presented at the Easter Sunrise Service. In his talk Professor Vetter told us about how Handel had composed the work in such a short time and how the work is organized to present the entire story of Christ -- from the promise of his coming to his birth to his death and finally to his resurrection. He even told us about the first performance. Toward the end of his lecture (for that is what it was) he urged us to find time to attend one of the performances. He told us that well-known guest soloists have been hired to sing with the large chorus.

Dr. Vetter indicated that the audience traditionally stands for the "Hallelujah Chorus." Why? Because George II when he attended an early performance of the work stood up supposedly because he was so overwhelmed with emotion. Later that day I saw Professor Donaldson and told him about what Dr. Vetter had said. Well, Dr. Donaldson just smiled and said that he had "to differ from Dr. Vetter's account." According to

Skating at Riverside

Professor Donaldson the king was "bored to tears with the work" and was assuming that the loud and dramatic "Hallelujah Chorus" marked the dramatic end of the performance. "Therefore," Dr. Donaldson exclaimed, "the king and his boxum German mistresses stood up to leave the theatre." According to Professor Donaldson, King George II probably thought to himself, "Thank God it is over!" When the people in the audience saw the royals standing, they all stood up too. Unfortunately for the king, the next part of the **Messiah** started and the king was unable to take his leave to his great disappointment. So, what is the truth? Who knows? I guess I'll wait until the performance to make up my own mind. It will depend upon my reaction to the work. Perhaps, I will find it very long, boring, and tiresome.

One happy event that happened this week was that I finally got up the nerve to ask Kara for a date. We were walking from the library to Old Main when I asked her to go to see **Meet Me In St. Louis.** She looked at me and said she would love to go. Dad let me borrow the car so that I could pick her up at her dorm and drive her to the Le Claire Theatre in Milltown where the movie is playing. We both enjoyed Judy Garland when she sang "The Boy Next Store" and "Have Yourself a Merry Little Christmas." Of course, Margaret O'Brien steals every scene she is in as little sister Tootie. We especially liked the Halloween segment with Tootie joining in with the other kids around the bonfire in the street and then pulling a prank on one of the neighbors that most of the kids feared.

169

After the film as we were leaving the theatre, we found that it was snowing again. We walked hand in hand down 5th Avenue to get to the car and as we did we talked about the film and how many holidays were included in it. When we went pass the office of **The Daily Herald,** I told Kara about some of my experiences working there and mentioned my desire to be a journalist. Then, we stopped a Hoffman's Ice Cream Parlor for a hot fudge sundae and coffee. After that we walked to the car, and I drove her back to the dorm. There, I walked her to the door and then turned to her and kissed her gently. She smiled and told me that she had had a wonderful time and that she would like to go it again some time. I only nodded, smiled and said, "I feel the same way."

[Code: That night I had another wet dream. I found myself in bed with Kara and we were nude. She was urging me to touch her. I found myself touching her breasts and her buttocks and reaching around her slim waist and down around her hips. Then, I imagined that I had entered her "hole of creation" and pumped vigorously as she locked her legs around my butt -- and then my "cob's head" experienced that great feeling before it released the "juice of creation." At that point, I woke up and found my loins and pajamas wet. "I laid there thinking to myself that I had had quite a dream. I showly got up and dried myself and put the wet pajama bottom on a chair to dry. I went to the dresser to get some long johns. As I got back into bed, I found myself being very relaxed and strangely happy and thankful at the same time. Of course, I was happy because of experiencing that "great feeling", and I guess I was thankful to have had such a dream that had given me so much happiness in celebrating the physical and emotional nature of my manhood. I thought to myself that this is the way that Dad must feel after he has made love with Mom. And, Mom must feel something like this too as a result of responding to the man she loves.]

The Passing Parade

News Stories: "Red Armies Close in on Budapest"
"Patton Advancing in Hard Fighting"
"B-29 View: Hirohito's Palace in Tokyo"

Song: "Harbor Lights" by Frances Langford

Movie: "Bowery to Broadway" with Donald O'Connor and Peggy Ryan

More Harassment, the Battle of the Bulge, and Handel's Messiah

A lot has happened since my last entry -- most of it disturbing and very different from the season known for "peace on Earth, good will toward men."

At the start of last week we received a Christmas card that turned out to be another poison pen letter or card in this case. Instead of using letters and numbers cut out of magazines, the sender had typed our address on the outside of the envelope. We should have been suspicious by that because most people write addresses on Christmas cards. Inside was a lovely card featuring the Holy Family but then when one opened the card, someone had spelled out with letters cut from magazines: "Get Thee Hence, Christ Killers."

Then, on the evening of the same day, someone decided to vandalize our "snow family" in the back yard. Of course, we didn't see who did it. We discovered what they had done the next morning. They had cut off all the heads and then with pieces of coal spelled out: "Death to all Christ Killers." Again, Dad decided to call the police and report the incidents. They told us that we should keep the poison pen note along with the others that we had received. Also, they told us to try to catch someone in the act of vandalism. They suggested that we tell some of the neighbors -- the ones we feel are really friendly -- to keep an eye out for any person who seems to be up to no good. Well, we did just that. We told all the people who rent apartments from Mr. Bishop along 18th Street to help us catch whoever is doing the vandalism. There was one exception -- the McCoys. We are very suspicious of them. Also, we told Dorothy Banister to be alert to anything suspicious. We thought about telling the Hansens but they are so far away that they probably wouldn't see anything. The ones we told all have a good view of our property.

If this wasn't enough to ruin our Christmas spirit, we then heard on the 17th by way of radio that the Germans had launched an offensive in the Ardennes Forest. Throughout the day it was reported that the Allied Forces had not repulsed the German offensive. In fact, by the end of the day, it was reported that the Germans had made significant breakthroughs. Some of the announcers are calling the conflict "the Battle of the Bulge." This renewed effort on the part of the Germans has caused many -- especially those with relatives fighting in France -- to be very anxious and fearful. The battle has certainly made this Christmas a different one. We are not looking forward to opening presents so much as to ending the German adance. Many have gone to churches and temples to pray to God to sustain our soliders in their fight against fascism and to bring an end to the slaughter. We realize that if the German offense is successful, that it will mean that the war will be prolonged.

Grandma Mendell feels that there are parallels between the struggle against Hitler and the situation that confronted Israel in its struggle against the forces of Antiochus Epiphanes. She prays for God to help our forces in Europe as He helped the Maccabees against the forces trying to destroy the Jewish faith so long ago. She reminded us that God saved the Jewish faith then, and she feels that He will save the Allied Forces now. "I can't think of a better time or reason to celebrate Chanukkah," she whispered as she placed the menorah on the mantel and lit the candles. "We pray for a miracle from God now as they did. It will happen. We have only to wait and have faith."

On Friday, December 16, one day before the German offensive, the entire family had gone out and purchased a Christmas tree at the Boy Scout tree lot up on 15th Street. Carol spotted it -- about 6 foot tall with plenty of branches evenly distributed on all sides. The price was fair too -- only $1.85. We took it home and decorated it that night. We put it directly in front of the wide window in the formal living room. Dad and I put on the lights first. We made sure that all the lights were working. We still have the kind that if one bulb is out, the entire string of lights won't work. Then, everyone added the ornaments and tinsel. We took a lot of time with the tinsel; each strip had to be placed two inches apart. Dad is adamant about this. He always says, "You can tell if people really know how to decorate a tree by how the tinsel is laid on the tree. If it is simply thrown haphazardly on the tree, the desired affect is entirely destroyed." You can't buy real tinsel now because of the war. We still have the real heavy thing. Why? Because we have carefully saved it from year to year. The tinsel we are now using goes back to 1940 and 1941. When we take the tree down, we will carefully save every strip of this rare commodity for next year.

After the tinsel, we placed the star at the top of the tree and made sure that it faced the front of the room and did not slant. Then, after Buddy placed a container of water under the trunk of the tree, we placed long strips of cotton around the bottom of the tree. After that we got out our manger set which includes Mary, Joseph, the baby Jesus, the three wisemen (one Negro) and a stable with animals -- two sheep, a horse, a cow, and a donkey. As I was helping to put the pieces in place, I noticed again where they had been made --in Japan. Unlike a lot of people we did not throw out everything that we had purchased before the war that had been made in Japan. But, it did seem ironic that these symbols of "peace on Earth, good will toward men" had been made by the Japs. After that, at long last, Dad plugged in the lights on the tree and turned off the overhead light fixture so that we could get the full affect. As usual, we thought that it was the most beautiful tree that we had ever had. And as usual, the trimming of the tree had helped us regain that Christmas feeling despite what had happened earlier in the week. Of course, after hearing about the German offensive, the brightly lighted tree with all its trimmings seemed at times out of place in a world that seemed so brutal. However, Dad pointed out that it is very appropriate because "it stands for the hopes of mankind and God's promise to concern himself with mankind's plight." He reminded us that when Christ was born, the world at that time was also filled with brutality. He explained, "Christ at that time came as God's gift to mankind -- a gift of hope for dealing with mankind's suffering. So, it is fitting that we continue to celebrate the arrival of that gift now even though it comes at a time when there is so much suffering in the world. What better time to remember and celebrate God's gift of love?"

On Sunday, I attended a performance of **Messiah**. It was held in the gym behind Old Main. I had a seat in the balcony where I could clearly see the entire production. The stage was decorated with large evergreen trees and laurels made up of branches from pine trees. They were not decorated or lighted in anyway. However, they made for a very natural -- like being in the woods-- sort of setting for the chorus and soloists. Dr. Vetter appeared at the podium and bowed to the audience and to the huge chorus that must have included about 200 people. He introduced the guest soloists: Richard Clark - bass, Henry Nelson - tenor, Victoria Reed - sophrano, and Catherine Albright - alto. Then, he told the audience that the performance that evening was dedicated to the men who were engaged in the Battle of the Bulge. He asked us to stand for a moment of silent prayer for those who were at this very hour fighting for our liberties in Europe.

As I mentioned earlier, I was not very familiar with Handel or his **Messiah.** I found the work to be filled with drama and emotion. Such musical numbers as "And the Glory of the Lord," "For Unto Us a Child is Born," "All We Like Sheep, Have Gone Astray," and "I Know My Redeemer Liveth" were powerful and moving. Of course, we all stood for the "Halleluj ah Chorus" and I found myself smiling as I thought about Dr. Donaldson's version of why King George II stood up. It was such a powerful and dramatic production that I felt that if I had been the King of England, I would have been moved to stand. However, I reminded myself that I was not George II. It could be that he was bored to death and wanted to leave. Well, does it really matter? I don't think so. What matters now at this moment to us is the safety of those fighting men and women who are at this very moment engaged in mortal combat with the Nazi forces. What matters at this moment to us is the hope that the God who has given us Jesus will also protect our forces and give them Victory over the forces of evil.

At the end of the performance and the long round of applause, Dr. Vetter turned to the audience and asked us to stand while President Bergman gave a departing prayer. In that prayer he asked God to embrace the souls of those who have died fighting in Europe and Asia for our freedom and to comfort their loved ones. Then, in a atmosphere of reverent silence we all departed.

The Passing Parade

News Story: "Nazi Push 20 Miles Into U.S. Lines"

Song: "I'm Dreaming of a White Christmas" by Bing Crosby

Movie: "Marriage Is A Private Affair" with Lana Turner

THE SHOOTINGS

Another experience -- and this time a terrible one -- happened on Wednesday evening. It has left the entire family shaken and worn out with worry and grief. Earlier that day Mom and Grandma had joined Mrs. Moore, Mrs. Wells, Mrs. Banister, Mrs. Thompson and yes even Mrs. McCoy in giving a surprise Christmas party for Grandma Jackson. They wanted to do something to cheer her up. She had been feeling as she calls it "poorly" and rather depressed. She said that she really missed her sister Rose; they usually had enjoyed Christmas together. She was hoping that Rose might be able to travel back to Milltown for the holiday season but this will not be possible. She has been hospitalized as a result of a fall and will be mending for some time.

The ladies wanted to do something to make sure that Grandma Jackson knew that her neighbors loved her and appreciated her. They planned to surprise her with a small tree for her upstairs apartment. Each had made something -- a casserole, a desert -- for the party. Mrs. Moore had telephoned Cora Jackson and told her what they were up to and she was really delighted when she heard about the surprise party. She told Mrs. Moore that she thought the party would really cheer up Grandma Jackson.

They went over to the Jackson farm at 3:00P.M. with the tree, decorations, and goodies. They really surprised Grandma; she told everyone that she had never had a real tree of her own -- even as a child. While she looked on with a child's delighted interest, "Santa's helpers" got busy and started putting up the tree and decorating it. As the lights were placed on the tree and each ornament was added, the more Grandma smiled and voiced her belief that "it was the most beautiful little tree in the world." She especially liked the homemade lacy snowflake ornaments and the large angel that had been placed at the top of the tree. Then, "Santa's helpers" set out the casseroles that they had made along with several deserts that they knew Grandma really loved -- orange nut bread and bread pudding. By that time Cora Jackson had brewed some coffee so that everyone could sit down and eat. After everyone had had their fill, they sang Christmas carols.

It was about 6:15 P.M. when the ladies were about to go home when "trouble" walked through the door. Kelly Jackson came home from work and didn't care for what he found there. He had stopped at the tavern with Jim Banister and had a few drinks after work. This gave him a lot of "courage" to say what he felt inside. When he saw Mom and Grandma, he immediately launched into a verbal attack on them. He wondered "how in the world two Jews could celebrate Christmas." He told them that he did not appreciate their coming over to see his mother. He told them not to come to his home again.

At first, everyone was so startled by this outburst that silence filled the room. Then, Grandma Mendell found her courage and told Kelly that they had come to see his mother -- not him -- and that it was his mother's decision to make with regard to their coming again. She also told him that for his information Jews and Christians share a lot in common -- like being concerned about people and wanting to express human kindness. Well, Kelly didn't like hearing this. He yelled, "Do Jews and Christians share Christ? No, I don't think so. You Jews do not love Jesus, you killed Him! You are nothing more than Christ killers -- and bloody-sucking bankers and money lenders. If it wasn't for the likes of you, we would not be at war today." Upon hearing this, Mom took Grandma Mendell aside and whispered to her, "We better leave. You can't argue with someone who has such distorted ideas." So, they left. As they were walking home, most of the ladies expressed how sorry they were that Kelly's outburst had marred an otherwise happy surprise party for Grandma Jackson.

When Mom and Grandma got home, they were very upset. Dad wanted to know all the details. After he heard their account, he became very quiet. I could see the anger rising in him. He told Mom and Grandma that he was going to talk to Kelly. Mom begged him not to. She pleaded, "You can't talk to someone like Kelly who has so many distorted ideas." Dad replied that he felt that he had to try. He explained, "I can't sit idly by and let him spread his poison." Grandma Mendell voiced her agreement with Dad that "the time has come when we must stand up to the likes of him." Then, Dad turned to me and asked me to go with him.

When dad and I got to the Jackson house, Kelly was there at the doorway. Dad told him to step outside where they could talk privately. Kelly stepped out onto his back porch which was lighted by one light fixture. Dad told him that he had heard what he had said to his wife and mother-in-law and that he felt that Kelly should apologize. Kelly refused. Then, he shouted that Dad was "a Jew lover -- a man who loved to fuck Jewish bitches -- a supporter of the Christ killing Jews." He then ordered, "Get the hell off my property!" Dad froze solid. I knew instinctively what he was thinking --"this is the person -- or at least one of them -- who has been sending the poison pen letters and vandalizing my property." Dad stood his ground and told Kelly that he would not leave until he received an apology. At that, Kelly disappeared into the house and returned with a rifle. Again he told Dad and me to leave. When Dad again refused, Kelly opened fire. Dad was thrown back by the power of the bullet and I could see blood appearing on his coat near his right shoulder. Instead of giving in to his injury, Dad rushed at Kelly and shouted to me, "Come on Mark lets tackle the son of a bitch!" I did as I was commanded. Dad and I lunged toward Kelly to grab his gun and bring him down. In the scuffle that followed Kelly got off another shot before Dad pinned him to the ground and got his rifle. The last shot hit me. I felt pain on the side of my head. The last thing I remembered was feeling blood dripping down my face and then seeing it spatter onto the snow covered ground.

The next thing that I remembered was coming to and finding myself side by side with Dad in a moving ambulance. I guess that the neighbors had heard the shots and had called the police. I remember looking at Dad who was conscious and hearing him say, "Good job Private Johnson." I wondered at the time if he thought that he was back on a battle field in World War I and that he was speaking to one of his men. Much later I found out from Dad that he had addressed me that way as a compliment for the courage that I had shown "under fire" sort of speak.

Dad and I were taken to the Milltown Public Hospital. When we reached the emergency room, it was determined that Dad had suffered a gun shot wound to his right shoulder. The bullet had to be taken out. I was lucky; the bullet had only grazed my head. They bandaged me up after sewing up the tear in my skin with about six stiches. Dad and I were kept in the hospital for two days and then discharged for a lot of bed rest at home.

Kelly was taken to Police Headquarters and charged with assault and battery with a deadly weapon after the police talked to the neighbors. Kelly denies the charge and has gotten a lawyer. He claims that Dad came at him first and that he was only trying to protect his property. There will be a hearing after Christmas. We heard that Kelly plans to post bail so he can get out of jail. Meanwhile, Aunt Sadie has come to stay with the family to help out. Naturally, other relatives on both sides have been told about the shootings and are keeping in close touch. The neighbors -- especially the Bishop girls, Dorothy Banister, and Mrs. Hansen -- have really tried to help.

The Passing Parade

News Story: "Nazi Drive Slowed 40 Miles Inside Belgium"

Song: "Have Yourself A Merry Little Christmas" by Judy Garland

Movie: "Meet Me In Saint Louis" with Margarite O'Brien and Judy Garland

CELEBRATING CHRISTMAS AND CHANUKAH

Christmas and Chanukah were certainly celebrated under different circumstances than we ever had imagined. Both Dad and I were home from the hospital but tired and sore. The doctor had given us both pain pills that we took every 3 hours. So, we took it easy and napped during the day. We all tried not to spoil Christmas day -- especially for Carol and Buddy -- by talking about what had happened and what might happen at the trial.

News of the war -- and especially the so-called Battle of the Bulge -- continued to be reported. The temperatures in the battle zone have been brutal; often the temperatures are 14 below zero. Lists of causalities from our local area appeared in the newspaper along with maps of the battle areas and huge photographs of men waiting for the enemy surrounded by deep snow. One of those killed was our good neighbor Bob Thompson. Ethel was informed two days ago by telegram. She hasn't received any details only that he was killed in the line of duty. Most feel that he was probably in the Battle of the Bulge. Naturally, our hearts go out to Ethel. Bob was such a good man. He and Ethel had hoped to start a family one day after the war.

We have also been barraged with news stories about the shootings. "Two Shot in Dispute;" "Councilman Johnson and Son Released from Hospital;" "Jackson Arrested in Shooting;" "A.C.L.U. [American Civil Liberties Union] Voices Concern Over Attacks on Jews." One photograph in the paper showed Kelly Jackson being led to the Milltown Police Station.

Since Dad and I were not able to do much to prepare for the big day, Aunt Sadie, Mom, and Grandma with the help of Carol and Buddy worked together to finish a lot of the last minute preparations. Besides finishing wrapping packages and preparing goodies, they also helped with a lot of practical chores like building the fire in the furnace, carrying out the cinders and trash, and bringing in the newspaper and milk bottles. Also, we had some more snow -- only about 3 inches -- so Carol and Buddy were given the job of clearing off the sidewalks. And, they did a good job of it too. While they were outside shoveling snow, Mom got busy and made something that she always did at Christmas -- popcorn balls. As usual she put them in cellophane paper of various colors -- red, green, yellow, and orange. Of course, she left unpapered about 8 so that Carol and Buddy and the rest of us could "have a taste" if we wanted. So, when Carol and Buddy came in after doing such a good shoveling job, they were surprised to find a popcorn ball surprise treat waiting for them. After that, they helped put the cellophaned wrapped balls on the tree.

On Christmas day, Dad and I got up later than the rest of the family. Those pain bills really worked but also they made us very sleepy. I remembered hearing voices and slowly remembered that it was Christmas Day. One of the voices that I heard was Uncle Ira's. In the early morning hours, he had arrived at our house. He had checked on the livestock at the farm and had taken off to be with us and his sister for Christmas. When Dad and I finally got dressed and came down stairs, we heard all about Carol and Buddy getting up very early and getting into their Christmas stockings that had been hung from the mantel. They had already enjoyed some of the candy and fruit that they had found in their stockings. We were told that Peggy had gotten into her stocking too (how I will never know) and was now enjoying a large soup bone.

When we sat down for breakfast, Dad asked us to bow our heads as he prayed that God would see us through our own difficult time and help our troops in their struggle to turn the tide and end the war. Then, we enjoyed a breakfast of eggs, orange juice, oatmeal with real cream brought from the farm by Ira, and a pecan stolen made by Aunt Sadie.

After breakfast we went into the formal living room where we plugged in the lights on the tree and also lit all the eight candles on the menorah. Then, we opened our packages. We followed our usual practice of rotating from one person to another; that way we could all enjoy seeing the person's reaction to a gift. Each opened about five gifts. Carol loved her new boots for riding while Buddy's favorite present was an electric military train. That train had cars built for all sorts of military uses -- from cars to transport cannons, tanks, and jeeps to one with a large search light on it to a railcar for the wounded. Buddy really loves it. Dad seemed to especially like a new calabash pipe like the fictitious Sherlock Homes smokes and an all-wool plaid shirt. I appreciated a new wallet and some argyle socks. Grandma was surprised to get a sewing cabinet; she said that now she will have a storage place for all of the flowers that she is crocheting for the table cloth. Mom liked her new pink chenille bathrobe too. Of course, the best gift she got was still having Dad -- alive and in one piece. Like all of us she realized that the bullet could have hit some other part of his body and either injured him permanently or killed him. She felt the same about me too only in a different way.

Aunt Sadie and Incle Ira really seemed to like the gifts that we got them. Sadie received fleeced-lined bedroom slippers and Ira got a wool lined winter cap with ear flaps to keep him warm when he goes out to check on the animals in the barn. They were surprised to find the presents under the tree for them. Of course, we told them that we appreciated them coming to help us and besides we knew that they had brought some special treats to serve with the Christmas dinner.

The rest of the day passed quietly. Dad and I took some more pain pills and then took another nap. Meanwhile, Aunt Sadie, Mom and Grandma were in the kitchen preparing dinner. Carol and Buddy along with Uncle Ira took off to look in on Celo and give her some carrots and cubes of sugar. We didn't eat until about 2:00 but by that time everyone had worked up an appetite. The main course for dinner -- a stand-up rib roast -- was supplied by Aunt Sadie and Uncle Ira. They had gotten the meat from a neighbor who had slaughtered one of his steers. That, plus baked potatoes, a corn souffle, a green-bean casserole, and warm corn biscuits made for a delicious Christmas dinner. For desert, we had our choice of mince meat pie or Aunt Sadie's famous bread pudding with whipped cream or some of both.

After the dishes were cleared away and washed, Mom and Grandma along with Aunt Sadie did some crocheting for the table cloth and visited in the front parlor. Buddy set up his electric train with the help of Uncle Ira and enjoyed seeing how all the cars looked as they sped along in an imaginary war zone. Buddy had gotten a lot of his toy soldiers out too and set up some encampments in the area of the railroad tracks. Carol seemed content to read a book that Uncle Ira and Aunt Sadie had gotten for her about her favorite topic -- yes, you guessed it - horses. The book contained photographs of all the breeds and an historical account of each. Dad still needed some rest and fell asleep on one of the sofas in the living room. After he woke up, someone -- I think it was Grandma -- suggested that we play Monopoly. She got most of us to participate except Mom and Aunt Sadie who seemed content to sit, crochet, and be observers. After two rounds of the game, we all had to admit that Grandma was hard to beat. She always managed to make sound real estate investments and have the best luck. She always got the cards to get herself out of jail or to collect some money from someone. Also, her investments in those small green houses and red hotels really paid off. The rest of us were always having to pay her a lot of rent. No wonder she likes to play Monopoly. When we asked her why she was so lucky, she smiled and said, "I never tell my strategy for winning."

Much later we had some left overs from dinner and then gathered in the front parlor to sing some carols while Mom played them on the piano. Then, we decided to turn in. Uncle Ira had to leave early in the morning to check on his farm animals. Besides, Dad and I had taken some more pain pills and were feeling tried. Before we went to bed, Dad asked us to join hands and again pray. This time he thanked the Lord for allowing us to have a wonderful Christmas Day and Chanukah and then he asked Him to watch over our troops as they fight to preserve our liberties Then, we joined hands and said in unsion, "May the Lord watch between me and thee while we are absent one from another." And, as usual, when we reached "from another" we pressed each other's hands.

The Passing Parade

News Story: "Nazis Drive on 11 Miles, Merge Two Wedges"

Song: "How Soon Will I Be Seeing You" by Dinah Shore

Movies: "Arsenic and Old Lace" with Gary Grant and Constance Bennett "National Velvet" with Mickey Rooney and Elizabeth Taylor (Carol saw this film twice - loved it!)

THE TRIAL

The press was there when the entire family entered the Court House in Andersonville for the trial. Dad was approached by Roy Morris from **The Daily Herald.** He asked Dad to comment on the case. Dad said, "I hope that Kelly Jackson will be found guilty of the charges." With that short comment we moved quickly into the court room. Shortly after that Kelly Jackson arrived with his wife Cora and Grandma Jackson at his side. On the advice of his attorney Daniel Cutter he declined to talk to the reporters.

The court room was filled with many of our neighbors. Dad whispered to me that we could have another 4th of July party right there because so many from Hilltop Place were present. On the left side of the room sat Professor Olsen, Mr. and Mrs. Patterson and Dave, Mrs. McCoy and her husband, Ethel Thompson, Mr. Phillips, and Mr. and Mrs. Hansen. To the right sat Mr. and Mrs. Montez and Maria, Dorothy Banister and her husband Jim, all the Bishops, most of the renters who live along 18th Street and 12th Avenue, and yes Mr & Mrs. Standstadt with Arvid and Caroline. They had taken a special flight back to Milltown to attend the trial. Way toward the back of the room sat Glen (in a wheelchair) and Anna Nelson with some of our friends from church -- Ruby Irwin and the Rev. & Mrs. Fritzgibbon.

All those present -- Prosecuting Attorney John Browning, Defense Attorney Daniel Cutter, Kelly Jackson, the jury, and the spectators -- rose as Judge Clifford Roberts entered the court room and took his seat. After the usual preliminaries, the trial began.

Prosecuting Attorney Browning called police officer Harold White to the stand to testify to what he found on the night of Dec. 20 outside of the Jackson house. He described the scene of the shootings and reported the injuries that Dad and I had sustained. He also told the court that he had immediately called for more police officers and for an ambulance. Next, Browning called for Dr. Logan from the Milltown Public Hospital to answer questions about the specific nature of the wounds that the "victims" (that's me and Dad) had sustained and how they were treated. Then, Browning called several neighbors. Since Jim Banister was the one who called the police after he heard gun shots, he was called to the witness stand to tell the jury what he had heard and saw that evening. He testified that he and Kelly had gone to a tavern after work and had a few drinks. Browning tried to get Jim Banister to verify that Kelly was very drunk when he got home and that he did have a temper. Jim refused to support that view of Kelly. However, Browning did get Jim to admit that the two men had had more than two beers each and shots of whiskey. Continuing, Jim testified to hearing angry voices and then gun shots followed by shouts for help from Cora Jackson.

Then, Browning called Mrs. Moore and Mrs. Thompson because they had witnessed the verbal confrontation between Kelly and Mom and Grandma Mendell. He tried though a series of questions to have the ladies testify to the nature of Kelly's remarks as well as how drunk he was. Kelly's attorney

Daniel Cutter tried to underplay Kelly's drinking. He tried through questions of the witnesses to portray Kelly as a man who could hold his liquor and not be terribly affected by it. Also, he tried to show that Kelly may have had some legitimate reasons to be upset with Mom and Grandma being in his home since he knew that they disapproved of how he had dealt with the situation involving Aunt Rose.

Finally, Dad and I were called to testify. We both stood by our account of the shootings. We told the jury that Kelly appeared to be drinking heavily and that he swore at us as he became more and more violent in his behavior. We testified that when he found that he could not intimidate us with words, he resorted to a gun. We both said that we had not made any moves against Kelly until after he had fired his gun.

In his cross-examination Kelly's attorney tried to portray Dad as being very protective of his family and hot-tempered. He reviewed Dad's military record of combat service during World War I. He suggested that Dad was capable of making a hostile move against Kelly that would cause him to feel that he needed to get a gun to defend himself. He tried to convince the jury that Dad had made the first move against Kelly after he aimed a gun at both of us. Cutter painted a picture for the jury of Dad (6'2") and his son threatening poor Kelly who only stood 5'8". Of course, Dad did his best to deflect these arguments.

When Cutter got to me, he tried to get me to admit that I would lie to protect my father. He did it so cleverly. The questions went like this:

"Mark, do you love your father?"

"You don't want any harm to come to your father do you?"

"Mark, you would lie to protect your father, won't you?"

Of course, I told the jury that I would not lie -- that I was telling the truth about the shooting. I said that I did not see Dad make any threatening moves toward Kelly before or after he got the rifle. Cutter tried to convince me that I did not have a clear view of my father because of the poor lighting that night. Again, I stood my ground and said that the light was adequate.

Finally, Cutter tried to rattle me by saying that I wanted to punish Kelly for his views toward Jews. Again, his questions were cleverly formulated:

"Mark, are you a Jew?"

"Mark, do you know how Mr. Jackson feels about Jews?"

"Tell the court what Mr. Jackson said about your mother and grandmother."

"Do you feel that people who express those ideas should be punished?"

"Would you lie to convict Mr. Jackson because of his anti-Jewish opinions?"

I found this line of questioning very upsetting. I guess I felt it was too personal. Cutter was opening up something that I had not totally resolved within myself. However, I responded to these questions by saying that although I found Kelly's views repugnant, I would not lie to convict or punish him. I repeated again that I would not lie to protect my father either if he had done something wrong. As I left the witness chair, I felt sweat running down my sides under my dress shirt.

Cutter called Mrs. McCoy as a defense witness and used her to make Kelly seem reasonable in his confrontation with Mom and Grandma. She tried to make Kelly out as the victim. She claimed that both Mom and Grandma knew how he felt about them and that they should not have participated in the party for Grandma Jackson. She claimed that Kelly was provoked by finding them in his home and by what Grandma Mendell said to him. In his cross examination Browning tried to get Mrs. McCoy to admit her hatred of Jews in order to explain why she was defending Kelly. She denied again and again feeling any resentment toward Jews.

Then, Cutter called Bill Phillips to the stand. He used his testimony to support the idea that Dad was hot-tempered and capable of doing bodily harm toward anyone who offended his family -- especially his wife. Phillips even testified that Dad had made erroneous charges against him with regard to his treatment of his step-daughter Irene and had threatened to "beat the hell out of him if he didn't shape up." While Mr. Phillips testified, I thought to myself and I'm sure Dad did too, that he was part of the group that had been harrassing us. The gang was probably composed of Bill Phillips, Jim Banister, Nell McCoy, and Kelly Jackson. It made me sick. I thought, "So many of them!"

Then Cutter called Kelly to the stand. Kelly claimed that Dad had refused to leave his property and challenged him to a fight. He claimed that I was lying to protect my father. He claimed that he got the gun to defend himself. He testified that Dad lunged at him and that it was then that he pulled the trigger. During cross examination Kelly was asked about his attitudes toward Jews. He was asked if he participated or organized a harassment compaign against the Johnson family. Of course, while he admitted his dislike toward Jews, he said that he would not do anything to harass anyone in his neighborhood -- this included Jews. He said that he just wanted to be left alone. He said that he did not want the Johnsons coming around his place, visiting his wife or mother.

After Kelly's testimony there was a short recess. We all expected that when we returned that the attorneys would give their summations to the jury. Instead of that happening, Prosecuting Attorney Browing called a surprise witness -- Grandma Jackson. During the recess she had gone to Browning and told him that she wanted to testify for the prosecution. She told him that her daughter-in-law had wanted to join her but was told that a wife could not testify against a husband. So, she had come by herself to do what she called "the right thing" despite the pain it would cause her own family. On the stand in response to questions she said that she felt morally obligated to take the stand to support the Johnsons. She testified that Kelly had been drinking heavily that night and that he had said horrible things to Mom and Grandma Mendell. She explained that while she had not actually seen the shootings, she did know that Kelly had been drinking heavily that evening and that he was furious after talking to Dad. She described how Kelly came into the house, reached for his rifle, looked to make sure it was loaded, and then proclaimed, "I'm going to shoot that son-of -a-bitch Jew lover if he doesn't get his ass home."

In his cross-examination Cutter tried to get Grandma Jackson to admit that she hated her son because he had sent her sister Rose away. While she admitted that that had been a "hard cross to bear," she said that she still loved her son -- but that she "loved the truth more."

The jury was only out for about two hours. The decision was "guilty as charged." The judge will sentence Kelly next week. Browning feels that Kelly will probably get between 2 to 5 years because he has no prior record.

After the verdict was read a sigh of relief could be heard throughout the court room. Then, as we (the entire family.) rose to go, there was a collective effort to reach out to us -- to reassure us that we had plenty of friends among our neighbors in Hilltop Place. It was an incredible feeling -- very moving, touching. Some of the men like Arvid wanted to shake our hands -- others simply wanted to pat us on our backs and shoulders. Some of the women like Ethel Thompson and yes even the self-contained Mrs. Wells hugged us with tears in their eyes.

The Passing Parade

News Stories: "Yank Counterdrives Cutting Into Nazi Flanks"
"F.D.R. Stands on Atlantic Charter Peace Basis"

Songs: "Always" by Deanna Durbin
"I Don't Want to Walk Without You" by Dinah Shore

Movie: "Laura" with Gene Tierney

WAITING FOR THE GOLDMANS

I am writing this as I sit at Union Station in Chicago with my family and Great Uncle Aaron and Aunt Ruth. We are waiting for the New York Central train to arrive with Joseph Goldman and his family.

Things seem to be working out. The German advance has been halted. Kelly Jackson has been punished. Joseph Goldman and his family will be here shortly.

As I sit here waiting, I wonder what to make of it all. Not only about Kelly and the Goldmans but the happenings of the entire year. A lot of good things have happen but a lot of bad and downright evil things have too. All the residents of Hilltop Place have had their lives changed forever by the course of events during the year. I for one have certainly discovered a lot about myself that I did not know a year ago. I'm thinking that life is very unpredictable. I guess the war has made that all the more of a reality to all of us.

All I know for certain is that it takes courage to live -- in peacetime and wartime. I have learned that it is important to have a family, neighbors, and friends to join together "to fight the good fight." However, I realize that often a person must stand alone. All we can do is our best and to stand with courage for what we believe -- for how we preceive the truth and the good. Sometimes we'll win -- other times we'll lose. The important thing is to be true to ourselves and the good that is within us and make an effort.

I am also certain about another thing -- evil exists. Perhaps it is Satan's work or more likely something innately wrong with some people or the circumstances of their lives. No matter what causes evil it is up to good people to deal with it. It is up to you and me. And, if something terrible happenes to us, we must be strong enough, brave enough to go on.

I must stop writing now. The stationmaster came on the PA system and has just announced that the train from New York is arriving on track 8.

ABOUT THE AUTHOR

This is a photo of the author
in 1939 -- shortly after
. being brought to the
U.S.A.

The author was born in Germany and was brought to this country after Kristallnacht -- the Night of the Broken Glass.

He grew up in Moline, IL and earned a B.A. in history from Augustana College and a M.A. in history from the University of Illinois.

He taught social studies for thirty -three years mainly at Webster Groves High School in St. Louis County.

This book is a result of a lifetime of reading about history -- especially social history -- and the presidency of Franklin Delano Roosevelt. That along with his intense concern for minorities and their rights helped stir his imagination to write this novel.

Besides publishing many educational articles about his his teaching methods, he also wrote several creative works of poetry and art. Author House published his following books: Echoes and Shadows of Life, Nights of the Black Moon and Days of Sunshine Among Common Folk and Dreams, Wishes and Fantasies of Common Folk.

IN MEMORIAL

DOROTHY IRENE WEBB
1909 - 1993

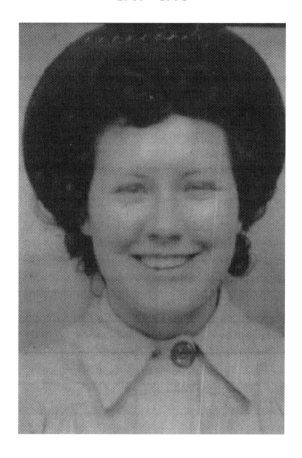

To the lady Irene who loved the small Jewish boy who was rescued from The Night of the Broken Glass.

She accepted the responsibility placed in her loving arms by her mother's people -- the Hirshmann -- to protect and raise the child of the night of burning torches and broken glass.

She also promised to keep secret the fact that members of the Hirshmann family were part of an underground group dedicated to trying to save Jews during Hitler's policy of ethnic cleansing.

Printed in the United States
By Bookmasters